Now You're Talking

Now You're Talking

Contemporary Welsh Dramatists

in conversation with

Hazel Walford Davies

Greg Cullen	Lucy Gough	Ian Rowlands
Lewis Davies	Mark Jenkins	Ed Thomas
Dic Edwards	Gareth Miles	Frank Vickery
Siôn Eirian	Alan Osborne	Charles Way
Siân Evans	Gary Owen	Roger Williams

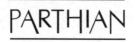

PARTHIAN

Parthian
The Old Surgery
Napier Street
Cardigan
SA43 1ED

www.parthianbooks.co.uk

First published in 2005
© The Contributors 2005
All Rights Reserved

ISBN 1-902638-48-4
    9 781902 638485

Cover design by Lucy Llewellyn
Inner design by type@lloydrobson.com
Printed and bound by Dinefwr Press, Llandybïe, Wales

Published with the financial support of the Welsh Books
Council

British Library Cataloguing in Publication Data

A cataloguing record for this book is available from the British
Library

Contents

Introduction

In 1993 members of the Drama Panel of the then Welsh Arts Council, concerned at the lack of a periodical that would provide English-medium theatre practitioners in Wales with a forum for debate, suggested that the Drama Officer, Michael Baker, and the panel's chair, Julian Mitchell, should look into the possibility of funding a theatre periodical. When it became apparent that the substantial sum necessary to establish and support such a periodical would not be forthcoming, a compromise was reached. There was a pattern that could be followed. Welsh-medium theatre had established a theatre supplement within the pages of the magazine *Barn*, then under the enlightened editorship of Menna Baines. It was decided to follow that example and to approach Tony Bianchi, Literature Officer of the Welsh Arts Council, and Robin Reeves, Editor of the *New Welsh Review*, with a view to incorporating a theatre supplement within the pages of that literary magazine. An agreement was reached and £5,000 was found to fund the supplement whose first appearance was in the Winter 1994-95 issue of the magazine.

It was in that issue the first interview in this present volume appeared. In the autumn of 1994 I was commissioned by Robin Reeves to write a series of 'portraits' of Welsh dramatists. It seemed to me at the time that what was needed was not filtered, Sunday-supplement style portraits but the voices of the dramatists themselves. I therefore suggested to Robin Reeves that the interview form would be more appropriate. Robin replied that he disliked interviews, that I would have to accept the portrait brief, and that the editor's decision was final.

I accepted the decision, and in October 1994 I went to talk to Ed Thomas at the Fiction Factory office in Cardiff, in preparation for the first portrait. Ten minutes into the tape, I knew that the portrait brief would have to be scrapped.

1

The dramatist had crucially important things to say about Wales and its theatre scene and these things would be inevitably diluted in paraphrase, and in being framed by the authorial analysis and comment that necessarily determines the shape of a portrait. 'The dramatist says or argues or urges that...' is not the same as the dramatist saying and arguing and urging. My thinking along these lines was prompted also by our particular situation in Wales, a situation which grew throughout the second half of the twentieth-century, and is perhaps only now beginning to change. Dramatists – the makers, after all, of the most central attitude-changing art – have tended to be more invisible than poets, novelists and visual artists as individuals, as people with a wide range of views fanning out from, as well as informing, their art. The portrait form suggests too easefully the notion of 'celebrity', and a further advantage of the interview is that, in having at length the dramatist's own words, it has spin-offs curving back towards the nature of the actual work itself. Literary or cultural analysis or portraits can draw on an interview to an extent that is not true to the same degree the other way round. The crux is the medium – the dramatist's own words.

As it happens, in the event I transcribed and edited an interview and wrote a portrait – and sent both to Robin. Within a few days I received a note from him saying that he was offering me a fresh commission – 'to provide a series of interviews with Welsh dramatists for the theatre supplement of the *New Welsh Review*'. There followed a postscript: 'The editor's decision is final!'

That was the genesis of the first ten interviews in *Now You're Talking*. Shortly before his untimely death, Robin wrote to ask whether I'd consider collecting the interviews into a volume, to be published under the aegis of the *New Welsh Review*. He had been struck by how many quotations from the interviews had already found their way into published essays and volumes that dealt, not only with theatre, but with wider aspects of the social, literary and political scene in Wales. An added incentive was that so little material was available on theatre in Wales. Sadly, I never got to work with Robin on the volume, but now that *Now You're Talking* is published by Parthian, it represents, amongst many other things, a tribute to Robin Reeves's flexible support and vision.

(2)

The original ten *New Welsh Review* interviews appear in this volume together with new updating interviews. Two other interviews are taken from the volume *State of Play: Four Playwrights of Wales* which I edited for Gomer in 1998. Interviews with five other dramatists were conducted specifically for this present volume. The interviews are placed in chronological order of the initial interview date. Naturally, I couldn't aim at comprehensiveness; I had regretfully to omit a few other dramatists who deserve to have their voices heard in this way, outside the voices of the characters they have placed on stage. The interviews were recorded face-to-face, and in each conversation I have sought to ration my own voice, delimiting my questioning in order to give primacy to the answers. I have also sought, through minimum editing, to retain the characteristic tones and emphases of the dramatists themselves.

They speak honestly, often sharply, about matters that concern them as both artists and people living ordinary lives in society. One, when asked to describe the state of Welsh theatre at the turn of the millennium, gave a one-word answer – 'Strangulated'. That is certainly not a word that could be applied to the voices and opinions in this volume. Indeed, it would be interesting to know whether the Boyden Report (2004) on English-medium theatre in Wales would have had a different emphasis had Peter Boyden had access to the informed but ununiformed opinions and descriptions registered in this volume. Also, would Joyce Macmillan, theatre critic of *The Scotsman*, have come to a different conclusion about the desirability of establishing a National Theatre for Wales had she had access to all the viewpoints contained here?

There is, for example, no consensus in *Now You're Talking* on the question of establishing a National Theatre, but the arguments for and against are made with equal conviction. More important still, these are the informed arguments, not of visiting luminaries and hired consultants, but of artists who know their Wales, and are therefore in a way to understanding Wales and, in its theatre history, its aspirations and possibilities. The interviews provide multiple perspectives on the Welsh theatre scene over the last two decades, from inside particular theatre crafts that are what make such perspectives possible in the first place. Amongst the many issues raised are the 'poor cousin' status of theatre in Wales ('Taffy knows his theatre better than he knows his plays'), the sorry state of theatre reviewing ('the low level of criticism here in Wales is unacceptable'), the enabling power of theatre ('theatre has the potential to influence the course of the nation') as against a view of the powerlessness of writers ('we can change nothing. Nothing at all'), the amateurism of Welsh culture ('Amateurism is largely what Welsh culture is about'), and the importance of new writing ('if there's no call for new writing, we may as well close our theatres and turn them into museums').

The theatre scene in Wales is examined from various perspectives: the need for 'joined-up thinking' in relationship to theatre policy in the Welsh and English language; the drama policies (or lack of them) of any national arts-funding body that survives; the dearth of opportunities for the dramatist to practise his or her craft; and the importance of Community Theatre and Young People's Theatre in Wales. These issues and others are aired all the more strikingly because in the dramatist's own voice, which naturally also brings to the fore different approaches to craft, to the

4

importance of language and experimentation in drama, to the role of those other experts who make possible the realization of a dramatist's play on the stage or on film, and to their own perceptions, as individuals, of what constitutes success or failure.

These are just a few of the topics covered or broached in *Now You're Talking*. I think the dramatists' answers throw a sharp light (they sometimes even change the lights for us) on the actual experience underlying what we often all too smoothly think of as the 'history' of the English-language theatre in Wales over the last two decades. In fact, in terms of theatre, that period has been largely unrecorded. The one thing certain is that the main staple of any reality that history has must be – I repeat the word – the actual *experience* of those who made, and continue to make, theatre possible.

I therefore hope that the volume will be taken as a salute to the talented artists who continue to work in Wales. When I asked one of the dramatists where Welsh theatre was at the turn of the millennium, he replied 'In the hands of the administrators, gatekeepers, Welsh-concept window designers (the hidden gorsedd). These are always in the forefront, it seems while the "real artists... are left down in the boiler room".' *Now You're Talking* celebrates the fact that the important and lasting voices are those of writers and artists, and that the place for the administrators, gatekeepers and Welsh-concept window designers is the boiler room.

Finally, I should like to record my gratitude to all fifteen playwrights for unfailing generosity with their time and for their friendship.

Hazel Walford Davies
Aberystwyth, November 2004

Russ Gomer in *Envy*, by Ed Thomas

Ed Thomas

Interview One
November 1994

HWD: *Over the last six years, your plays have received exhilarating reviews from theatre critics,* Y Cwmni *has won awards for nearly every year of its existence, and you yourself have been described as 'the most exciting playwright in Wales'. When did you first become interested in the theatre and in writing for the stage?*

ET: I went from school to study English at the University of Wales, Cardiff, but my interest in theatre certainly didn't start while I was there. I went to Cardiff mainly to play rugby, but I dislocated my shoulder four times, and realized in my second year that I would have to have an operation, and I decided then that I would have to find something different to do. I joined a band, couldn't sing, couldn't play, and so I started writing the lyrics. I left college, went to

France, had a bit of a breakdown and recovered by picking Golden Delicious. I learned I could get more money holding the apple in the palm of my hand, picking it by the stalk and placing it down unbruised. Then I returned to Wales, worked in my dad's butcher shop for three days, met a friend who said he was going to London, and four pints later I went with him. I stayed there for seven years. Then I started writing.

HWD: *In London you worked in fringe theatre for three years and participated in various productions – as actor, stage-manager and director. Did you find time for scripting during this period?*

ET: Yes, but the first *play* I wrote was a forty-minute piece for Made in Wales. It was called *When the River Runs Dry*, and it wasn't very good. I probably had two pages of good drama in it and the rest was dodgy – very Welsh I thought. Then I left London for Cardiff since I was acting in *Pobol y Cwm* at the time. Made in Wales took an interest in my work and I began writing another play, *The Last Order in The Hope*, but although this unfinished play was better than the first, Made in Wales in the end decided not to commission me to write a full-length play. I went off in a fit of pique probably, and wrote *House of America* which is my most successful play in terms of the number of times we've performed it and in terms of audiences. We played for two weeks in London and *House of America* won the 'Time Out/01 for London' award for 1989 for one of the best new plays. I was very proud of this because the company did the play on a budget of £26 with five actors and no pay. We played to full houses in London and in Cardiff at Chapter, and it also did very well at the Edinburgh Festival. My second full-length play, *Adar Heb Adenydd*, which I did in the Welsh language for the theatre company Dalier Sylw, did much better in Edinburgh than in Wales. Here at home, audiences found it difficult to believe that the same dramatist had written these two very different plays. *House of America* is very naturalistic, or a play

8

of heightened realism, while *Adar Heb Adenydd* is an obvious, self-conscious search for style.

HWD: *You have claimed that the failure of Welsh theatre is one of style and form, and that for far too long, writers and theatre practitioners in Wales have embraced Naturalism. Why did you, after* Adar Heb Adenydd, *decide to question the appropriateness of the naturalistic style in the creation of a new Welsh theatre?*

ET: Because I believe that Naturalism and the Welsh language are incompatible. *Pobol y Cwm* is only a boom shadow away from being an absurdist play. But of course, when I'm talking about Wales, I'm only talking about myself. My desire to be Welsh is complicated by the insecurity of being a Welshman, and the fact that we can't be that confident that Wales exists. Wales is only an idea, a desire, a sense of something. As a country it doesn't exist inasmuch as it's not a territory governed by its own people. Since Wales therefore is only an idea, it is one that anyone can claim or invent, and any person can be the author of his or her own Welshness.

In the plays I've written since *Adar Heb Adenydd* what you have is an invented Wales. Not that I think for a moment of myself as a spokesman for a nation. But I do believe that there is no longer a hundred per cent Welsh-speaking monoglot community in this country, and I'm also convinced that the reality of Welsh-speaking Wales is very much more selective than the reality of English-speaking Wales. You couldn't set a play in Ebbw Vale and write in the naturalistic style in the Welsh language because it wouldn't ring true. The style, instead of liberating the language, makes it appear ridiculous, because the premise upon which it is based is false. And so the dramatist has to be very selective. Probably the only play you could write naturalistically is one about the media in Cardiff. But then you couldn't go into a taxi in Cardiff and expect the driver to be a Welsh-speaker. And so I come back to my point that Naturalism and the Welsh language are incompatible. Since there isn't a one hundred per cent Welsh community Realism becomes something of an absurdist concept, and because of that, the Welsh-language play *Adar Heb Adenydd* became an absurdist play. Every time I tried to write in the same style as *House of America* I failed, because the premise wouldn't hold. I come back to my belief that Wales is an invented country because in reality it doesn't exist.

HWD: *Doesn't this sound a little too fluid? Every construct that purports to be that of a community is a personal one to* some *degree, obviously, but I would have thought that writing as if it was* totally *personal flirts with the danger of giving your Welsh audience too much disbelief to suspend. Doesn't your dogmatic emphasis on the non-existence of Wales run the danger of alienating your audience through sheer disagreement?*

ET: If people disagree with what I say, that's fine by me. Maybe my sense of my own country isn't as secure as theirs. Although my parents speak Welsh, and I myself am a Welsh-speaker, Cwmgiedd in the Swansea Valley where I grew up wasn't particularly Welsh, and in the last ten years what little Welshness was there has vanished, and I'm not talking only about the Welsh language, but about the whole tone and tempo of the place. It feels like a bypass town in a bypass country. If people want to watch *Pobol y Cwm* and believe that it's real, then so be it. It's just that I don't believe in its reality. But if their suspension of disbelief extends to the absurd, then it's their business.

HWD: *But isn't your own use of the theme of the American Dream in* House of America, *for example, itself the use of a construct whose very nature is to contradict reality springing indeed from dichotomy, from the feeling that this pluralistic reality won't do, that it abandons too easily an inherited single identity? So why did you choose to employ the American Dream as an idea?*

ET: Because I envied it, probably. I envy America for its space and the fact that dramatists like Sam Shepard have inherited a culture which they can reject and attack. Arthur Miller, David Mamet and Sam Shepard can look at the American Dream, dismantle it and create another mythology, and so the American Dream contains within itself numerous mythologies. America also has the immense advantage that the whole world hears about it, and that it is *the* land of the 'Go West' mythology. If you're Welsh you have no mythology. Furthermore, outside its confines, very few people know about Wales. It's no accident that when Ian Woosnam won the American Masters in golf, he was asked in which part of Scotland Wales was situated. I find that shameful and embarrassing, and it hurts me more than I like.

And so I envy America, and I envy the fact that it has a blueprint on popular culture, popular music and film. American dramatists can play around with iconography. When I was looking for heroes, I realized that I'd inherited a batch which could be looked at subjectively as heroes, but not as a whole iconography, unless of course, you're very protected, nationalistic or patriotic. But you couldn't use the heroes I'd inherited as a way of going from the particular to the general. And so in *House of America* the particular was a family in a bypass town; next to them was the hugeness of the American Dream, and the family was made sexy by their pursuit of a dream. They are dreamers, but beautiful dreamers, and the play shows that without the network of a mythology, which for Wales needs to be a modern one, all things fall apart.

HWD: House of America, Flowers of the Dead Red Sea *and* East From the Gantry *form a trilogy and each one explores the experience of living on the edge, the pain of cultural dislocation and the shame of Wales's invisibility. Do you think of modern Wales in terms of defeat and invisibility?*

ET: I very much agree with Gwyn Alf Williams's view of the history of South Wales. He has spoken eloquently of its history as one of rupture and reinvention rather than one of old Celtic myths and legends. People in the Valleys lost the language two or three generations ago. Their desire to retain their Welshness is a credit to the resilience of an idea, yet it is an idea that is constantly being reinvented. I believe that the Welsh are paralysed by a lack of self-esteem and lack of confidence. The way we live our culture doesn't mean anything to anyone else, and moreover, we've never seen that culture reflected back at us. We've never seen in the last thirty years an English-language film made in Wales on a big 35 millimetre screen with a Welsh hero and heroine in the centre of the frame. Wales has no English-language soap opera which can transport itself outside Wales, it hasn't got a sitcom, it hasn't a fifty-minute drama, it hasn't got anything. All we have here in Wales are failures and defeats. If everybody grows up thinking we're no good, then that breeds a massive lack of self-confidence and we'll never have our culture reflected back.

HWD: *You're talking here of course about the media and theatre. What about literature? Don't Raymond Williams's or Emyr Humphreys's novels, for example, contradict your point about Wales not getting its own reflection back from works with currency beyond the border? And of course behind Williams and Humphreys lies the older first wave of more deeply Anglo-Welsh twentieth-century prose writers, Gwyn Thomas and Glyn Jones for example. Anglo-Welsh poetry is perhaps an even stronger suit with which to come back at you, even if we symbolize it only with the amazing 'external' currency of the two Thomases, Dylan and R S.*

ET: I know that a few Welsh poets writing in English have that confidence and currency, maybe because as a nation we have more confidence in the fact that Taffy knows his poetry better than that he knows his plays. Theatre hasn't got a rooted tradition in Wales; it's not central to the cultural life. When dramatists started writing for the theatre in Wales what they did was '*efelychu yn slafaidd*', that is they 'slavishly imitated' English and European styles and traditions. Welsh theatre is a theatre of adoption. The result is that we haven't got a style that characterises our theatre, and I very much doubt whether such a style is possible in this postmodernist age. But theatre in Wales could be a powerful forum for language and ideas, as well as a place for spectacle and the physical.

Theatre, however, is a difficult medium for the writer. In the English language the more successful writers leave Wales. And then theatre, especially Welsh theatre, is not the sexiest animal in the world. I very rarely go. I'd love to be dragged by my hair to see something in the theatre that's really going to blow my head off, especially if it's Welsh. But theatre here is a non-event. In America, Mamet and Shepard and Peter Handke are creating a new theatre tradition at the end of the century. But in Wales, in order to create a new tradition, and in order to sell a Welsh play in England, you would have to begin with the year zero. Very rarely does anyone show an interest in Wales. We can attack English indifference and the metro-centric approach, but some of it is our own fault because we don't protest enough, and we don't have the aptitude to make other nations interested in our work.

HWD: *Y Cwmni, however, has this year been acclaimed yet again over the border by winning the prestigious Barclays New Stages Award with a subsequent invitation to perform at the Royal Court in May 1995. Do you see this as an opportunity to convince a British audience that Wales does have a distinctive voice?*

ET: The irony is that Y Cwmni is only in existence as a company this year because we get a project grant from the Arts Council of Wales. We are in fact not a company but a rag-bag of individuals. Richard Lynch for example is Richard Lynch Inc and has his own career to fashion. For the last two years, the company has been funded and it has a full-time administrator – full stop. But I'm not interested in lambasting the Arts Council for lack of funding, because it, too, is only a player in the game. The Arts Council cannot change the lack of desire in Welsh cities, towns and villages to see and experiment with new forms. But the project grant we've received this year is very much appreciated because it enables us to put a new play together. The prospect of touring in Wales to half-empty houses isn't the first thing to stimulate you to get out of bed in the morning. But winning the Arts Council of Wales funding and the Barclays New Stages Award provided the company with a platform. This time if we can't cut it in Wales, and if the Royal Court audiences don't think we're good, then we'll pack it up and finish. And so I'm motivated to get together the body of actors I've always worked well with and we'll put the play together with dynamism and energy – and, yes, we do hope we'll convey *Y Cwmni's* distinctive voice.

HWD: *Can you tell me something about your new play?*

ET: It's called *A Song from a Forgotten City* and I've nearly finished it. It's about people who are well aware that they live in a forgotten city in a forgotten country. They're homeless, but they imagine a city, they imagine a landscape, and they nearly succeed in creating it before they destroy themselves. The idea is that these people live in fiction, in story-land, because that is the only bit of Wales they can imagine. Everything else has been wrecked, raped, damaged, destroyed, so their only sense of themselves is romantic. Their life is desperate but the idea is that they become poets by not even knowing they are.

HWD: *Your characters in* A Song From a Forgotten City *live in story-land and you've been quoted as saying that you yourself live in myth. What is the nature of this myth?*

ET: It is true that the only reality for me is the reality of myth. The only thing I see in Wales is defeat, and I personally find defeat difficult to live with. I have therefore constructed my own Wales in order to convince myself that I and the culture and the city in which I live have any value, because I know only too well that outside Wales we don't feature on any map.

HWD: *Sam Shepard whose work I know you greatly admire confessed that he had 'American scars' on his brain, but he admitted that it was only when he came to live in England that he found out what it really meant to be an American. Did 'exile' at any time provide you with a sense of identity?*

ET: Yes indeed. In London I realized how invisible the Welsh really were. In London you could be Scots, Irish, Jamaican, Asian – anything in the street – but if you were Welsh you didn't exist. And nearly every Welsh person I knew in London had changed his or her accent in some way. Every other culture had street currency, but for the Welsh to mean anything they had to disappear into Britishness. In England the Scots and the Irish hold on to their identities more tenaciously than the Welsh. I'd like to think that if my plays are any good at all, they will breed a generation of young people who will want to throw stones at us, a generation with more savvy and greater confidence in their Welshness.

HWD: *In your article 'Wales and a Theatre of Invention', published by* The Guardian *to mark the 'Whose Nation, Whose Theatre?' conference at* The Tramway *in 1991, you mention that the prerequisite for a new Welsh theatre of invention is the will and desire to create it. Three years later, are you convinced that the will and desire exist here in Wales?*

ET: We are in danger in this country of seeing theatre as a mere preparation or platform for film or television. Most Welsh theatre is small-town theatre with small stages and small audiences. Theatre here is a mere stepping-stone, whereas in London the stage can still be attractive to major actors because of the special dynamics it offers a performer, and because of the prestige which theatre there still offers. In Wales, on the other hand, especially in the Welsh language, theatre is what you do when you're 'resting', or when you can't get a good role in film or television.

Money of course is a major contributory factor. We've all learned an enormous amount from the cross-fertilization of theatre, film and television because of the existence of S4C, but the demands of television are voracious. Television isn't interested in experimentation. It goes for formula, because formula makes a great deal of money. It certainly makes a lot of money for people in suits. You've got to be very clever when writing for television if you want to slip something into the script which has the arrogance to call itself art. The men in suits don't want that on television. Film is different, but film is expensive, and the British film industry is on its knees. In Wales all we've got is what S4C puts into it, although *Hedd Wyn* and *Gadael Lenin* have done remarkably well to compete internationally. But we also need an English-language film culture. Film isn't as text-driven as theatre. I've adapted *House of America* as a screen play, and I hope the BBC and British Screen will do it at the beginning of next year.

HWD: *Yours is very much a text-based theatre. To what degree is that text negotiable during rehearsals and beyond?*

ET: If the casting process works well and you trust your actors, then there's something wrong if they don't feel comfortable with a line. I am constantly aware that without actors and without a stage, plays are dramas of possibilities rather than dramas of certainties. For me actors are collaborators, and my trust in the actors I've worked with has allowed me to experiment with form and style in the

English language. In writing I start with the word, and that word is joined to another and makes a sentence which makes the idea which makes the play. Some dramatists, however, start the other way round because they want to talk 'about' something. They become issue-led, and the drama lies in the way that the issue is split into an argument and a counter-argument and then into a synthesis. I've always looked at that construction as something I'm not particularly good at or interested in. I deal, as I said earlier, with an invented landscape, and then it has to be invented in terms of its language and its form. The form is sometimes difficult, but I think the awkward form sometimes, particularly in the first version of *Flowers of the Dead Red Sea*, threw up more truths than I could explain. The flaw sometimes, the accident, is more interesting than the well-made construct.

Of course any experiment with language, form and style can lead to black holes, and the dramatist has to collaborate with the actors and designers who are sophisticated in the possibilities of theatre. If it's obvious that the shape the dramatist envisaged is not working, the team can then find ways of re-engineering it into a complete whole. And in my case, since the plays are usually written in the space of two or three months and then performed immediately, the published text, which comes much later, is generally the third or fourth draft of the play. There's a version of *East from the Gantry* which appears in Methuen which is not the version we toured earlier this year. The new version appears in the Seren text and I'm not sure which one I prefer. *Flowers of the Dead Red Sea* started as a six-hander, but the printed text will be a two-hander. There will be changes too in the printed version of *Adar Heb Adenydd* and *The Myth of Michael Roderick*.

HWD: *You're Welsh-speaking and yet* Adar Heb Adenydd *is the only Welsh-language play you've written. Is this a reflection of how more comfortable you feel in English in terms of writing for the theatre?*

ET: I've had more opportunities to write in English. I'm not a poet like Saunders Lewis and Siôn Eirian. I think Saunders Lewis is a great poet primarily, not a great dramatist. Dramatists like Siôn Eirian and Gareth Miles have a richness of language in Welsh that I don't possess. They have a rooted sense of themselves which makes them use the Welsh language eloquently. I could never be a Welsh poet, yet I would argue that my English-language plays are more poetic than realistic. I'm a dramatic poet if you like, but my Welsh is too limiting to convey what I want to say. When we took *Adar Heb Adenydd* to Edinburgh the use of the Welsh language became a political statement in its own right, and it looked and felt wrong. I'm very interested in putting the Welsh language into the right vehicles.

I'm interested in writing a film, set in a city where Welsh is spoken as if the English language didn't exist. But it would be a very selective city, a 'phantasyland' city. But that wouldn't make it anything like Phantasy Island – it would be more *Twin Peaks* than Max Boyce. When I came to write *The Myth of Michael Roderick*, the English adaptation of *Adar Heb Adenydd*, I found the Welsh language too fragile to translate directly. And at the time I thought *The Myth* needed to be far more physical and spectacular than *Adar Heb Adenydd*. As a result the English version became more outrageous, too outrageous for some people, but I thought it was an adaptation of the same spirit that characterised the Welsh play.

HWD: *Several critics have written about your employment of the 'chaos theory'. What are the implications of this term for the plays themselves, as you see them?*

ET: I really like the fact that potassium in water does not always burst into lilac flame and that the 'controlled experiment' is not always secure, and that seems to be a convenient way to look at drama. Rules are there to be broken, but not broken willy-nilly to shock. It's easy to shock by having sex on the stage or masturbating in the first five minutes. But no dramatist is going to spend four months constructing language to shock. The chaos theory is convenient to me because everything seems to be that way. I myself am confused. I've never written a play where I know at the beginning exactly what I'm going to write about. I discover that through the process of writing, and in the process of rewriting I present the ideas in a more consistent way. And then the shape follows. Because butterfly wings in Abercwmboi can cause a whirlwind in Colorado – sometimes, not always – then it gives you more confidence in the fact that things are there to be played with. My imagination is eclectic but I'm also stubborn, and part of the process of writing involves sifting through six hundred pages based around a theme which seems to be more prevalent than anything else in the work. For example, when I started *A Song from a Forgotten City*, all I knew was that it was to be set in a city and how many characters it needed. How it would look would come out through the language. I've started it about forty times, but it all breaks down after thirty pages. To get into eighty pages is what I'm doing at the moment and I find it very difficult, because there are all kinds of things which are contradictory. When I was writing I didn't know whether my characters were male or female. The way I write is chaotic, but I look at it as a way of constructing one dramatic moment next to another in exactly the same way as you write one sentence after another.

I come back to the point that for me the use of language is the liberator and not the plot. The theme is inherent in the language and repeated in the motifs and in the style that characters and actors choose for that language. I'm pleased with *House of America*, but I'm not pleased with its language. Its only interest is what happens next. That's nothing to be embarrassed about, but I'm infinitely more interested in a play when language dictates in a way that is not the everyday.

And that language can be interpreted by the audience, by each individual member, and not by a collective, cajoled by the dramatist into thinking one thing and one thing only. I'm quite happy for an audience to say that a play of mine is crap, but I also like to think that perhaps there are people in the audience who are interested enough to want to take away an interpretation and who are prepared to wrestle with language. That wrestling process is for me more dynamic than saying one little thing that's as clear as a bell to a thousand people. That of course is not to say that my themes are difficult, but they collide accidentally with other themes, and they go off in different directions. I like Sam Shepard because I think some of the plays are impossible and inexplicable. Why does the mother show up right at the end of *True West*? What does she do? A lot of script editors for television would say, 'Out with her, she fulfils no useful purpose at all.' I often get the same criticism, and some of it is justified, but more often the shape of the play which emerges through the process of writing, angular and random though it may be, carries its own meaning. I'm not interested in pre-plotting a play and writing it out in neat three-act structures.

HWD: *To what degree, then, can you rely on being able to create a taste by which your plays are to be enjoyed? Are you conscious of creating an audience in Wales?*

ET: Is there a Welsh audience? Is there a theatrical community in Wales? I don't know what it is any more. There is no Welsh audience, only a rag-bag of individuals, some bigoted, some enlightened, and others who just want a good night out. I am well aware of where my plays will fit in and what kind of audience will be attracted to them, and then how, as a company, we have to pitch them. This makes for a fairly narrow marketing band, but I believe with Howard Barker that you should educate an audience. I find it difficult to think in terms of an 'audience', because there was a time when the only people who came to my plays were friends and friends of friends. What pleases me now is that the people who come to see my work, particularly in Cardiff, are strangers.

If an audience is created in Cardiff and proves to places like the Sherman theatre and Chapter centre that there is enthusiasm for new writing, then my work will have served its purpose; and if there is a hunger then for that kind of theatre, it might encourage other playwrights to go off and write. The audience then might look at a glass half-full and not half-empty. However, I believe that most people still want plays they can easily understand. But I prefer epiphany to comprehension. That's not to say that I see my plays as epiphanies. Sometimes they're very ugly and they don't follow a pattern of cause and effect. I don't believe in cause and effect – nothing is organized. But what I do believe in is that a work of art has to have the possibility to inspire people to create a new landscape, but of course theatre alone cannot do that.

HWD: *Theatre alone can't inspire people but is your aim, nevertheless, to inspire – not only people, but a people?*

ET: If in the next ten years Wales were to produce three major novels, five acclaimed English-language films, six plays and superb work by two visual artists, and if all these became known throughout Britain and Europe, then you could really say that the total of all these things would have invented a landscape for a new Welsh culture. A new Welsh mythology cannot be created by one artist alone, but by the accident of all artists coming at it from different directions and being perceived and digested by a world that thinks that this culture is worth something. I want to see a Wales at ease with itself and a people with confidence in their own worth and in their own identity. At the moment, our silence is embarrassing.

Interview Two
July 1997

HWD: *You and I drove last night from the airport in Columbus, to the University of Rio Grande, Ohio.[1] En route we passed houses that were mirror images of the one constructed for the film* House of America. *Today, however, here in Gallipolis, within a stone's throw of the spot where the Welsh immigrants from Ceredigion disembarked at the beginning of the last century, we see nothing that kindles the imagination or reinforces the myth of America as the land of the Dream. As Boyo says to Sid in* House of America, *'Not much of a dream then is it?'*

ET: Too right. This is my first visit to rural Ohio, and after our bizarre journey from Columbus down here, the line between fiction and reality is really blurred. We had a burger and French fries last night in a diner where the table-mats illustrated Jesus on the Cross and a tableaux of praying hands. Well after midnight, we arrived at Gallipolis to find that there was no room for you at the inn [The Holiday Inn, Gallipolis]. And then, this morning I went on a journey that made me think I was really existing in a dream-world. On the banks of the Ohio here in Gallipolis there's a notice indicating 'Beach Front'. That's a joke. In Europe, or indeed, even in Wales, such a magnificent riverfront would boast a pub, a restaurant, a viewing area, but all you see on this 'beach front' is a convoy of lorries delivering iron or steel bolts to large factories. Along the front, too, is a ribbon of cheap diners and dime stores. I despise the 'Happy Shopper' mentality of America. American functionalism is the exact opposite of my aesthetic concerning fiction and the imagination. Here in Gallipolis the banks of the Ohio are full of elongated trucks – penis extensions to the male machismo. They're functional. America itself has a functionalism, a concreteness that has a reality overload.

Take this town. Gallipolis has a population of 30,000, but it hasn't a restaurant worth the name. All you have is a strip of fast-food shops, cheap mini-malls, a gun-store and economy motels. These Americans live in bulk. On my hotel television this morning the list of the ten American best-sellers were as follows: Pamper nappies, peptic indigestion tablets, Scotowels, acid tablets, another brand of nappies, acid tablets again, yet another brand of acid tablets, the fifth brand of acid tablets, nappies again, the sixth brand of acid tablets. Americans seem to be living on indigestion tablets, and it seems to me, from the television advertisements, that all their problems can be solved by acid tablets and nappies. But the way of life here has no hips, no romance, no imagination, no possibilities. It's functional and false. Language doesn't mean anything over here. I don't think people listen when others say, 'Have a nice day.' I just heard you say 'Thank you' to the woman who filled your coffee cup and told you to have a nice day. I myself felt like saying 'Fuck off' or 'Wash my socks'. But of course the answer would be 'Pardon sir? Have a *really* nice day.' Here in Wales we are far more impolite than the Americans, but when we are polite, we mean what we say.

HWD: *The Dream then is certainly dead and buried?*

ET: For me it's a fiction. But look around us. Everywhere in this town we see the American flag flying, which means it's very much alive here. And the American Dream is still a hugely concrete exportable myth. But the idea of the Dream of freedom and equality is wrapped in crass commercialism. The Dream is still a global phenomenon and America is eminently successful at exporting crap all over the world – Mickey Mouse, Macdonald and KFC. I am both attracted and repelled by America. American dramatists are lucky in having an exportable mythology. Take Sam Shepard, for instance. He can go to a caravan in the Midwest and write what appears to be a pretty domestic play, but somehow its branches can reach out, and it becomes a dramatic counter-argument to the American Dream. A dramatist writing in Wales has no global myths, although we do have myths and stories that sustain us at home. But, unlike Sam Shepard, we have no *exportable* myths. And so a dramatist who works from a country without global myths has to work with primary colours. Either you create a myth and export it, or you work in pastel shades which nobody can relate to or understand. What people want to buy are British myths. When we as a Company travel abroad, what our audiences expect is a British kind of theatre, but we seek to define our theatre as Welsh theatre.

HWD: *You're due to lecture tomorrow to a large group of Celtic scholars, some from Wales but most of them from America. No doubt you'll tell the audience that Wales has no exportable myths. Do you think they'll agree with you?*

ET: No. But you'd have the same problem with any group of exiles. The Conference is entitled 'Visions of Wales', and I'm aware before I give the lecture, that the American vision of Wales is a million miles away from what real Wales is like in the 1990s. I'm not interested in smashing their vision, but what I'd like to emphasise tomorrow is that the Wales of the future – and I hope Wales has a future – will be an eclectic, modern European society, where 'Britain' has become an anachronism. In the Wales of the future the coalmines will have disappeared, our ability to compete internationally on the rugby field may or may not exist, the Eisteddfod may or may not exist, but I hope that the image of Wales that the Welsh Tourist Board currently exports will have disappeared for ever. Rivers, mountains, the Druids, the Mabinogion and the Gymanfa Ganu do not represent my Wales. I want a Wales at ease with itself and rejoicing in its natural eclecticism. I don't want to see a Wales locked in a debate about Welsh and English. I want a multicultural Wales with a myriad of sustainable myths. The old Wales is a country without an architecture, without a symbol such as an opera house. The new Wales has to be fast, maverick and imaginative, and innovative and inventive in its aim to be a small, interesting country within an European context, a country where the albatross of Britain has finally fallen from its neck. It certainly has fallen from my neck. I like England, but not Britain.

But the important thing for me is to see a grown-up Wales, which is self-defined and not stereotypical. It's healthy to have self-defined myths. I find that our culture is sometimes very servile to stereotypes, and my argument is that we have to have the confidence to construct our own sense of who we are. Wales has never had a self-conscious Modernist or Postmodernist age which means that Welsh people can wear flowers, a red beach jumper, have spiky hair, listen to Margaret Williams and hymns and drop acid all at the same time without any contradictions. Wales is all inside-out, back-to-front and postmodern without even knowing it. Take this as an example. Ritchie James from Manic Street Preachers one day went whistling along Pontypool High Street and then his car was discovered abandoned on the Severn Bridge. Do you know that some people in America think that Ritchie James is a mythical figure? Pontypool High Street then becomes like James Morris's grave in Paris or the Chelsea Hotel in New York where Dylan Thomas stayed. It's wonderful seeing Americans walking Pontypool High Street looking for the grave of Ritchie James. So you don't have to have your 'hero' in the Chelsea Hotel in New York any more. You can find him in Kwik Save in Ponty, asphyxiated auto-erotically!

HWD: *Early on in your career, however, you went to America for your mythology. In* House of America *Sid says, 'I wish I'd been born someone else, somewhere else.' For you, America was that 'somewhere else'.*

25

ET: I grew up wanting to be someone else and it seemed to me that there was a possibility of being that someone else in America. America was hip and Wales was the opposite of that. Most of the people I went to school with wanted to clear off out of Wales because Wales had no contemporary mythology. I became Jack Kerouac for a short period of time and I ran a fringe theatre in Fulham. I shared a flat and a girl-friend with an American. He was a bisexual and I was heterosexual and she was, well, disappointed. In our fiction he was Neal Cassady because he didn't have an education, and I was Jack, because I had graduated from the University of Wales, Cardiff. We lived a fantasy life. He wrote sub-Neal Cassady poems and I wrote sub-Jack Kerouac poems and Roger McGough liked them. During a read-out I realised I wasn't Jack Kerouak and I saw clearly that the poems were crap. I stopped playing the Kerouac game there and then.

I realised also how false the larger mythology of the American Dream was. If Russia had been 'cool' at the time I wrote *House of America*, I could have written about the 'Russian Dream'. But in 1989 the concept of the American Dream was in the ascendant – baseball hats were being worn back-to-front, bowling alleys, Kentucky Fried Chicken, Macdonalds – all these were being peddled over here, and the multiplex cinemas, based on American models, gave us the impression that America wasn't over there but all around. The truth is that I have a love-hate relationship with America. My concern is that it exports a kind of monoglot culture, a dangerous simplicity, a facile world which, as an European, I find counterproductive. I was twenty-seven when I wrote *House of America*. Now I'm looking for a different kind of theatre.

HWD: *Can you describe your kind of theatre?*

ET: I've often said that I write dramas of possibilities, inasmuch as my plays don't begin from a certainty. To be

Welsh at the end of the Twentieth Century you need to have imagination. The one thing you need on your birth certificate is the word 'imagination'. I call my plays 'dramas of possibilities' because I, as much as any other person, am searching for a path, for meaning. My job as fiction-maker is to make up fictions because good fictions tell good truths. Sometimes, to kick off a play, I have only a landscape, not a particular theme. But I'd probably argue that all my plays have the same theme, and I probably will have to put up with that theme for the rest of my career. However, I don't think that's necessarily a bad thing since variations on a particular theme can be interesting.

HWD: *What, then, is that particular theme?*

ET: I suppose my main aim is to try to discover what mythology means in contemporary society and especially in contemporary Welsh society. I'm happy to be a Welsh writer, but there has to be universality as well. I'm content to work from a small area in South Wales as long as my plays have relevance to, say, Barcelona or to Ohio where we're having this conversation. It gives me considerable confidence that people choose to translate my plays into other languages, although no one to date has done a translation into Welsh of *House of America*.[2] The British Council don't pay for my plays to be translated so I'm delighted that people from different cultures in France, Germany, Spain and Montreal choose to translate my plays when they have a wide range of international plays from which to choose. And when they do translate it they place it within a Welsh context. They don't adapt it to a Catalan or Quebec context. So the central theme, the central metaphor of my plays means something to them; the themes therefore are universal and not locked into a parochial view of the world.

But on the question of 'theme' I'd have to add that I'm pretty obsessed in my plays with absent fathers. I can't analyse that. Playwrights aren't the best people to deconstruct and describe the nature of their plays.

HWD: *Why do the Catalans, although they like* House of America, *prefer* East from the Gantry?

ET: *House of America*, as I've often said, felt for a time like yet another albatross around my neck. I'd written one good play in *House*, but the subsequent ones were not as good, but they were different. *House of America* is easy to get your head around since it's heightened naturalism, but the plays I wrote subsequently don't follow the same strong narrative. Rather, they experiment with form and style. The Catalans, although they liked *House of America*, preferred *East from the Gantry* because of its shape and the gaps it had. What I mean by 'gaps' is that in my theory of 'drama of possibility', they found more possibilities of fitting their own Catalan version into my text. In *House of America*, because the metaphor and narrative are so strong, you take it or leave it, so there's less room for manoeuvre. When I work with Y Cwmni, now Fiction Factory, the plays serve me and we work within our own interpretation. When other people and nations do the play they are free to see other possibilities within the text. It pleased me that the Catalans chose to do *East from the Gantry* rather than *House of America*. That albatross has also finally dropped from my neck.

House of America is the least translated work of all my plays, and the French translation, to be performed in Montreal this summer, will be the first translation of *House of America*. To come back to your question, I think the Catalans relate to the themes of my plays – the theme of shifting identity, of how to be a small but significant voice in a changing Europe and a changing world, and maybe, how to reclaim and reconstruct the past and make it your own, and also how to create an attitude and a confidence. I'd probably argue that all my plays have the same theme and that I probably will have to put up with that theme for the rest of my career, but I don't think that's necessarily a bad thing. The important thing is to have variations on the theme.

HWD: *You're clearly not prescriptive about the way your plays should be produced. What is it, then, that makes your plays 'plastic' or 'dramas of possibilities'?*

ET: Part of the explanation is that the process of writing plays is a journey of discovery for me. When I begin writing I have no idea what I want to write. Initially, I just write three to four hundred pages of dialogue without male or female characters. The characters, then, are sexless and stateless. What I have are words and rhythms and at least two hundred pages have to be scrapped. I might start with a landscape. Often that's enough of a kick-off. And I like having deadlines. But even after writing the three hundred pages I don't know exactly where I'm going. I construct a narrative out of those pages and after that I do a careful re-write. It's very rarely that I'll use more than probably a page of complete dialogue from the initial pages.

HWD: *Indeed, there's no such thing as a 'final re-write' in your case. The plays are continually updated.*

ET: Yes, I'll be updating *House of America* for the 1997 Autumn tour and, who knows, I may revise it even during the tour. *Flowers of the Dead Red Sea* started with six characters and that's how we did it when it opened in The Tramway, Glasgow. There was a whole sequence about linking art and killing, but I saw that the strength of the play was the landscape and the two slaughtermen. In the original play I had an artist who was the lover of one, or possibly of both, of the slaughtermen. But I didn't think that the scenes with the artist worked. So when I directed and adapted it to a radio version, I had two men and a woman. The woman was the conscience, the chorus. When it came to publishing the play I felt that what I was really after were the two slaughtermen. And they weren't really two slaughtermen. It was a much stronger metaphor than that. *Flowers* could be set anywhere because it's about story-telling, memory. What I was conscious of doing was developing a dialogue which takes us beyond the rhetoric of 'Ry'n ni yma o hyd' (We are still here). I wanted to say that Welsh identity is as fragile as Tom Jones's dicky-bow. I also wanted to convey that we were living in a world we don't comprehend and I wished to explore the idea of being good as opposed to being bad. Mock and Joe could be two men in hell or two men in heaven. When we staged *Flowers* in The Tramway, it was absolutely slated by the Scottish critics. We then took it to London and back to Glasgow again. The second time the play was transformed.

HWD: *What did the critics have to say about* Flowers *the first time round in Glasgow?*

ET: Rough, tough, brutal, violent, nasty – they used all those adjectives. They also stated, 'it grapples with the guts of theatre'. I have no idea what that means. *Flowers* isn't a well-made play. I think my plays are well-made from another point of view. I don't like 'well-made' plays that have an argument and a counter-argument and a message relayed to a sheep-like audience. I find that very problematic. I like layered plays that suggest possibilities, plays that are open to different interpretations from different audiences and cultures. For example, *Flowers* was performed at the Castle Theatre, Aberystwyth last year and two women played Mock and Joe. I'm really pleased when somebody produces an unexpected and fresh version of my play. In Barcelona, Madrid and Montreal people do my plays in different ways. They are all equally valid. It means that my plays can be about different things to different cultures while still maintaining a coherent flow. I hope there's something in the text of the play that liberates the imagination.

My job as a writer is to write about the world I know, and if the themes and metaphors become universal, that's for someone else to decide. In some productions of *House of America*, for example, the names I gave the characters are retained. In Barcelona they kept the Welsh names and Welsh places even though the play was in Catalan. In the Montreal production they changed the names to Jean Claude, Alvarez, Maria and Maman; they appropriated the play to their culture. In Quebec they think *House* is the play that Quebec never wrote because they're surrounded by North America, and the American Dream is far more pertinent to them than it is to us. They thought it very strange that a Celtic country across the Atlantic should be obsessed with the American Dream. Small nations understand the themes of *House of America*, they understand the invisibility, they understand what a huge culture like the American one can do to small cultures and nations. But if, during performances in various countries, the play loses its Welshness, it probably gains in some other way. I distrust art that tells you what to think. If my plays are only the assertion of my point of view, then they cannot be good plays. I, as dramatist, am a flawed man and I'm as confused by the world as any watcher of my plays. I am a fiction-maker and I don't claim to be prescriptive. My job is to be imaginative, to make things up. Maybe the way I work has been conditioned by the fact that I was interested first of all, not in the character, but in the actor.

HWD: *In writing your plays are you thinking of particular actors?*

ET: Yes, maybe. It has something to do with the way Y Cwmni was established. We were all unemployed, and the first play we did was *House of America*. I was lucky enough to have a body of actors who were committed to my way of looking at things and who wanted to do my plays.

In collaboration with people like Russell Gomer and Richard Lynch I learned certain theatrical possibilities. They never treated my text as if it were a 'new play' or 'new work'. There's nothing more off-putting than 'New Writing'. It means, 'Don't go to see that play, it will be crap.' Members of Y Cwmni collaborated to solve acting and directing problems, and we didn't cut the text willy-nilly. But we weren't overprotective of the text, either. The main thing was that we never sat down and discussed 'the meaning of the play' or the policy of 'how can we work together?' Indeed, when we started doing workshops three or four years ago we felt quite nervous and diffident about it because we were trying to respond to people who were asking us to 'describe our process.' But we didn't have a process, except the one that declared, 'I'll throw it, you catch it.' My process has got to have hips. I'm the scrum-half, and I like actors with hips. By that I mean that I like actors who can glide through defences with an ease. My job as director is to release that 'ease'.

What pleases me is that, in the plays I've written, the actors have been free to see that there are enough clues in the text to construct the characters that they want to enact on stage. That, of course, is often based on the kind of people the actors are. So, inevitably, there's a Richard Lynch part and a Russell Gomer part. I hope that in my plays there's a gap for the actors to take on board the possibilities of the play, and to feel that they're expressing their own words, rather than using their acting skills as a vehicle for expressing Edward Thomas's world-view. My world-view is as confused as anybody else's. Richard Lynch and Russell Gomer have used their own voices in constructing characters.

HWD: *Russell and Richard are now working for the RSC, and you will have to work with new actors. Is your process of writing going to change?*

ET: Not radically, but I will of course have to work with new actors. I've just had a play accepted for the Royal Court. I have ten actors, and when we did the reading in the Duke of York I deliberately chose people I hadn't worked with before. I chose Philip Madoc, Jason Hughes, Simon Harris, Michael Sheen. We did a very quick private reading in the morning and we had only an hour and a half to discuss the plans for the 'official' reading in the afternoon. The afternoon reading was terrific and Stephen Daldry thought it was the most exciting reading he'd heard for two or three years. I'm thankful the actors got the spirit of the play. Working with new people therefore will be a welcome challenge. We all have to grow up and move on.

HWD: *In moving on you've reinvented your company. It is now Fiction Factory.*

ET: In 1989 we were called The Company. Then we changed our name to Y Cwmni, because we were a Welsh company. But because the scale of our work was increasing, and because on our travels to Germany, Australia and England, and indeed within Wales, people couldn't pronounce 'Y Cwmni', we had to re-think. Anyway, what did the name mean? 'Fiction Factory' seemed to be an umbrella name for all our work. If you place the emphasis on 'factory' it appears as if we churn things out willy-nilly and make nuts and bolts. The word 'fiction' changes all that. We've often re-invented the focus of the company, and changing its name was actually much easier than I thought it would be.

HWD: *Tell me about the play that has just been accepted by the Royal Court.*

ET: At the moment it's called *The Aces of Gaerlishe* or '*Where do you go when you drive a blue-tinted glass Marina 1800cc into the heart of Saturday Night?*' Or the title might be *Gas Station Angel*.

I'll probably stick to the third title. It's probably the closest thing to a straight narrative I've written since *House of America*. It's a kaleidoscopic road journey between a man whose house has fallen into the sea and a dancer who has missing brothers. It's a strong story, the language is heightened and it's got a voice-over. In fact the whole play is heightened. I like the absurd. All you have to do to see absurdity is to look out of the window. But I wouldn't define myself as an absurdist writer in the Ionesco sense. What I like about the absurdist tradition is its enquiry about the world, between order and chaos. In art, we're not recording reality, we as dramatists are not journalists discussing the issue of unemployment in the South Wales valleys or the use of heroin or ecstasy in Cardiff or London. As dramatists we don't discuss issue-based things. We weave fictions, reveal issues which exist only in fiction, but fictions which contain possibilities of telling certain truths or reflections about the world.

Take *Song from a Forgotten City*. If I'd put a narrative to that play I'd say it was about a lonely smack addict who lives in this city, hasn't got any confidence, but wants to become a hero, to be centre frame. The only thing he knows about the films he's seen, like the film noir, is that you start at the end and work back, so if he places himself in his own fiction, 'Man shot dead in a hotel room and discovered by bell boy', he naturally becomes a hero. The narrative interest of the play, therefore concerns itself with the question of 'How did this character get to be shot in this hotel room?' You realise at the end of the play that it's all fiction anyway. But, during the course of the play, that doesn't stop you from believing that what you are watching is something with which you can legitimately engage.

HWD: *Recently Seren published the play* Hiraeth *in a volume of selected one-act plays. Do you think* Hiraeth *could be performed without the context for which it was first written?*

ET: I certainly wouldn't be comfortable about performing it without that particular context, although the editor of the selection of the volume of one-act plays must have been of the opinion that it could stand on its own two feet. *Hiraeth/Strangers in Conversation* was an installation piece, a collaboration between myself and the artist Iwan Bala. When *Flowers* was first produced Iwan painted seven canvases for the production and in 1993 he suggested to Jenny Spencer Davies that he and I should work together. My play would be there, not to describe his paintings but to recreate imaginatively what the themes were. He'd done a lot of work in Zimbabwe and when he was there he had a dream about Wales being the mainland that he could never reach. And then, when he was in Wales, he had a dream about Zimbabwe in ruins, and again he couldn't reach it. The dream had mythic meanings.

In his work he tried to convey the sense of 'hiraeth', of never being in a place, but always longing for it. In the background you might see a canvas he had painted three years previously, and then he'd pull the glass a foot or two away from the canvas and start painting on the glass. It became something like a palimpsest. I had to write something about that gap between the canvas and the glass. The only thing I could come up with was this idea of two disembodied heads that appear above a parapet in a landscape of nothing. These heads don't know who they are. In forty-five minutes they have to make up a past for themselves and imagine a future. They have to invent on a blank canvas. They begin to talk and express fear of the landscape in which they find themselves. One of them tells a story about a trip in America and both have visions of absence and presence. In Iwan's work there were, as I say, canvases he had painted three years previously, and I therefore deliberately used characters from my previous plays *House of America* and *Flowers of the Dead Red Sea*. It was a self-conscious mélange, and I shall probably never perform it again. I directed a Welsh-language version of the play, and acted in it. We performed the play in Oriel Gallery, Cardiff and then took it to Swansea.

HWD: *You've just mentioned that you're a director and an actor as well as a playwright. Do you find that your skills as actor and director have helped your work as a dramatist?*

ET: Well, I use the term 'actor' loosely. I'm not a very good actor and I don't enjoy it. I became an actor through financial necessity. Although I'd never acted before, I was offered a job in *Pobol y Cwm* and I did it for three years. But, yes, my experience as an actor has helped in practical terms. Knowing my limitations as an actor means that I'm well aware of what's difficult about acting. Also, in order to allow me to make a living as a writer, I've been lucky enough to have had the opportunity to direct a lot of television and I've directed three films. This means that I can cross-fertilise my ideas between film, television, radio and theatre. I've done an opera with John Hardy and Music Theatre Wales, and I've worked a great deal with John since then. He scored *Double Indemnity* which we did in the Royal Court and which we'll do in the West End next year. He also created the soundtrack for *Song from a Forgotten City*. We're lucky in Wales because we can cross-fertilise between the different media without self-consciousness.

HWD: *In the case of your work, of course, you've adapted your plays for radio, television and film. Is it difficult for you to transpose a theatre piece into a film?*

ET: *House of America*, for example, has a strong narrative but we had a hell of a battle to make it acceptable as a film. I wrote the script but the director Mark Evans collaborated closely with me inasmuch as he and I worked on realising the film and defining the images. The film we both imagined became the script. Mark Evans is probably the only director

I'd trust with my work, and it would be great if we could collaborate every two or three years. Mark was probably more protective of the words of the original play than I was. We worked on the film for six years and eventually we got the money to make it. What attracted Mark to *House of America* was the metaphor that the play says more strongly than the film – the metaphor concerning the American Dream and the lack of contemporary Welsh mythology. There is in *House*, too, the idea of Welsh characters being cool dreamers. There is nothing wrong with Sid, he just selects the wrong dream. But the quality of his imagination is terrific. In the play the choice of the wrong dream becomes a tragedy. In the film, however, as soon as you put Sid Lewis on a motor-bike, the loser becomes the hero. We use the South Wales landscape in the film and Wales appears as the big little country. Wales is shot in colour and America in black and white, and America appears quite small. While complaining about Wales's lack of heroes, we have in the film created one. Wales wins by doing a double-con.

In the first production of *House of America* it was a case of 'Let's make something up before it's too late.' But my autumn production of House will be fuelled by the ideas and the thinking that were developed while making the film. The film and the play will co-run, and at the same time there will be a Galician version, a Spanish version and a French version. What puzzles me is that nobody is particularly interested in doing a Welsh version of it.[3] I'd like to do most of my plays one day in Welsh, but I'd be interested if somebody else translated some of the English texts into Welsh. In fact, one-eighth of *Aces of Gaerlishe* [*Gas Station Angel*] is in Welsh. I don't know whether the Royal Court will use sub-titles – they've never had the Welsh language on that stage before. There's another 'first' in the play. It's the first time that anybody has good heterosexual sex in a play of mine. So, being a heterosexual man, I am after seven years as a fiction maker, writing good heterosexual sex! At the end of the new play the characters re-invent a sex language in Welsh, which is very healthy I think. I've yet to meet anybody who can have exciting sex in Welsh – it's either overridden by guilt or it's completely unromantic.

HWD: *How would you define yourself – as a writer or a Welsh writer?*

ET: Oh, as a Welsh writer with international aspirations. A Welsh writer is primarily one who writes about his own square mile. For me, the idea of Wales as an imagined nation is a really interesting one. But in Wales, and certainly in Welsh-language theatre, there is still a perverse kind of naturalism. In the 1970s naturalism was big in Britain, and in Welsh-language theatre it is still the dominant factor at the end of the 1990s. And naturalism isn't the best model to express Welsh ideals, especially in the Welsh language. If you watch *EastEnders* or *Coronation Street* you can accept the premise on which they're based, you can accept that life can be like that. But I've said to you before that in *Pobol y Cwm*, the reality is so selective that it's almost like Phantasy Island.[4] If in *Pobol y Cwm* a hooker turned up to see a gynaecologist and wanted legal representation, that scene would be a brilliant absurdist scene because you couldn't identify the reality of it. It would be Theatre of the Absurd at its most brilliant, and I think that's liberating rather than confining. In Wales only about a fifth of the population speak Welsh and so the premise on which *Pobol y Cwm* is based is completely unbelievable. If you dropped the sound boom into the frame and revealed the cameras, then potentially, you've got an interesting way of showing what the real Wales is. In the Welsh-language real Wales probably exists in the Television Studio rather than in the rural areas.

It needs a master of style to liberate the Welsh language. On S4C the language is made into a laughing stock because it has no mastery of style. S4C style is borrowed and copied from elsewhere and appropriated to a Welsh context and expression that demeans the language. That offends me greatly. If you create fictions you have to know what style means in terms of culture, expression and in terms of your reality and perceived reality. Style is the most important thing. People who practise in the Welsh language need to understand what style suits the language in order to liberate it. Let's not ridicule the Welsh language with the use of naturalism. Naturalism is a joke.

HWD: *You said to me earlier that you enjoy creating pictures on the stage and that you will aim at this in your future directing ventures. Is this because you've been involved with film which is picture-driven?*

ET: The dynamic of cinema is the picture, the dynamic of the stage is still the picture, but the words have to carry more weight. I enjoy writing for the theatre because I like words, but words without a picture are meaningless. I think my directing for the stage is getting to be more cinematic and more sophisticated. I know how to construct a screen play and I know how the cuts work. You can use the same techniques in theatre and have numerous narratives going on at the same time. Many people think that *Aces of Gaerlishe* [*Gas Station Angel*] is cinematic and I'm very keen to do a cinema version of the play. The landscape, characters and narrative will be the same, but I will provide a different dynamic. Some people will call it an 'adaptation' of the play. I call it 'a pretty much full realisation of something woven around the same theme.'

Working on a film has taught me a great deal. You have to communicate ideas very clearly to fifty or sixty people and you've got to prepare carefully. It's no good going on the set at 8.00 a.m. and saying 'Oh, wouldn't it be a good idea if we had this or that prop here?' I think theatre people could learn a great deal from the rigour, the preparation and the communication that is needed to work on a film. You've also got to be pretty humble about yourself and your abilities, and you've got to find a system whereby you can creatively gloss over the weaknesses and maximise your strengths. It's much more rigorous than theatre or television.

HWD: *You have often described television as 'the bastard child'? Why?*

ET: What I mean is that film and theatre have become the forum of adventure and ideas. Television doesn't interest me that much, not because of any snob value, but because of the nature of broadcasting at the moment. It's more formulaic than it's ever been. It needs international sales to sustain a thirty-minute drama or a fifteen-minute sitcom. And television drama needs world-wide sales. That means that it *has* to be formulaic, and the individuality of the author is submerged. There are some talented writers who can survive this straight-jacket, Jimmy McGovern in particular.

HWD: *Will you, while over here in America, go to the theatre in, say, Boston or New York?*

ET: Theatre is dead in America. I'm amazed how low it's sunk. Broadway is fast disappearing and 'Real Estate' is taking over. Independent American cinema is taking over the role of our fringe theatre. The forum for powerful and exciting ideas in America is not the theatre but the Independent American Cinema. In Britain, however, I think that theatre is undergoing a renaissance. There's a buzz there. Stephen Daldry is doing a great job at the Royal Court. Welsh theatre, however, is in the doldrums.

HWD: *Is that why you are looking beyond Wales, to Europe?*

ET: Yes. In Wales, there's not enough investment in theatre. Maybe it's not the fault of the Arts Council of Wales. It's probably to do with the Welsh Office. Seven years ago when

Y Cwmni was starting out we were the young Turks. In Welsh theatre there were people who were more experienced than us – Moving Being, Made in Wales and Brith Gof. They were funded as revenue clients. We were not. We were not 'The Establishment'. In the last seven years Volcano, Brith Gof and Y Cwmni, were the companies that toured most extensively outside Wales, but these three companies cannot, in reality, be regarded as 'Establishment' companies, by the very nature of their work.

What worries me is that there are no young Turks coming up behind our companies now. There is no energy, no enthusiasm, no bright young things with gusto and élan. There's no 'New Wave'. I think that theatre in Wales is an abject failure, or rather that the reception of theatre *within* Wales is depressing. The companies I've mentioned have received acclaim, not by touring Wales, but by presenting their work in Europe and the UK. There is, after all, only a limited number of theatres in Wales where we can tour. The cost of productions prohibits doing things from the back of a lorry. I'd much rather be a Welsh artist plying my trade in the world than belong to a struggling 'Welsh Theatre Company' with access only to touring Wales. In Wales, too, it's a failure of the imagination from venue managers. More worrying, perhaps, is the fact that dramatists in Wales have not been able to attract the imagination of Welsh audiences. Sustaining an audience in Wales has always been a problem. Do Shakespeare and the classics and you have a full house. Do something challenging and new and you have half-empty houses. I myself am an optimist as long as I can tour internationally.

HWD: *You talk of 'empty houses' in Wales but you yourself aren't a great frequenter of the theatre.*

ET: No, I'm not. Classical theatre doesn't appeal to me. Too often I see plays that are journalistic in their expression.

What I've enjoyed are circus groups, Théâtre de Complicité performances and the scale of Brith Gof's work. I'm not a Thespian. I like the 'possibilities' of theatre. I think that theatre should release the imagination for people who want to be taken on a journey. I don't think anyone wants sensible footwear. Nobody wants to espouse mediocrity. Nobody wants to part with ten quid for an evening that doesn't take them to a landscape or fire them up. I dislike the kind of theatre, represented by the theatre of the 1970s and the 1980s, that tries to bring everything down to ordinariness. Theatre of the ordinary is like washing up. Nobody likes washing up unless he or she is high on drugs. Washing up isn't interesting.

I enjoy the theatre of the imagination, the theatre of possibilities. Bridging the gap between the actor and the audience to me is paramount. The actor knows what is going to happen next, the audience doesn't. The actors are the fiction-makers and the audience are the collaborators. To refuse to acknowledge this fundamental difference is to create the theatre of the ordinary. In my kind of theatre I aim at the extraordinary.

[1] In 1997 Ed Thomas was invited to deliver a lecture on Welsh Theatre at the annual conference of the North American Association for the Study of Welsh Culture and History, held at the University of Rio Grande, Ohio.

[2] In October 1997 Iwan England translated *House of America* into Welsh (*Tŷ'r Amerig*, unpublished).

[3] The Welsh version, *Tŷr Amerig*, was performed by Cwmni Seithug at The Cabin, Aberystwyth, 14 and 15 December, 1997. The performance was reviewed in *Y Cymro*, 24 December 1997; in *Golwg*, 8 January 1998; *The Big Issue Cymru*, 26 January 1998; and in *Barn*, March 1998. See also Iwan England, 'Lladd America', *Golwg*, 11 December, 1997.

[4] See previous interview.

Ed Thomas

Interview Three
December 2003

HWD: *I last interviewed you five years ago in America on the banks of the Ohio river. Then you were in the middle of writing* Gas Station Angel, *a play that, in the final scene, heralds and salutes a new, confident Wales. In the same period you declared that 'old Wales is dead, and new Wales is already a possibility, an eclectic, self-defined Wales, with attitude.' Post-devolution, do you retain that confidence?*

ET: That last quote now sounds like the raving of a lunatic for the simple reason that, by now, all that confidence has been completely destroyed. They do say that the smaller the country, the bigger the tyranny. I'm not here to speak to you about Health or Education. I'm here to speak of Culture. The optimism many of us felt in the late 1990s about the cultural possibilities for Wales has by now evaporated.

When I speak to my colleagues in theatre they convey a sense of desperation because of the lack of authority, vision and leadership from the top. We have no real leadership whatsoever, and what happens within the English-language theatre scene in Wales happens once again 'despite' not because of the structures that exist. Effectively, we're back to where we were ten years ago, except now we're paying the travelling expenses and funding the Cardiff pads of a whole bunch of politicians.

HWD: *I hear what you're saying and I wouldn't disagree with you. However, in terms of your own career in the theatre, what has changed since the pro-devolution vote and your play* Gas Station Angel?

ET: When I first started writing, the entire theatre scene was different. When Y Cwmni was established it was very much like a band, and we were free to make the kind of theatre that we wanted. It was very much an individual enterprise rather than a formally-funded bright idea of a Wales Arts Council quango. We were a company of individuals. I was the playwright and the director, and Richard Lynch, for example, was Richard Lynch Inc and everything else besides. *Gas Station Angel* was definitely the last play we were going to do as a company, because, in the late 1990s we were all involved in other projects.

At that time I felt optimistic because of the winning, though depressingly narrow pro-devolution vote. I've often quoted Gwyn Alf Williams who proclaimed, 'Wales is dead', since, as he saw it, politics died the death in Wales after the failure of the 'Yes' vote in the 1979 devolution referendum. I should have known better, but I felt misguidedly optimistic when I was writing *Gas Station Angel*. I'd decided that this was a play that would be more magical than what I'd written before. In the play I was searching for a new form, and it's certainly a departure from my other plays, but no more of a departure than *Song from a Forgotten City* was from *East from the Gantry*. *Song* was about a writer who creates his own fiction in a city which doesn't exist.

When *Gas Station Angel* was staged we had a devolved government. Also, in terms of popular culture, Wales had moved on and we had Super Furry Animals, Catatonia, Cool Cymru and so forth. We had a flourishing film industry, and *Twin Town* and *House of America* got made, and actors like Rhys Ifans and others gained prominence. But that flourishing film industry meant that *Gas Station Angel* was very difficult to cast. Many of the actors I wanted were much more interested in doing film, and it seemed to me at the time that producing *Gas Station Angel* was like pushing a boulder up a hill. It's fair to say that by 1998 I was pretty burnt out and moving away from theatre.

HWD: *You moved away from theatre to do exciting work in film and television. What, apart from the theatre 'burn-out', attracted you to film and television?*

ET: The money, of course, and the fact that there was opportunity there for innovation and progress. In order to earn a living as a playwright you have to turn our five or six plays a year and that just isn't possible. I like working in film and television, and I've directed and produced several drama series and films for S4C including, for example, *Fondue*, *Sex and Dinosaurs*, *Brad yn y Bae*, *Triongl*, *Four Short Films* and *Gwyfyn*. I particularly enjoyed producing the poetry documentary feature *Dal: Yma/Nawr* and directing one of the short films, and directing and producing *Mind to Kill* for S4C, HTV and C5.

HWD: *In the late 1990s it was inevitable that several artists abandoned the sinking theatre ship for the opportunities offered by the film and television industries. Did that sad theatre scene at the turn of the century also keep you away from writing for the stage?*

ET: It certainly did because in theatre at the turn of the century there were no opportunities whatsoever. The Arts Council was doing nothing to encourage theatre in that period. What it was busy doing was salvage-work in the aftermath of the crippling drama strategy perpetrated by members of the pre-2000 Council.

The theatre scene in Wales in 2000 was radically different from the one I knew in the late 1980s and early and mid 1990s. What we had then was virtually a national theatre of many voices. That theatre had a loyal audience. When, because of lack of funding and opportunities those companies disappeared, and when new writing was disregarded, theatre in Wales sank into the doldrums. I've no idea what level of funding Sgript Cymru now receives to encourage new writers, but my guess is that it's woefully inadequate. In Wales 2004 we shall need to start from scratch again and seek to establish an eclectic, broad choice of physical language theatre, imagistic theatre and text-based theatre that will be muscular and fresh enough to attract new audiences. At the moment, unfortunately, all we can depend on is the presence of a safe, mainstream audience who frequent safe, mainstream productions.

Take, for example, the New Theatre in Cardiff. The people who go there enjoy mid-scale, family-safe stuff. It's unchallenging theatre. I'm not saying that that kind of theatre shouldn't exist. What I am saying is that it's only one kind of theatre, and that it's sad that it is all Wales seems to have in the new millennium. I'm also concerned that if an English-medium 'National Theatre' is estab-lished here without wide consultation, it will become the 'National Theatre of Shakespeare'. That is, in order to attract a safe audience, it will do the classics and only the classics. Quite frankly there's an abundance of Shakespeare already at the Royal Shakespeare Theatre in Stratford and in London. Let's have something distinctive here in Wales. I agree with Joyce Macmillan, theatre critic for *The Scotsman*, that a massive National Theatre Company has no proper justification unless it knows what exactly it is and to whom it is meant to be speaking.

HWD: *You mention there the need to create a new, eclectic audience. How would you go about doing that?*

ET: You have to be prepared to market a play energetically. You can't just put up posters and expect immediate ticket sales. By now, venue managers in Wales should recognize the fact that you have to nurture an audience over a period of time. But, in terms of nurturing an audience and promoting theatre, the main thing that's lacking in Wales at the moment is the presence of a central drive and vision from an organization that can fund and take risks. The task of filling in forms and ticking boxes has replaced imaginative policy and vision.

If a play, particularly a new play, doesn't do well at the box office that doesn't necessarily mean that the play is a flop. The fault could be in the venue, in the placing of the play in the wrong space at the wrong time; it could be in the marketing or it could be in the failure of a venue manager or company to do the right work in attracting an audience in the first place. You hear some directors and managers claiming that there is no call for new writing. That's simply not true. Indeed, if there's no call for new writing, we may as well close our theatres and turn them into museums. Let's do our plays in St Fagans and let's turn our backs on exciting, vibrant theatre spaces. The fact is that the health of theatre in Wales depends on new writing and fresh ways of presentation. To quote John Berger, new writing offers us 'ways of seeing'. In Wales now we prefer to be blind. The lack of opportunity and the lack of the strong presence of theatre here in 2003 is an embarrassment. Good established playwrights and good young playwrights have no hope of getting breakthroughs in Wales, but they are warmly welcomed abroad. What is of value in Wales happens on the margins. It's that 'despite' culture again.

HWD: *Do you think there should be in Wales a Creative Writing Centre solely for playwrights?*

ET: A drop-in centre for the already destroyed you mean? What I'd like to see first and foremost is a public forum where the question of new writing could be aired and discussed openly. If and when the Welsh Assembly Government gets its act together and comes up with a coherent cultural policy, divorced from party-politics, then there may just be a chance that theatre can once again play a vital role in the cultural life of the nation. I believe Sgript

Cymru should play a central part in that regeneration. It could, with proper funding, be a vigorous new writing centre, and it could also devolve some of the production work to other companies or individuals.

But from the viewpoint of a forty-two year old playwright who has written ten plays, I've got enormous sympathy for experienced dramatists with proven track records who have to do work on the margins. In England, the Royal Court has an established tradition of new writing, and Scotland has the Traverse. We haven't got any place whatsoever in Wales that can be identified with regular performances of new writing. Plays at the Traverse can be whacky, crazy, disgusting, beautiful or inspiring. The important thing is that Scotland can boast of a venue that is clearly identified with what is fresh and new.

HWD: *A few years ago I heard you argue in a lecture you gave at an American university that 'the plague of the Welsh artist was the expectation that he or she would explore over and over again the question of national identity.' Is that still an expectation and does it, by now, point to a lack of confidence in our 'Welshness'?*

ET: Yes, to both questions. In Wales everything has to be about self-definition. Playwrights, of course, can help a nation define itself. A few months ago I read a piece by Joyce Macmillan where she claims to have discovered her Scottishness through some of John McGrath's plays. I feel that if a young playwright wants to write a state-of-the nation play, then he or she should get on with it. I've done it, and the subject holds no interest for me any more. The plain fact is that we are no more confident as a nation than we were pre-devolution. If we were enabled to have some faith in the credibility of our politicians maybe that confidence would begin to grow. The reality is that when it comes to our profile in the UK, nobody cares whether we exist or not. I said the same thing in the 1997 interview.

That invisibility is ongoing, and our theatre today suffers because of it.

HWD: *Despite the far-from-enabling theatre situation in Wales, you have decided to devote some time recently to writing a new play for Theatr Clwyd.*

ET: I have, but it's not as optimistic as *Gas Station Angel*. But once again, what interests me in this new play is the language and the form. Some people saw *Gas Station Angel* as belonging to the 'magic realism' genre, but I myself thought of it as 'poetic'. The new play is also poetic. It's an odyssey and takes place in a city, but again it's like tectonic plates and the ground is never firmly present. You don't really know whether you're in a hotel in Antwerp, in hell, in the real world or in the characters' imagined world. People come and go discussing one another's dreams and then they disappear. I'm a writer who enjoys weaving voices.

The draft I'll send to Terry Hands in Clwyd won't have any characters because I haven't yet decided what the voices represent. They could well represent the different sides of a single consciousness. It will be interesting when the play goes from the initial script into the hands of a body of actors. It will then become a collective consciousness. This is a way of working with a script which is similar to what Y Cwmni did in the early 1990s. I have always accessed and trusted the imagination and consciousness of the actors so that they're free to construct what they see as the quintessence of a character. For this technique to work you have to have a body of actors who can interpret the text in a muscular way and who are totally familiar with the requirements of theatre.

HWD: *Have you decided on a title for the new play?*

ET: I once wrote a poem called 'Stone City Blue'. It was about throwing a stone into a pond and seeing the rings spread out. I saw those rings or ripples as representing the generations. The poem went on to explore the fact that the world, as I see it, has forgotten the existence of those rings and generations, so that modern man is bereft of memory. I've mentioned in my second interview with you my fascination with the palimpsest. In this play the stone and the rings form the palimpsest. The idea of memory, or the absence of it, fascinates me and that idea becomes the central concern of the play. I was going to call it *Stone Dead in the River of Time* but I'm beginning to think that that title is a little over-poetic. I think I'll opt for *Stone City Blue*. The stone and the rings are the palimpsest, the city is the location, and blue is the colour of the emotion in the play.

HWD: *Clearly the concept of the city itself fascinates you and* Rain Dogs, *the performance you did last year in collaboration with Mike Pearson, is a work that explores the many facets of a city. That work throughout asks the question, 'What is a city?'*

ET: Mike Pearson and I will continue to ask the question without arriving at a clear definition. Both of us like cities. When I began to collaborate with Mike he was at the stage where he was fed up with being a professor in academe. He's first and foremost a practitioner, a talented artist. Academe was confining and stifling his talent, and I too was imprisoned by the tyranny of custom and the prescriptive requirements of the three-act structure and the television series. And so Mike and I decided to write the monologues that became *Rain Dogs*. In February 2005 we'll perform Part Two of *Rain Dogs* in Chapter, this time with five women. It will be a very different thing from our initial production and it will not adopt the monologue form. But we'll continue to explore the mysteries and possibilities of the city.

HWD: Rain Dogs *had a strong narrative. Does* Stone City Blue *adopt the narrative form?*

ET: The text that I'll submit to Terry Hands in a few days will be almost like a long narrative poem. In this poem a character wanders through a city looking for himself. As a result of a car-crash he has lost his memory and thinks that God has substituted him for someone else. He's a street-drifter who goes around the city leaving photographs of his old self on walls. Eventually he stops his search, but in the meantime we have gone on the journey with him. The play is actually a dramatization of a bloke who lives in his own mind. That takes you back to *Song from a Forgotten City* where the character constructs his own city. You could say that in this new play too what the character is doing is making it all up and admitting 'I live in a world of my own. That's OK, because everyone knows me there.' The character presents us with what he saw and the people he met during his city drifting, but it's not at all an *Under Milk Wood*-type odyssey of a night and day in a city.

I've told you before that when I'm writing a play I don't really know what I'm writing 'about', but that the same themes crop up over and over again, and the only way I can justify that to myself is to trust that, during the process, the nature of the writing changes, and that the context and form change as well. If I was an egotistical theatre manager I would put on a performance of *Song for a Forgotten City*, followed by a performance of *Stone City Blue*, and then I'd ask the audience, 'Well, what's different'? Are *Song* and *Stone* basically the same play? What, if anything, has changed?

HWD: *From your account of the play it seems that you are dealing once again with fiction and myth. There's no 'concrete playwriting' here.*

ET: What's interesting about fiction is that you can move around in the realm of the mind and in the world of half-remembered things. These things have no 'meaning' and cannot be clearly defined. For me the things we don't understand are far more interesting to dramatise than the things that are crystal-clear. There's a certain kind of concrete playwriting which is very effective inasmuch as it develops a clear idea and nails it. I'm not at all interested in nailing an idea. I'm far more interested in fiction and myth. I like to think of language as an endless confusion of memory, and that the narrative only really works in the audience's mind. The language allows the audience to drift in and out of the play, and the play's narrative is just a background to the audience's personal narrative thinking. The play allows the audience to weave their own stories. The audience, in a way, writes the play. I just provide the musak in Little Chef.

You could say that what I'm writing is a load of guff, but it's far more interesting than writing about the fluctuation in the interest rate. I also think that there's a hunger in audiences to see things they don't immediately understand. In the new millennium we inhabit a relentlessly concrete world and there are fundamentals we no longer connect with. During a recent holiday in St Ives I used to take my dog down to the harbour every lunch time, and there was always someone there staring silently out to sea. I liked to think that these individuals were trying hard to connect with that certain something that remained a mystery to them.

HWD: *It reminds me of Robert Frost's lines,*

> *They cannot look out far.*
> *They cannot look in deep.*
> *But when was that ever a bar*
> *To any watch they keep?*

ET: Yes exactly, and in my new play I try to convey that failure to understand, that confusion. I'm not advocating wilful obscurity on the part of the playwright, but in plays of possibilities everybody can celebrate that moment when the imagination of the audience hits the imagination of the performer and the performance. That is the kind of celebratory moment that I aim for in my fiction.

Siôn Eirian

Interview One
May 1995

HWD: *As a first question, I'm tempted to put two very different propositions to you, but I also realise that they may be close to being the same proposition. On one occasion, prompted in a similar interview, you quoted one of Newton's laws, that 'To every action there is an equal and opposite reaction'. At the same time, I feel I want to ask you something more obviously related to your situation as a writer in Wales – whether seeing and hearing your father preach every Sunday was a 'theatrical' experience that gave you a sense of theatre itself. I wonder which particular handle you'll take on that question now.*

SE: Let me take the more autobiographical one and say *No, not at all*. The idea that Welsh sermons, in the amphitheatres of Welsh chapels, were in any way 'theatre' was only true in a sense that left me gob-smacked and wide-eyed when, in due course, I encountered *real* theatres. To me, the chapel was something so deadly that, now that I look back on it, it simply begged to be caricatured, hated even. That sounds a Caradoc Evans point of view. But what I found in that upbringing as the son of a minister, with the regulation two or three attendances on Sunday, was that it stultified anything creative. So I certainly didn't see anything dramatically alive or vibrant in my background that I could associate with when I was writing. The writing was more to do with what I escaped *from*. When I was studying, there were little private enclaves of the mind that I would escape to, to create my own little daydreams and fantasies, and that's what theatre was about, it seemed to me, not what you *have* to attend and be dressed up for in the regulation starched shirt and tie. So my work is a movement *away* from that.

HWD: *But were you conscious of that 'moving away' very early? When, in fact, did you first become interested in real live theatre, or have that opportunity to be 'gob-smacked' by it?*

SE: There were no theatres as buildings or as centres of pilgrimage then. Theatr Clwyd wasn't there when I was growing up in Mold. The drama we saw in the late 1960s and early 1970s was what took place in the school hall in Ysgol Maes Garmon or Mold Alun School, so you saw plays on the same stage as you'd seen the headmaster take the morning service and prayers earlier that day. Seeing theatre displacing that kind of regulated activity gave it a thrilling resonance that you only rediscover when you yourself are working in it, because theatre can be anarchic and so dangerous. You suddenly remember the people who look in on it when they are 13, 14, 15 years of age, in school, and you realise where the electricity, where the danger comes from – that is when you yourself now have something to do in shaping it. Those venues now appear absurdly clichéd, ill-suited and ill-equipped. Today school pupils are bused in to proper theatres.

Siôn Eirian

HWD: *After your childhood and schooldays in north-east Wales, you went to the University of Wales at Aberystwyth. Was that an improvement in your opportunity to see 'theatre'?*

SE: No. Certainly there was a building there. Theatr y Werin was built by then, part of the grand design of five great concrete blocks on the skyline – the usual Arts Council scheme of finding the place before finding the product. This was in 1972-75. But in my time at Aberystwyth what I remember, above all else in Theatr y Werin, is doing make-up for student productions. I only did that because I'd been with the Flintshire Youth Theatre where it was something I'd dabbled in, and I thought I had acquired some expertise in putting No 9 and No 5 and Base on people's faces. I also translated a couple of plays, and even acted in one, on the assumption that the theatre could take someone on board who could dabble in everything. It's only as the years go by that you begin to understand that the theatre isn't just supposed to be fun. With the cold winds blowing, and with the necessity to earn a living and to take yourself more seriously, you realise that the theatre you experienced in school or university may have been great to watch or partake in, but that it isn't enough. By the time you get to your thirties you have either to make a proper living out of it – and I do mean a proper living, not just scrimping and scraping a living – or you just have to give it up and do something else.

The difficulty for me was that, once I'd started indulging my passion for theatre – mainly writing, but with some acting as well – I lost the discipline to do anything else. I could not then work from nine to five, I couldn't even be a teacher, because I'd lost that self-discipline totally. Some days I can't even get out of bed; other days I get up at six in the morning. That's fine for me, but if somebody was actually employing me, it just wouldn't be acceptable. Sometimes you feel that adrenalin rush, and you've got no other choice but to do what you *are* doing. It allows you to be lazy half the time, but it also pressurises you to be hyper-energised, and occasionally brilliant, some parts of the other time. It's a corner I've got myself into. It's not comfortable, not easy.

HWD: *And yet the subjects you chose to read at Aberystwyth – English, Welsh, Philosophy – were ones that required a great deal of discipline. They are in any case an interesting mix. Did you find they instilled discipline at least in your urge to be a creative writer?*

SE: Yes, they focused me, Philosophy in particular. They focused me, not in the sense of a future career, but in the way philosophy especially helps one to train and structure ideas and in the dialectic that exists always within dialogue itself, let alone within the general shape of a play. It is something I've been able to fall back on – the general shape of ideas. More important, the immediacy of it was something that enabled me to sort out what and where I'd come *from*. You mentioned the Newtonian 'To every action there is an equal and opposite reaction'. Well, possibly. Looking back on the way I was brought up, I would quote something else. It's Philip Larkin –

> They fuck you up, your mum and dad.
> > They may not mean to, but they do.
> They fill you with the faults they had
> > And add some extra, just for you.

HWD: *Though, of course, Larkin adds –*

> *But they were fucked up in their turn*
> > *By fools in old-style hats and coats,*
> *Who half the time were soppy-stern*
> > *And half at one another's throats.*

SE: Exactly. Studying philosophy at university was a way of trying to disentangle myself from the Sargasso Sea of *any* preconceived ideas, not just the religious ones of my own background. As it happens, my parents weren't in any way puritanical, but there was a lot of baggage that came with growing up in a manse, not just of a religious kind but also in terms of Welsh culture, which is a separate thing. There is a term in Welsh, '*Y Pethe*', 'The Things'. It sounds rather silly when you say it in English, but it means something great and all-encompassing in Welsh. It's what *worth* and *value* are attached to when they're not merely financial. In such a society you're able to discuss and debate, and probably write poetry. It's a kind of cultural meritocracy.

Now, that in itself was not inherently bad, but it was something I desperately wanted to shake my hair free from. It's like when you walk out of a shower, and there's no towel, and you just want to be free of discomfort, like a dog coming out of a river, and you just want to spray away all that is putting things in your eyes, blurring you. Philosophy showed me why and how people make moral decisions, what morality is. You don't get that through religion. Religion was the *antithesis* of morality, as far as I could see, because you have to adhere to things that don't help you, don't propel you to brave decisions. For me, philosophy was a great push forward towards something else, and away from something which I distrusted.

HWD: *So at university philosophy absorbed you more than literature as such. On graduating, you proceeded to the College of Music and Drama in Cardiff. Was it some kind of career decision that determined that move?*

SE: I went there absolutely be default. This is going to sound implausible and unreal, but when I was leaving Aberystwyth in the summer of 1975, I did ask about the possibility of postgraduate work in the Philosophy Department. I was told, because I had not been a good attender and had not got my proper stripes, that I wasn't a strong applicant. Much though I would have liked it at the time, they made it clear that that flight-path was not open. Just as oddly, I had also written to the Shotton Steel Works, as it was then, because I'd worked a summer there in the coke ovens as a student. It was just manual labour, but the money was so good that, as a student, I couldn't believe it. I'm glad I didn't get in there because, however brief, interesting and romantic, it would have been so different from my upbringing and the expectations of my family. There were no jobs going in the coke ovens and it was as a last resort that I applied to the Welsh College of Music and Drama, did a year as an actor and got an Equity card. I then worked as an actor with Theatr Cymru in Bangor for a year. It was at the end of that year that I realised I was a god-awful actor, and I had to look yet again for something else.

HWD: *Sam Shepard once said that the very process of trying to act taught him how to write – and what not to write – for the theatre. Did at least being an actor help you to write?*

SE: I don't think being an actor opened my eyes or ears to anything in terms of writing, but your question makes a valid point because other writers – I can think of Meic Povey and Ed Thomas – are still actors if they wish to be. Acting is a discipline that allows you to speak the lines out loud, and pace about as you say them. So the fact that you are an actor helps you think of your writing as a spoken, as well as a written, thing. If you're an actor you also get into a fraternity where most of your friends are actors anyway. There aren't many of us around who are full-time writers. Ed Thomas would say that his soul-mates are actors. He works very closely with Richard Lynch and Russell Gomer, and I'm sure that, as a writer, he draws a tremendous amount from them, from their speech-patterns, from their humour. You see it in his plays. Myself, though, I've had no truck with acting for over twelve years now, though most of my friends are actors.

HWD: *Let me press you a little further on this. Ed Thomas works with a company and a group of actors. Have you ever felt that you would like to work with actors you could script for – a small ensemble? Would your own work benefit from that?*

SE: It probably would benefit. There's something very attractive in it. But at the same time I'm sick of thinking of how Ed Thomas, by setting up his own ensemble, his own company, has done the right thing, and got it right. Best of luck to Ed, but it's rather tiresome that Ed has got it so right, because in no other country would you be asking people who are writers, simply writers, 'Why can't you get your act together, find your own performance space, and tour your stuff to Kiev?' It's only in Wales, because of the lack of back-up, lack of support and stretch from the Arts Council and various other sponsorships, and because of the lack of intelligent critical back-up in newspapers and periodicals, that it behoves the writer (if he wishes to have fair treatment) to do it all himself. Ed's done it, but I don't want to learn lessons from Ed.

HWD: *Given whether or not 'the Foundation will Bear your Expenses' – Larkin again – I suppose, whatever the format, the difficulty is the lack of proper funding. But do you find that it's even more difficult to get sponsorship on the Welsh-language side? Welsh-medium theatre presumably doesn't allow you as much freedom to tour, etc, as English-medium writing in Wales.*

SE: No, not at all. The Welsh-medium theatre has been, and still is, tremendously supportive. The companies I've worked for – Hwyl a Fflag and, more recently, Dalier Sylw – have been writer-friendly companies, not only in the sense of trying to wean you through the script stage, but doing their best in terms of getting money. It doesn't come down to the resources behind Welsh-medium as opposed to English-medium theatre; if anything it can be a bleaker experience with an English-language play.

HWD: *In that case, which do you feel the more comfortable with, a Welsh-medium play or an English-medium one. Or doesn't it matter?*

SE: I'm as comfortable with the English medium as with the Welsh. It's not a case of two caps on one head because those heads talk differently within each cranium, except, perhaps, when I'm translating a play like Saunders Lewis's *Blodeuwedd*. The last original English play I did was for the Sherman – based on Bram Stoker's *Dracula* story. I never once thought 'How would this be if it were in Welsh?' The last Welsh-language play I did was about three prostitutes and a slum landlord, and again I never once thought 'How would this turn out if it were an English play?' It just doesn't occur to me. It's not real for me. I'm able to jump like a flea from one cap to another – live on two caps and find deep, or enjoy quite shallow, fur.

HWD: *That's an interesting metaphor...*

SE: Well, it's all about language, you know.

HWD: *But, in whatever language, you're on record as saying that you're afraid of theatre. Now that's an interesting word – 'afraid'. Why?*

SE: The reason I fear theatre more than any other medium – not that I approach any drama commission with sweaty palms and sleepless nights; it's not that kind of nightmare – is that, compared to film or TV and radio, I haven't quite got my anchor down in the style of theatre. In some ways, it's hit or miss for me. I'm concerned enough to appreciate that, when it comes to a film script or television script, it eases my way, I know what they want and feel I can deliver. When I get a theatre commission, it's 'Oh, hell, here we go again!' and 'Where the hell *are* we going?' It's frightening on that helter-skelter, on that big-dipper. With the best will in the world, you see the play in your head, but on stage what is it going to be like? That happened with my play *Dracula* for the Sherman, even though that was adapted from Bram Stoker's novel. The *idea*, the ambition of that was tremendous but, well, let me tell you a story the theatre director Huw Thomas told me. Somebody or other was not able to appear on stage, so they got someone from the audience to come up instead. And then the joke goes: 'He had had no tuition, had never been to Drama School, had no experience, hadn't even seen the script properly, but when he got up on that stage he was – *crap*!'

Writing some plays is like that – not plays you're in total control of, but *Dracula* certainly. You set out to write something that involves people flying, that involves all those special effects, stakes through hearts and beheadings, and then you find that your script isn't working properly anyway, that the budget of the Sherman is only half there and, instead of Dracula flying, he's winched up slowly, jerkily, and you just want to hide under your seat. It's nobody's fault, it's just how theatre is chugging along on its budgets, how the grand ideas of writers don't quite get there to the right place at the right time. That's the thing about the fear of theatre.

But it didn't scare me. Where theatre would scare me involves a different example. I'm thinking of a Welsh-language play I wrote, called *Elvis, y Blew a Fi*, written for the Newport National Eisteddfod. That didn't work out at all, and I didn't know why. At least with *Dracula* I knew, and Phil Clark the Director knew, and everyone else knew, designers, cast and all. To write something, with you yourself not knowing why it's a failure, is just traumatic. *Elvis, y Blew a Fi* was a very schematic, fractured play. I now know, with hindsight, that I was so rooted in television at the time that every break between scenes, every time a character went off stage or entered again, I was looking for camera-angles to pick them up. It was terrible.

HWD: *This sense in which television stands in the way of writing effectively for live theatre seems to me important, and a timely warning. Can you think of some other examples? When a dramatist works for television, is it impossible for him to work successfully for the two media, side by side?*

SE: Yes, absolutely. I can give you other examples without citing myself. I think that if you take three different writers who have never worked for television – say, Ed Thomas, Alan Osborne and Dic Edwards – the only TV work that Ed Thomas, for example, is trying to set up is a tele-visualisation of *House of America*, which I hope gets on television round Britain because it deserves to be seen again and again. But Dic Edwards, and Alan Osborne haven't had a sniff at television, or much radio, I shouldn't think. Alan had one of the 'Wales Playhouse' slots – but we can discount those; they're not artistically serious. Other than that, you have there three true theatre writers. You then get writers like Meic Povey, Gareth Miles and myself, and Geraint Lewis – and this happens mainly in the Welsh language because the opportunity is there for us – where we are spoilt for choice. We turn back to theatre all the time because there's an artistic purity there, a cleansing of the soul, a use of drama as a diuretic form.

We need to go through that because at least we respect the people with whom we work in theatre, and that's why your best television writers turn back to theatre. Some people think it's a masochistic thing because we do it for no money. But the incentive there is not at all to see your work on the stage or to get a fat cheque – it is simply to test yourself against yourself.

HWD: *What else is it about theatre that draws playwrights back from television, or indeed why do playwrights who appreciate the 'artistic purity' of theatre write so much for television?*

SE: You get in television, not a purity of form – I think that has disappeared – but a purity of person, the ghost in the machine, the new value in what has been a grey old constant. You get inspired by the fact that someone like Dai Smith is suddenly dragged in to these big offices in Llandaff, and you think, 'Now that's someone I'd like to have a pint with'. And Geraint Morris – he's now working for HTV. And suddenly you start discounting the organizations that are behind them and get inspired by the people there. But you never find ongoing values in those places; that's how they are.

With theatre it's different because, there, the personnel can change week by week, but the graft and sweat of the people who work with you is utterly admirable. It's the diametric opposite of what you have in television. Television has to have that one occasional inspiring person like Dai Smith – and I refer to him again because I think he's someone important in what BBC Wales has set up here. But theatre is not dependent on the personnel. It's dependent on people who are earning very little but who will shout at you about your script, who will want you in the rehearsal room next morning. Television is so anodyne, so superficial in terms of creativity. Theatre is still rough. It's like a badger's arse; stick your nose in that, and you've lived a bit.

HWD: *If you react that strongly to the medium itself as message, I wonder what your response will be to the critical view that prompts my next question. Critics have talked about your work as being concerned with the fringe of society, as being 'on the edge', How do you react to that?*

SE: The idea of some experiences being on the fringe of things – I don't know if that is a particularly Welsh view or not.

If it's thought anywhere that homosexuality and prostitution are on the fringes of life, then what is the core that sees them as fringe elements? These things are central to me in my understanding of how society organises itself, how values, including sexual values, are put in place. I think it's as much a generation thing as a moral thing. A great many of my friends are gay and that's as it happens to fall. Prostitution is peripheral to the lives of most of us, although before a rugby match in Cardiff, I'll always suggest we go down to the Custom House – it's quieter there, and the prostitutes are far better company than those yobs from North Wales and the Valleys who flock to the big match.

Yes, there are some people who think that my themes and concerns lie outside their particular paddock. But I grew up in that field where these things were meant, for me too, to be outside my world. But I'm trying to get out of that in a big and fast way. I would rather the company of prostitutes and gays than that of people in suits and the 'big seats' in chapels.

HWD: *Caradoc Evans again. But do you think that, at base, it's the difference between rural Wales and urban or Cardiff Wales?*

SE: Yes, many of us have grown up on coming to the city because we've found a place where we can turn our backs on something else. Meic Povey has come from Porthmadog, Gareth Miles is from Waunfawr and Wrecsam, but the point is that all of us have come to seek something, something more real, relaxed and lovely than this 'Welsh' upbringing has given us. I don't mean 'Welsh-language'. What I'm talking about is that people who have an interest in the darker or seamier side of life, like Michael Povey and myself, must go and seek it out, because the dishonesty is not inside Cardiff as a city, but outside. It's like ripples in a pond: the further out you go, there's *less* honesty.

HWD: *And yet the reaction to* Epa yn y Parlwr Cefn *was much the same, in terms of shock-factor, in Cardiff as in Aberystwyth. In either place, might not the use of consciously 'dirty' language be legitimately seen as simply passé? Or is it that Welsh-language theatre is fifty years behind in that respect?*

SE: My intention with the language – the play was as much about language as about prostitution – was to replicate as much as I could of the way the prostitutes were talking. I wanted to be true to them; I wanted the play itself to be true to them, and to reflect their world. When you go and spend an afternoon talking to these girls, and when you dig into their world, you just don't think about using a different, sanitised, language or ask whether the language you *are* using is going to shock. It's only when you've written the play that you think, 'Ah, this might be a bit strong'. You do the writing first and then only think 'This might be a bit heavy'. In any case, I wanted that play to be like a long broken-up poem. Yes, the four-letter word was there throughout.... But then I didn't do a body count like a Vietnam general. I think there are probably two to three hundred four-letter expletives in the play – I'd imagine so. To me, that was fine – it was every other word when I met the prostitutes in Roath. So it wasn't an issue when I was writing the play. But that issue did arise when the play was going out – to Carmarthen, Tal-y-bont, Dolgellau, Bangor. To be honest, when the director Eryl Philips and I sat down to discuss the matter, the only worry we had was, 'Are the people going to walk out?' or 'Is it going to disrupt the actors?'

HWD: *So the fear was different from that of 'doing it in the streets and frightening the horses'?*

SE: Yes – we felt protective, above all, of the actors, not of what was in the script as such.

HWD: *So a writer writing in Wales, in Welsh Wales, doesn't need to worry about the crudity of the language as such?*

SE: The writers writing in English Wales don't tour to Tal-y-bont and Dolgellau. Anyway, the interesting thing for me wasn't the language. The first word of the play is 'cunt', and that was never a worry, because I wasn't emblazoning it, I wasn't saying, 'This dirty word is here'. What interested me was what went on *in between* the 'f' word and the 'c' word. Those telling, emotional moments, for example, when a prostitute talks about masturbating a thalidomide. For me, that was a speech at the core of the play – that a prostitute can do that, whereas the pimp, the slum landlord would not be capable of doing anything so generous, for any person. So much for its morality, or sentimentality. Then there was another scene that I took out initially, then in the final rehearsal put back in – with the consent of the actors and the director. And even if it struck someone as an awful image, it wasn't like shooting someone in Bosnia. Now that's got nothing to do with Welsh-speakers and English-speakers. But, of course, for the Welsh-language-speaker, it's going to set off much more reverberation than would happen in English-language Wales – not that the latter is more mature, but that its people are less conscious of whom they fear meeting in the interval, or on the way out, or in chapel the next day.

HWD: *Being Welsh in a predominantly English literary world is by definition a complicated experience. But let's take the substantive example that you've now raised: you want, in your plays, to represent prostitutes as a central slice of life. We see them as prostitutes in Eugene O'Neill's* The Iceman Cometh, *and are firmly convinced of what they are – but they don't there use tape-recorder language.*

SE: If Eugene O'Neill were writing now, he would be writing a different play. The people who write today use an abrasive

68

and a come-hither language, people like Jim Cartwright. In America dramatists have no qualms about breaking barriers. Howard Barker is the most brilliant poet and linguist, but he does it using the vernacular as well, though choicely. I just bombarded. I out-blued *Utah Blue*. Those prostitutes in a little house in Roath, in Donald Street, that was their language in trade. Not using that language may be fine artistically, but it's far removed from the world that I really sat in on, and listened to. We can draw tramlines about the words we use, but if you sit with prostitutes in Cardiff, you think it's a bit immaterial what their sensibilities to words are. I went ahead because they just talked like that. And, of course, to do it in Welsh was even more beautiful.

HWD: *But, of course, there will be a wider loyalty to your own language, too. Several other dramatists have said that they envy you because you're a 'poet in the theatre'. You yourself have said that there is no formal structure for your plays. Is that because the words themselves impose the structure? Could you expand on this?*

SE: Yes, I can in both a positive and a negative way. I consider *Epa yn y Parlwr Cefn* to be a long long poem, but containing lots of action. It was through the poetry, I think, that the two actresses, Siân Rivers and Maria Pride, discovered characters in my play that they could weep into. Playing the part of the prostitutes was difficult for the two actresses – but their emotional journey, their little odyssey, was one of the most precious experiences that I've had in theatre. But, in a more cynical vein, I would say that the only part of the theatre that allows poetry is the rehearsal room. You can in a rehearsal room, without the detritus of the set and props, have the essence of the dramatic moment with Siân and Maria and the tears in your eyes. Poetry is alive in rehearsal room performances, in scripts and in directorial values. But poetry comes to grief in the realisation of the script on stage. We get it right in the rehearsal room, but on the stage things don't work out as envisioned. It's the cranking-up of Dracula, inch by inch, again.

HWD: *So, given that you have things to say, do you view theatre as a medium that can change society?*

SE: Nobody can change society, not even by a vote. I think that Ed Thomas, who is probably the best young theatre writer in Wales at the moment, may think that he might change something. He can't. We who are slightly older – Dic Edwards, Alan Osborne, myself – would probably say that we can change nothing. Nothing at all.

**Interview Two
October 2004**

HWD: *Is there any theme or experience you would like to select to evoke your work in the period since we last discussed things?*

SE: I find that I'm still banging on about some of the same themes as I was ten years ago. How language shapes experience, and shapes perception, is still an issue in much of my work. In *Cegin y Diafol* I tried to mesh-in Waldo Williams's mystical and primal poem 'O Bridd' with a fantasy located in a cyberspace surreality. That sounds like a frivolous exercise but it attempted to juxtapose the deep yet narrow confines of Waldo's huge vision with the shallow yet vast expanse of internet culture, which is eclectic without being very erudite, where irony is absent and insight hard to come by.

In the one short play I was able to touch upon religion and belonging, as things beyond language (Waldo), and sexuality as something often created from within language and transient iconography (cyberspace). This was a definitive last incursion into this territory for me. It's not by chance that I chose to write it for the Royal Welsh College of Music and Drama. At its best and most generous, that place can give you the resources and dedication to realise a theatrical grand design. I remember seeing Greg Cullen's huge play about Shostakovich and Stalin – *An Informer's Duty* – there in the early 1990s, where he had a huge cast and a whole orchestra on stage. The result was exhilarating. Because there is an access to resources there, without the constraint of box-office expectation or grant finance justification, you can sometimes get an environment far more enabling than most professional theatre companies can offer. I had a fantastic set and costume design by Max Jones and Laura Thomas, there was a crop of precociously-talented Welsh-language acting students, and Tim Baker came in to direct it with a risk-taking bravura. It worked.

HWD: *Your experience with* Cegin y Diafol *was obviously a heartening one...*

SE: Yes, you are indeed heartened by individual reassurances of craft and insight, as in, for example, Lewis Davies's ambitious and intense writing in *Sex and Power at the Beau Rivage* for Theatr y Byd or, in a very different vein, Charlie Way's consummately-crafted *The Borrowers* for the Sherman. But these are instances in isolation. Generally I still despair about where theatre in Wales has led the writer over the last ten years, though I've disengaged largely from the debate now. The general map of Welsh theatre with its linguistic bisecting and its geographical quartering is still like the old Marcher lords jousting over their bits of principality. Personal fiefdoms and feuds. The writers are rich in lip service but starved in all other ways. And there's less of note being written or said now than there was ten or twenty years ago. But maybe that's a fair if sad reflection of how difficult it always is to speak up and agitate about society itself. When dialectic has been debased by the voices in power – one thinks of course of George Bush and Tony Blair – and truth is no more, and rhetoric rings hollow, 'I only know what I believe'. Logical debate seems to be dead in the political arena. Narrow personal agendas masquerade as far-sighted policy. So too in the arts in Wales. And there are times when it seems sensible, thoroughly excusable, to withdraw from the debate and concentrate on your own little concerns.

Dic Edwards

HWD: *Obviously, the area in which this interview will move is that of your view of your experience as a dramatist living and writing in Wales. But I was intrigued to read that you are also a published poet. Did the poetry come first?*

DE: Yes, and my first poetry success was in 1974 when I read one of my poems on a Radio Four programme, 'Wales, where are your poets?', a programme which was introduced by John Wain who was Professor of Poetry at Oxford. I find the title of this radio programme a good way in, actually, to this interview which could well bear the title 'Wales, where is your culture?' John Wain's 1974 question was absurdly rhetorical. Would anybody have dared to ask the question 'Sweden, where are your poets?' The question was inappropriate and the BBC

73

got an Englishman to ask it. On that programme I read a poem called 'Dead Leaves' and recorded it in a small studio in Aberystwyth. In rehearsal I declaimed it in a Dylan Thomas style but the producer at the studio persuaded me to 'read it naturally'. I knew even then that I wouldn't advance as a poet, and certainly hadn't begun to write poetry at a very early age. Gillian Clarke for example claims that she wrote her first poem at the age of four. Does one really envy people who are *that* precocious? I don't think so. Except Mozart, perhaps, who wrote symphonies at the age of four or five.

I was watching a programme on television recently on Gore Vidal and he recounted how Tennessee Williams had told him that he, Vidal, had become a success at far too early an age, and had therefore always seen the world through the eyes of someone who had 'made it' and not through the eyes of someone who had known what it was to fail. This is something Americans do – they see things in terms of success, of achievement. American artists – whatever their background, the families of the Gores and the Vidals, or the lowest of the low – American artists seem able to keep to their humanity and their embodiment of that fantastic ingredient that makes us human. It's something to do with American culture. I find Wales, and I'm sorry to say it, the exact opposite. Here, we deny the great fundamental rising of the spirit. We always feel – I don't, and I'm sure you don't, but a great many people do feel – that they need to be *somewhere else* to fulfil themselves. We're not confident in ourselves, in our own culture. If you're American you're full of that confidence – but certainly not if you're Welsh. Eighteen months ago I wrote *Utah Blue*, a play based upon the story of Gary Gilmore who shot two men in cold blood and then fought to be executed. The play was performed at The Point, Cardiff early this year, and people complained that it wasn't about Wales. They complained, too, that it was about violence and that it was sexual. And yet these very same people love Tarantino. I myself find Tarantino fascinating for

74

many reasons, not for cultural reasons, but ones that have to do with sheer entertainment.

HWD: *Well, that certainly got us somewhere. Apart from the relative merits of early or later 'success', there is, then, the question of which countries or nations actually foster that sense of applause or esteem. If you'll forgive, after a lead-in question, another leading one, why do you think Wales has denied you the welcome given to your work elsewhere? After all, no less a figure than Edward Bond has said that he is 'in awe' of your plays, and they have been welcomed in places like Glasgow and Leicester and by English reviewers generally.*

DE: The easiest thing to do in answer to that is to repeat that the plays haven't been specifically about Wales. Wales is such a complicated culture, but I think the less than whole-hearted welcome given to my plays has been partly to do with Welsh amateurism. Amateurism is largely what Welsh culture is about. Welsh-language culture is rooted in the Eisteddfod, the *Noson Lawen* – which is an important and positive thing inasmuch as anyone can belong to it; you don't have to be artistic or famous to belong to the culture. But, on the other hand, that kind of amateurism can become a part of the psychology of a people to an extent that it becomes a psychosis, so that people envy anything that is successful. They regard anything that is good or excellent grudgingly.

And I really do believe that there is such a thing as Welsh clumsiness. I can understand why R S Thomas described Wales as a country 'sick with inbreeding'. It is almost as if we see ourselves as a nation of village idiots – it's horrendous, outrageous. We latch on to a figure – say Dylan Thomas – and make him into an icon. Dylan will in fact pay a heavy price for being the poet on whom the people who 'run' our culture rely to represent Wales. I myself feel sorry for people like John Tripp, Raymond Garlick and Emyr Humphreys who came in the wake of Dylan. Where is their status? It's true that a 'John Tripp Award' has been instituted by the Welsh Academy, but who exactly is John Tripp in the world of letters in Wales today? He was one of the first victims of whatever it is that is at the heart of the Welsh cultural establishment that denies a living, growing culture, and that denies, too, the development and encouragement of writers. Now that encouragement and support is exactly what the Welsh Playwrights Company seeks to provide. The Welsh Playwrights Company is an enabling body which seeks to create an environment whereby the playwrights of the *next* generation will flourish.

HWD: *I suppose that, on some scale or other, the Welsh Playwrights Company could be described as an institution. It is at least an organized body. What about bodies that are clearly 'institutions' in the national sense? For example, do you think that the current movement to create a Welsh National Theatre might form what you call an 'encouraging' medium for promoting playwrights?*

DE: I think that a Welsh National Theatre would be a disaster. We've got a Welsh National Theatre. There is, for instance, the work of the Welsh Playwrights Company. The work we've done in a year or two is phenomenal, and playwrights who belong to the Company have had their work performed all over the world. Peter Lloyd's plays, for instance, have been performed in California and Australia; Greg Cullen's work has been seen in America and Scandinavia; Lucy Gough's plays have toured the UK; and with luck, my work will be seen soon in New York. We don't need centralized theatre. Wales is a place where 'touring' works well. We don't need buildings based in Bangor, Swansea or Clwyd to give us an identity, because they can't possibly house all the enthusiasm and endeavour in Wales. Buildings by definition need to be maintained – just think of the drain the Welsh National Opera makes on the Arts Council budget. My fear is that a grandiose 'Welsh National Theatre' would mop up money that could be allocated to serious Theatre in Education companies such as Spectacle, a company that does such important work in the Valleys. Theatr Iolo, Arad Goch, Theatr Powys – all these important companies would be threatened. Even companies like Made in Wales would inevitably be sucked up into this horrendous 'National Theatre'.

In Wales we are not amenable to giving ultimate authority to one person because we are not in the business of centralization. Do people who support devolution for the nation support centralization for its own theatres? Twenty years down the road we'll end up with these big buildings, with theatres, but with nobody who will have an ongoing relationship with those theatres. And what exactly would be the nature of a National Theatre? Would it be a theatre that would give due emphasis to Welsh plays and Welsh playwrights? I don't think so. I don't think its advocates are interested in Welsh plays. They are interested in doing Goethe, Ibsen and Shakespeare. We've been down this road before in Wales and we've seen that it doesn't work. Theatre isn't in the business of boosting the ego and reputation of individuals. The right road is the one that the Welsh Playwrights Company is taking, the road of collaboration, the road that's an encouraging and democratic one and the road that will lead to Wales having a strong and confident voice in the cultural market-place of the UK.

HWD: *I'm sure you'd agree, on reflection, that even your own phrase 'cultural market-place' is a contradiction in terms. But it is true, of course, that your own plays are not in any case written for grand operatic spaces. They demand an intimate relationship between stage and audience. They've been often described as challenging because they don't fit comfortably into specific genres in 'conventional' theatres. Quite apart from the 'National Theatre' question, how do you yourself view your work in this respect?*

DE: There are a couple of issues here. It's true that my plays are not written for the proscenium arch approach. They are not representational paintings. The proscenium arch anticipated film. In this kind of theatre you're looking at 'distanced' spectacle. It's so very different from what my plays demand and from what the Brechtian alienation theory implied. I try to bring the Brechtian distancing technique into my work. It's not a distancing between stage and audience but a distancing of the audience from any bourgeois representation passing itself off as a 'slice of life' on the stage. The proscenium arch play glorifies an artificial picture of bourgeois life. Personally, I find proscenium arch theatre bizarre. Attic theatre didn't stick a play in a box – Greek theatre was a forum. For me the fundamental notion of theatre is that it is a debate and the audience has therefore to be a creative part of the performance. They must feel that they are part of action and argument.

HWD: *Yet you've been very specific, not only about the physical nature of your kind of theatre, but also about the ways in which actors handle and mishandle your actual text. Indeed, you've often said that acting – that's interesting, acting, the medium itself – can get in the way of the text.*

DE: Yes indeed it can. My starting point is that a play exists because I've written it. That's not an arrogant statement. It's a simple fact. I begin my plays from argument. This again may sound pompous, but one of my early influences was Socrates – certainly the Platonic Dialogues, which fascinated me while I was at university in Cardiff. Socrates is a paradox. On the one hand he was extremely clever, and on the other he hated cleverness even to the extent of undermining cleverness. That's astonishing, and so dramatic. And playwrights who worked from argument influenced me – Eugene O'Neill, Edward Bond and Oscar Wilde, for example. *The Importance of Being Earnest* is an incredible play, a Socratic play in the built-in sense of paradox.

In my work what's important is to understand the argument, and actors especially have to understand that argument. If actors were to have, say, a month of rehearsal time, I'd tell them to spend three weeks understanding the *argument* of the play, and then to spend one week blocking. At the same time, they shouldn't have to do any of this nonsense about finding where characters in my plays 'come from'. If an actor wants to know where characters in my plays come from, just ask me. They come from my head. The exist because I've put them on paper. If an actor needs some information about them as human beings, then they also have their own personal humanity to draw on. I have always found the Stanislavsky approach to acting a very strange one. Marlon Brando, for instance, in preparing for his role in the film *On the Waterfront*, would have gone to spend some of his time in the company of a docker, a longshoreman. This is quite arbitrary. What if an actor bumped into the wrong docker? The character is a creation of the dramatist's imagination. You won't find him on any street.

The important thing to understand is the *argument* of the play and to see how you, as a human being, relate to it. If an actor plays his own interpretation then he has taken away the writer's authority, with the result that the audience is looking at the actor rather than at the play. And then, of course, the audience is let off the hook, because it doesn't have to make decisions. The actor has made the decisions. Theatre is not a passive experience as in the case of film and television. A television programme or a film has inevitably been edited, and the audience are passive watchers. But theatre can present arguments and allow the audience to participate in the debate. Dramatists can employ devices like irony to engage and undermine an audience. I believe that actors should not present a play in a way that prevents the audience from taking part in the argument because it is essential that theatre is a creative experience for the audience, too.

HWD: *I find what you've just said interesting notably in its analogy with film. Arthur Miller, one of the modern playwrights I know you admire, has said recently that screenwriting doesn't require you to write very well, that language in the process of film-making is 'skinned alive'. Do you agree with Miller that film has only a tenuous connection with conventional ideas of what 'literature' is, and what writing is?*

DE: Yes, indeed I do, though this is not to say that I don't find film an absolutely fascinating medium. When I was following an MA course in Cardiff under the inspiring tutelage of Norman Schwenk, I watched a lot of films and film versions of plays. I found that the versions that worked, that did least violence to the plays, were those which were filmed as stage productions, where the power and primacy of the *word* is upheld. Take Tarantino again: now he has introduced into film what can almost be called playwriting techniques. He's not shy of the word. In fact his works are word-bound, word-placed pieces.

HWD: *On top of which, of course, many of your own plays deal directly with the power of words, of language itself. One of your characters says of another, 'Your face became like a perfect sentence'.*

DE: I didn't fully understand the nature of language until I had read Wittgenstein. My play *Wittgenstein's Daughter* is not about philosophy. It's a play that alludes to Wittgenstein's philosophy for reasons that are to do with the fact that he was a philosopher of language. A playwright has to structure language dramatically. After an experience I had two years ago which is as close as you can get to a nervous breakdown without having one, I began to try to understand the way we structure our own lives and values. Because everything that is done is defined by how we *talk* about it, I needed to know more about the *way* we talked about it. I needed to know whether, in talking about what we were doing, we were just simply describing rather than actually defining it. There's a distinction there. When you're writing plays you can't be casual about language. If you're writing an 'argument' play and if you're putting characters on the stage, you have a responsibility in the artistic sense for the structuring of the dialogue, and you have a further responsibility to understand why the characters are saying what they say. In writing dialogue you have to understand not only the argument, but where the *language* of the argument is coming from in the first place.

HWD: *In the light of your cultural and philosophical emphases so far, do I dare raise the short-hand tag that so often tends to subsume these – when people describe a writer who presents arguments as being 'political'? Would you yourself say your plays were 'political'?*

DE: Oh yes. I'm a very political person, but in the Aristotelian sense. I don't exist without politics. I believe passionately in democracy and I've discovered that the more a political party talks about democracy, the more it's likely to take it away. If I'm an 'ist' at all, I'm a class-ist. I'm from the working class and I rejoice in that. If a working-class person can tell a middle-class director these days a truth of which he wasn't aware, then you can be certain that that director won't stage that playwright's work. In the eighties the paradox about London theatres was that they were radical theatres which were rejecting radical writers. Now, of course, London theatres have finally made the transition to a Thatcherite Director's Theatre, and they certainly don't use writers who have views, who have opinions. They would rather use writers who kowtow, who would do anything to have their play staged.

HWD: *And kowtowing, of course, is not something one could accuse you of doing. In fact, two years ago, you wrote a libretto which fluttered the Conservative, as well as the conservative, dovecotes of opera-goers in Kent, many of whom walked out of the performance. Did the experience unnerve you?*

DE: Not at all. This kind of thing has happened quite often to me. I quite enjoyed the Kent experience, and so did the actors and the other members of the audience at Broomhill. Broomhill is a wonderful country house outside Tonbridge in Kent where Jonathan Miller set up a centre for opera when Kent Opera collapsed. Broomhill is seen as a new Glyndebourne. I was commissioned to write the libretto for *The Beggar's New Clothes*, a reworking of *The Beggar's Opera* by John Gay. *The Beggar's New Clothes* offended the Tories of Tunbridge Wells in particular because there's a scene where a black heroin addict has a fix on stage and, to compound the insult to the Conservatives in the audience, in the opera that addict is also a local Tory Councillor. In fact when I saw the blue-rinse brigade arriving for the performance at Broomhill I knew they weren't going to like it, and they did indeed orchestrate a walkout. The last one to walk out was the Mayor. *The Beggar's New Clothes* transferred to the Cockpit Theatre in London and, to my added (you might say 'political') gratification, it received several very good reviews and was chosen as the 'Pick of the Week' in *What's On*.

HWD: *Let's take the 'political' a little bit further. When Time Out reviewed your play* Casanova Undone, *which was first performed at the Citizens' Theatre, Glasgow, the reviews praised your 'intellectually zestful writing' and stated that 'Edwards's "oeuvre" is shamefully avoided by mainstream London venues' because 'People don't want Truth, they want entertainment'. Recently BBC Wales turned down a play they had commissioned from you. What are your thoughts on BBC Wales's decision?*

DE: It seems to me that people will now be queuing up to deny that they were at all responsible for not broadcasting my play. I was told that Alan Yentob, Head of BBC1, was unhappy about the quality of the work appearing on BBC Wales and that a decision had been taken to look for new plays. I was commissioned to write one, but I didn't really think the BBC would be able to do a work of mine, because I believe that the BBC in Wales is an agent of trivilisation. It's all about presentation. You have these trailers which should be of no ultimate consequence but are better than the programmes themselves. There are a few people in the Drama Department whom I admire and who admire my work, and therefore I agreed to write a play which went through four drafts. There was no doubt about the quality of the work – nobody complained about that. But eventually I had a telephone call to say that the BBC wasn't going to do the play. I was given the impression that the decision came from the top – whoever or whatever 'the top' is.

The BBC is an institution, and individuals within it get institutionalized. They can't make decisions for themselves and therefore end up blaming others. My play was about racism in the Valleys. I'm from the Valleys, they're my cultural home. I've spent a large part of my life there. It's a dear place to me. Living now in Llanon, Cardiganshire, I heard on *Wales Today* that drug-taking in the Valleys has reached horrendous proportions and that the Valleys have become the most racist part of Great Britain. I naturally want to write about it. It is in any case the duty of any playwright to address the issues that are addressing us. The News – with the capital 'N' of the media – is a passive experience because you can't argue with it; but a play allows an audience to try and understand the issues. But BBC Wales didn't want that. I was told by a member of the Drama Department that the BBC, in refusing to do the play, had gone for safety. I find that disgusting. The BBC is an agent of pessimism because it is perfectly prepared to let us worry ourselves over the horror stories on its 'News' about the state of affairs in the Valleys, but it is not prepared to allow us, through our own creative skills, through our art, through our imagination, to try and *understand* these things. Pessimism leads to fascism, and paradoxically the BBC becomes an agent for the very fascism that it described in its report on racism in the Valleys.

HWD: *This autumn, the College of Further Education at Milford Haven also decided not to stage your new play,* Lola Brecht. *Why was that?*

DE: They banned the play without even reading or seeing it. All they'd seen was the flyer which said that the play contained language and imagery of a sexual or explicit nature. They decided they didn't want that in their college. What they were doing of course was protecting the grant they receive from Tory Councils. The whole ethos that Thatcher created is anti-art. Thatcherism is Fascism because it is deeply reactionary. Eric Heffer referred to Thatcher's 'jack-booted fascism' and it's exactly this that has led to the fear of creativity and the fear of people responding to creativity. Culture has become afraid of art – it's a paradox. People often think of my plays as bizarre, but when you think of the speech given by Michael Portillo, a government minister, at this year's Conservative Party Conference, you begin to see that my plays are not bizarre at all. In his speech Portillo was so obviously destructive, so obviously bowing to the lowest common denominator, and going deliberately for the most base and heinous instincts in people. His speech was like something out of a Ionesco play, and yet this man holds a leading government post. Now, *that's* bizarre. What's beyond the pale in any moral sense is not my work, but the society in which we live. It's dangerous when people have become so scared of art and creativity that they ban plays without even knowing what they're about.

HWD: *The irony of seeing a College of Further Education ban your play must have been very personally felt in your case. You have, after all, declared a very firm belief in the liberating influence of education. Is it this belief that makes you so committed to Theatre in Education?*

DE: I believe totally that education empowers people. I work with Spectacle Theatre Company in the Valleys, a company that is unjustly underrated, as is their extremely talented artistic director, Steve Davis. Spectacle addresses the various age groups in schools accurately, and the company most certainly meets the needs of schools in the Valleys where children cannot possibly afford to go to the theatre, not even to see a pantomime. But it's shameful that Spectacle has to do all this wonderful work on a shoestring. Before long they'll have to do it on profit share! Theatre in Education is the most difficult kind of theatre, at the cutting edge. Wales should rejoice in the fact that it has maintained its Theatre in Education tradition and that it is heading the world in this field. Kevin Lewis from Theatr Iolo goes to Prague to share his skills in this field and companies like Arad Goch, Outreach and Theatr Powys are all contributing marvellously.

Theatre in Education is theatre as education, and theatre as *counselling* too. It's the greatest kind of theatre. I don't envy David Hare at the National, playing to his pompous audiences. He should envy me, playing to an audience of school children.

HWD: *You've also had contact with university teaching and you continue to teach various Creative Writing courses within the University of Wales. Can you actually teach people how to write plays?*

DE: When I attended a workshop recently with Music Theatre Wales, I advised those who wished to attempt a libretto to listen to a great deal of music. I can hear the drama in Beethoven's *Eroica*, in Prokofiev's *Second Symphony* and in Shostakovich's *Fifth*. I know that when I write a libretto that fact comes across because composers have told me that I make it very easy for them. On the other hand, you can't write plays by watching programmes like *Neighbours* or *EastEnders*. You've got to read and re-read good plays, and understand how they're structured, how the masters have done it. For a play to be worth anything, the playwright has to have commitment, and has to have something worthwhile to say. There's no sense in which anything comes from nothing. But I come back to my first point. To write a worthwhile play you have to read the masters. I myself this summer have been reading Chekhov. It was an incredible experience.

HWD: *A private master-class through reading Chekhov, therefore. Does that mean we'll be detecting a Chekhovian note in your next play?*

DE: Absolutely. I feel a great need to interpret Chekhov because I feel the humanity of the man very strongly in the work. I've just written *Desire* for Theatr Powys in which I try to employ the same kind of techniques you find in Chekhov's magnetic speeches. I think it's the duty of every generation of playwrights to interpret previous dramatists in their own way, and, as I say, I feel the need to interpret Chekhov. I also feel a real affinity with him in his insistence that *The Cherry Orchard* is not a tragedy.

HWD: *This exact relationship to classic dramatic forms is interesting. You have, for example, described tragedy as 'undemocratic' and have insisted that your own* Lola Brecht, *which is touring at present, is an anti-tragic play: that's an interesting term. What does it mean?*

DE: Tragedy flourished during undemocratic times, when people had no authority over their lives. The tragic hero is essentially someone who has no power over his destiny – a notion that challenges the very precepts of a democratic age. *Lola Brecht* argues against the notion that destiny is important or that our death is in any way in the hands of 'the gods'. Very few modern playwrights claim to write 'tragedies'. Tragi-comedy is the genre for a democratic age. In *Death of a Salesman*, Arthur Miller sees Willy Loman as a tragic hero, but if I think of him that way I can't understand the play. Willy is something like my hero Gary Gilmore in *Utah Blue*. He's in search of the American Dream. But that

Dream is a paradox. In theory you can have everything, but if you don't have the dollars, you can't have anything. Willy's life is unfulfilled. This is not tragedy. We have to have a meaningful destination for our lives in each day. We don't find a meaningful destination in a fridge. I find it ironic that Willy Loman at the end of the play kills himself by driving into a wall. You can't say that the failure to realize the American Dream is tragic. It's a dead-end. That Dream has nothing to do with humanity, with values, or any of those things that make our lives meaningful in terms of a living, vibrant culture.

HWD: *So this brings us back somewhere near where we started. You have strong doubts regarding the creative confidence of any culture or cultures at present existing in Wales. On the other hand, I can't imagine you claiming that we could, even if we needed to, 'invent' a new Welsh culture.*

DE: But there are, apparently, people going round – proselytizers of one kind or another, Messiahs – declaring that we need a new culture here in Wales. The first thing I'd like to say in response to that question is that if you're born into a non-Welsh-speaking background, you're cursed. Napoleon tried to 'invent' culture, designed to unite Europe, and the very notion seems to me megalomanic. No, you can't invent a culture. Culture is what people respond to in their lives and the way they lead their lives. I would have loved to have been brought up Welsh-speaking. It must be great to have some kind of home to go to in the language. Instead, I'm categorized as Anglo-Welsh – that disgusting epithet. I object to that description of my culture because it makes me neither one thing nor the other. It's a kind of euphemism for saying you're a nobody. Just imagine 'The Diary of an Anglo-Welshman' – that is, 'The Diary of a Nobody'.

In the English-language parts of Wales you don't, unfortunately, have a cultural expression. You can quote rugby or choirs, of course, but I'm not particularly into those things, and English-language television in Wales doesn't help. In fact, it's almost the worst English-language television in the world. Most of the programmes people watch come, in any case, from outside Wales, programmes such as *Coronation Street* and *EastEnders*. And the aspirations of Welsh viewers are then trapped within the compass of those imported programmes. Young people in Wales, in both languages, are at home with Oasis, Pulp or Michael Jackson. It's pompous to suggest that we should 'invent' a culture for them. And by culture do the proselytizers, the Messiahs, mean culture with a capital 'C'? I despise High Culture, Establishment Culture, Freemasonary Culture. The important thing is to create a society wherein everybody can become part of the actual cultural experience. No, the idea of *inventing* a culture is far too arrogant.

HWD: *Lastly, then, how important is theatre, in particular, in the kind of situation you've been describing?*

DE: I think it's the most important thing. The last event that will take place before the world ends will be a theatre performance. Someone, somewhere, knowing the world is coming to an end, will want to stage a performance concerning the event. It would take too long to shoot a film. Someone will want to get up on stage and shout 'Please don't do this'. Theatre is about the only place left now where you can debate things publicly. You can't do that in television because you've got editors, sub-editors and sub-sub-editors, demi sub-editors, and, above them, super-editors, producers and directors, many of them with very little talent. The structure of television won't allow talented people to express themselves and, with deregulation, the smallest minds will get into the biggest places. I don't worry about that because we'll always have theatre. In Bosnia, for example, the one thing, in the middle of that catastrophe, that artists have

88

been determined to preserve is theatre. They've continued to put on their theatre shows. Theatre is one thing you cannot destroy and ultimately it's the one thing that will sustain us and keep us optimistic in a world where television is doing its best to drive us into states of despair and pessimism. A morally responsible theatre, presenting argument and encouraging debate, will never die.

Interview Two
April 1998

HWD: *You've often said that you are a working-class Welshman. But your plays deal with middle-class subjects in a highly intellectual way. This is true especially of a play like* Wittgenstein's Daughter.

DE: The severe reality is that the vast majority of people who go to the theatre are middle-class people, because theatre is too expensive for the working-class to afford. Culturally of course it's more complex than that. My audience is a middle-class audience, and if I were to write a play for them about a working-class situation in an analytical way it would come over as something of a complaint, a harangue or just anger. It would be dismissible in dramatic terms. Working-class plays of course *are* written, and written mostly by middle-class people, but they tend to be what I'd call 'chocolate-box' plays which just paint a picture of working-class life. You can imagine a middle-class photographer from New York going to the Dust Bowl in Oklahoma back in the 1930s during the depression, and taking photographs of these startled, almost unbearably lost people there, and taking the photographs back for the middle-classes of New York and Washington to see. These middle-classes would probably marvel at the quality of the photographs, but would do nothing to help the people who were starving out there in the Dust Bowl. But the photographs would do a hell of a lot for the reputation of the photographer. In a sense that is what theatre for the working-class is like in this country.

The kitchen sink, slice-of-life stuff is, in my opinion, just sentimental nonsense. What I'm interested in is looking at the condition of the working-class in all its complexity, and trying to analyse the complexity. The lives of the working-class are largely shaped by the middle-classes. It's probably no coincidence that the same people run the theatres, too, and so they are perfectly happy with a middle-class portrayal of the working-class. If the middle-classes shape the lives of the working-class, I want to know how responsible they are. I'm very critical of the people who govern us, namely the middle-classes, and that's why I write plays about them. But I'm a dramatist, not a politician or a propagandist. I think we live in a society, even under New Labour, where debate is marginalized once again. I've explained my views to you elsewhere about theatre as a forum for debate, the idea being that theatre can help us to progress as a society.[1] I think that in the overwhelming sea of creativity there is these days in film, television and literature, there is very little which deals with any kind of analysis of society. I think it's not too much to ask that there be a little island or a space in this ocean where people can debate the nature of society.

HWD: *In your Introduction to* Wittgenstein's Daughter *there's a note on 'real language' and 'apparent language'. Are these the languages of the two classes?*

DE: The 'apparent language' is the language of everyday discourse and the 'real language' is the language of being human. In the note, I qualify that by adding that the language of everyday discourse in our society is the language of the bourgeois classes, and the 'real language' is the language of the humanity tortured by the language of bourgeois politics. No, it's not exactly the language of the two classes. I find that the working-class speak a kind of language that derives from that of the middle-classes. The real language should really be the language of theatre – that's the point. In life, as in kitchen-sink drama, language isn't fulfilling its role properly.

There is of course a fundamental difference between the language of the two classes. Working-class people say 'We can't do that, we're not allowed to', whereas the middle-class, collectively, would be more inclined to say, 'We must be able to do that, we must find a way of overcoming our inability to do it'. Language is so important. The literary arts don't just *use* language, they are actually *about* language. I take Gertrude Stein's famous line, 'A rose is a rose is a rose', to be a line about language because it implies that there is a constancy about language that in more fanciful moments we might like to call truth. To me the whole point about language is that it begs for truth, and it's only the practice of language that gives us the idea of truth. It's a bit like colour. Colour only exists because we can see, but in another sense it exists because of light. And language demands of us access to the light. If we don't want truth, why speak? To use language for a purpose other than to tell the truth is to waste language, it's anti-language.

Some of our leading, most famous dramatists use language in the service of the ego, either to show what great representational painters they are or, in other cases, to show off their facility at the witty aside. They use language, and consequently theatre, falsely. Oscar Wilde was witty, but what makes a play like *The Importance of Being Earnest* so important is that the wit implies the serious, luminous core and the truth of the language he's using. It's not merely a superficial blessing as in the case of some of Wilde's imitators today who aren't even witty. Wit, to work, has to have an intellectual depth. I'm currently reading *Arcadia* by Tom Stoppard, and it's so superficial. You simply can't believe any of it. It's a dereliction of duty in some ways. It was the 'best play of the year' some years ago, but the stuff is empty. I do think that it's related to the proliferation of television and cinema writing. And I think it's going to get worse.

HWD: *I know you have strong views about the relationship between film and theatre. Could you talk about this relationship?*

DE: Well, there *isn't* a relationship. Two things couldn't be more different. I'm alarmed at the ease with which the plays of, say, someone like David Hare translate from stage to screen. I'm ashamed because he's regarded as a playwright. For an audience, cinema is essentially a passive experience, whereas theatre is an active and creative experience. Cinema and television are, of course, primarily entertainment. What a cinema audience sees is what comes through the camera, which is one way of seeing and which the director controls. So ultimately you're seeing what the director sees. This clearly precludes the notion of debate. In the theatre the situation is absolutely different, or should be. Of course, one of the failings of modern theatre in Britain is that it has become 'Director's Theatre', and the tendency now is to have the director's vision. This is appallingly reactionary. It's like living in a dictatorship where you do what the dictator wants you to do. In British theatre you see what the director wants you to see. The director looks at a text, chooses what he wants to see and then directs in a dictatorial, fascistic way. Under such circumstances real theatre can't happen.

In theatre you have live people on stage and live people in the audience, and the gap between the audience and the stage is full and fraught. It's like the aura at a political meeting where everybody is putting forward a point of view. The gap that exists between the screen and the audience is a dead gap. Its only business is to carry as much light as is needed to see the film. This reality about theatre suggests a society, people in one place, and the society progresses, develops and advances out of debate. It seems to me to be a negation of society if all we're concerned with in theatre is being titillated in some way. If in any circumstances in history, a group of people in a society come together for the sole purpose of being titillated then you can say that this is a society in collapse. The obvious example is Roman society in decline. It may be argued, of course, that in a restaurant you can have a corporate body of people. But there's no debate going on there, because in a restaurant people are separate at their own tables. There's only an illusion of people being together. In a restaurant you're distracted by people coming and going, by the waiter, by the food. In theatre there's no such distraction. The experience in the theatre is focused and intense. To waste that on trivial joke-telling as in West End comedy is a dereliction of duty.

Of course, some big theatres are designed to help you forget that you're in the theatre and make you believe you're in a cinema. Cinemas came out of, in many respects, Victorian melodrama which was really just entertainment with some heavily plotted story which used music very often – hence melodrama – to elicit emotive responses. And, of course, Victorian melodrama has been in many ways discredited. It's an aberration. Theatre should be looking back to find its roots. Also, I think there are some kinds of theatres where you can even have a meal while you're watching the play. What an outrage. It sounds as if all the people in that space, the actors and the audience, are two separate species. But there should be an interaction between the actor and the audience; in a sense it should be as if the actor had just stepped out of the audience. Edward Bond says that society sends the audience to the theatre. This makes so much sense. This means that in the theatre space we recognise an intensity of experience going on, which does what all art does, which is to enable us to look at our lives and our society in a new way and a way that helps us to progress.

HWD: *You've talked about your view of theatre. What about your view of yourself as a Welsh dramatist? You've recently declared that you're not a Welsh writer, indeed not even a Welshman.*

DE: No I'm not, and it's a pity. It's a conclusion I've arrived at from the application of logical thought. Is Norman Mailer an American or a Jew? If I were living in America and someone asked Is Dic Edwards an American or a Welshman, I would have to say 'I'm American.'

HWD: *Why couldn't you say that you're a Welsh American?*

DE: If anyone asked 'Is Dic Edwards Welsh or British?' I'd have to say 'I'm British', because there's something about being Welsh that's a little like being Jewish. There's an intensity about it that can be compared to the racial intensity of being Jewish. And, I suppose, historically, some of the experiences have been the same. I suppose I'm a bit like Bob Dylan who was once a Jew and became a Christian. Presumably he felt that he couldn't, with justification, call himself Jewish. I was once Welsh, and now am British, because I can't with justification call myself Welsh. I don't speak the language. I suppose I'm a bit of a purist. There's this anomaly that's taken place in Welsh culture. So much, by definition, of what is truly Welsh is predicated now on the language. During the last fifteen or twenty years so many people have come into Wales because they haven't been able to get work in England, and they've learnt the Welsh language, and taken positions in the media and the arts, and so on. These are basically middle-class English people who are filling cultural positions in Wales. So the major influence in Wales is that of middle-class English filtered through the Welsh language.

There are serious implications here, devastating ones, because we are creating outside Welsh-speaking Wales – which will always have a cultural identity of its own – a cultural waste land. So you will understand that my argument about not being Welsh is an intellectual one and not an emotional one. If you want to see this anomaly on a grand scale look at the so-called Welsh Theatre – theatre outside Welsh-language Theatre. It's not Welsh at all. What's Welsh about the Torch Theatre in Milford Haven? It hasn't, I don't think, ever had a Welsh artistic director. Or take Theatr Clwyd. Has that theatre ever had a Welsh artistic director? It looks as if Theatr Clwyd, as I understand it, is to be regarded as the National Theatre of Wales. When I went up there, not so long ago, out of the repertoire of plays they were doing at the time, one was a 1960s proto-gay play, which isn't a gay play anyway, and is in fact a supercilious commentary on the situation of gays before the legislation which freed them. I'm talking about *Entertaining Mr Sloane* which isn't funny any more because the joke has been blown anyway. The other play was *Equus* which is an entirely superficial play about someone who stabs horses. It has, I suppose, some interesting if not very original psychological notions. It's most notable for its superficial spectacle rather than for a true theatrical experience. And then there was *Abigail's Party* which isn't a play, but a television piece, which is one of those insulting pieces in terms of humanity, written by Mike Leigh, a master of insults. He hasn't anything remotely to do with Wales. A theatre like Theatr Clwyd, situated in Wales, won't produce plays by Welsh playwrights.

HWD: *So how should Welsh theatre proceed?*

DE: That's an interesting choice of word, 'proceed', because it is rather a procession rather than a progression of the kind of plays I've talked about. It's a procession of plays that are irrelevant even to their cultural origins, but which are, for some reason, felt to be appropriate in a Welsh context. I voted for the Welsh Assembly because I was hoping that, when it's instituted, the playwrights of Wales, within the Welsh Playwrights Company, which we hope to enlarge, will be able to join a debate about theatre that ultimately could possibly lead to a theatre that is *about* debate in Wales. How can any theatre in Wales claim to be reflecting a Welsh culture when it refuses to use the playwrights of Wales? Many of those playwrights have had to work outside Wales. There's a whole list of writers living in Wales whose plays have been done throughout Britain, in London, Leicester, Glasgow, Northern Ireland, Europe and North America. There's no trace of them in mainstream Welsh theatre like Theatr Clwyd.

HWD: *You've just mentioned the 'Welsh Playwrights Company'. Are you a member?*

DE: I'm an honorary member. I claim refugee status, a kind of temporary citizenship. Yes, I'm a refugee in Wales. Incidentally I spell my name now with a 'k' instead of 'c', to mark the change that logic has brought to my status.

[1] See previous interview.

Interview Three
October 2004

HWD: *I had anticipated that in this interview we would discuss the exciting responses to your play* Franco's Bastard *and the equally public response to the libretto of* Manifest Destiny *on which you collaborated with Keith Burstein and Corin and Vanessa Redgrave. I would also have valued your views on your important involvement with Spectacle. However, I appreciate your wish to devote this interview to some wider thoughts.*

DE: Yes, I'll tell you why. I think what a lot of people don't understand about theatre is its power to transcend. You probably need to think about it a lot to realise that, and most people who hold the cultural purse strings neither frequent much serious theatre nor think often about cultural things, let alone think about the transcendent nature of it all. So what difference does it make? The difference is that it can raise you up. It can take you beyond yourself. We live in a small country, and that produces an intensity of experience that confuses us: it makes us think that somehow we need to identify with the country itself in order to have identity ourselves. As long as we think that's the case then we're not ready for theatre. Theatre is the antidote to small country angst.

HWD: *But even angst presupposes that you* have *an identity, and an identity presupposes location, a country, not least because it presupposes a language.*

DE: But you can't see unless you can get beyond yourself. No lasting or unimpeachable truth was ever discovered in the unalloyed service of self. Any truth arrived at subjectively is an accident. We live in a culture which glories in its proselytizing of comfort. All our predispositions are amoral because we accept the comfort and cushioning of received judgements as a kind of civic or social or national duty. To rise above these practised positions, and the certainty they carry, is to encourage eviction and outlaw-dom. In many ways theatre is the natural hideout of the outlaw. I've talked in my previous interview with you about the Theatre of the Evicted – this is the only worthwhile theatre. We need to separate theatre even from the grant-giver – whether it is Arts Council or government.

HWD: *But governance isn't society.*

DE: Yet we need to write as if it were. We need to treat theatre as prisons and see them, as we see prisons, as places that need to be urgently built and manned in order to protect bourgeois society from the outlaws who gather there. To gain entry you ought to be prepared to commit crimes against order and propriety – the offspring of malfeasance. All modern, especially Western, societies are built on malfeasance.

Lincoln, the first Republican President, made a poem in the blood and dirt of Gettysburg which included the marvellous peroration:

> It is rather for us, the living, we here be dedicated to the great task remaining before us – that, from these honored dead we take increased devotion to that cause for which they here, gave the last full measure of devotion – that we here highly resolve these dead shall not have died in vain; that the nation shall have a new birth of freedom, and that government of the people by the people for the people, shall not perish from the earth.

HWD: *A great testament indeed – and interestingly the shortest and only memorable speech made that day.*

DE: Lincoln's oration was already theatre: the words expressed truths which transcended Lincoln himself. Ever since, instead of those words being used as a guide for a responsible society with a yearning for freedom while acknowledging Rousseau's chains, they have been used in the service of malfeasance – at an almost philosophical level – as though the idea had been too big for the mere 244 words which held it.

The theatrical and cultural establishment in Britain is a reflection of the malfeasance practised by the political class. Theatre should militate against this corruption. But how can it when it's become its metaphor? Theatre which serves the comfort of a self-happy culture is pointless and should be shunned, its buildings emptied of theatrical accessories and given over to the mad. When *Wittgenstein's Daughter* was produced at The Citizen's Theatre in Glasgow, the best audience was one which turned up one free Monday evening from the asylum (as we called it then). They loved the play, totally understood it. This is a paradigm of how theatre works that should be followed.

HWD: *Theatre as merely the reflection of 'that which it was nourished by': it would be a sad pass. Is the same true of Wales?*

DE: Indeed, Wales must be one of the few cultures in which the marketing of what's perceived as that culture and its arts has a higher priority than the supporting of the creation of the art itself. The effect of this is that there's less and less actually to market, and so it becomes a culture in which the marketers market the marketers. It's like television becoming its own justification. TV is more and more about TV than the world it broadcasts in. Weather women turn up as items on the news!

BBC Wales is very strong on promoting itself and its cultural values which are a kind of cultural sub-species to which belong phenomena like Macdonalds and film stars with their dubious auras. When these sub-species of culture dominate culture itself we get nihilism. It appears to be revolutionary. A dialectical historical process has taken place in which theatre is displaced and becomes meaningless for most people. This is why those who run theatres produce shows which simply mimic TV. There's been no revolution – more a fascistic take-over of culture.

HWD: *It's a depressing scenario. But you spoke at the outset about theatre's available power to transcend.*

DE: For theatre to transcend, the writers need to write transcending theatre. I don't know whether my plays do this. Maybe they do, which is why they're not often produced beyond a first, usually quite short, run. But I do know that I use my imagination and creativity to get there. This is the main thing: creativity. It's an easy word to say but saying it doesn't mean you've achieved it. Creativity has become a marketer's word, but the marketers know nothing about it. Creativity is about going beyond the boundaries – all of them. A bit as an outlaw does. If I hadn't become a writer I might have become a criminal. This is a common enough notion – I wrote about it in *Utah Blue* – but whether it's commonly realised is another thing. Creativity ought to be like breaking and entering: the racing of the pulse and the pumping adrenalin got going by the not knowing what's coming next – it could be a guy with an axe. If it's too easy to burgle a house, you lose the drama – you might get the loot but you lose the thrill. It's the same when you write a play.

HWD: *And true of the role of drama in Wales no less than anywhere else?*

DE: Exactly so. I'm glad you reminded me of one thing. *Kaleidoscope*, the BBC Arts programme, did one of its last shows, and one of the few live ones, on the set of my play *Utah Blue*. I was asked on the show what a play about a murderer in Utah had to do with Wales. I shouldn't have destroyed the moment with an answer. I probably said that it had everything to do with Wales and everywhere else, and I'd hold to that. This being confined by the obvious and the facile is unfortunately at the heart of any cultural administration's relationship with creativity. They're imprisoned by walls and rubrics and endless documents listing targets and cutting-edge demands and bad conversation and office posturing and just wanting to go home.

Wittgenstein's Daughter exists beyond these boundaries – that's why those mad people in Glasgow could enjoy it. Most of my produced plays are commissioned. I've only rarely had an unsolicited play accepted. I can understand this. I comfort myself with the thought that if these people bound so strongly by their limitations were able to see the totality of my play on the page, I would probably have failed. Anyone able to see such a play on the page is creative in his or her own right.

HWD: *That reminds us of others, beyond the writing. Directors, for example.*

DE: The most creative director I know and therefore the best is Steve Davis the director of Spectacle Theatre. He's like a George Devine – an exception that proves the rule that most directors are self-servers. One other exception to this is Simon Harris of Sgript Cymru who valiantly attempts to meet the Arts Council brief set him and badly needs a building. As it is, Spectacle is the best new writing theatre company in Wales with its history and fearlessness, though it's hardly recognised as such by the authorities.

So much of the theatre that's produced in the West (outside the commercial sector, where you *expect* the worst) is tedious. I mean, of course, the stuff that's produced by companies like Theatr Clwyd in Wales – like a school timetable for a child which weighs you down with the expectedness of it all at exactly the age when you need adventure; or a job you don't question on the long haul to retirement or one of those car alarms that go off in the deep of your night and irritate like chilblains. I say this as a playwright in the thick of it and not as someone who occasionally goes out for a couple of hours of entertainment as a part of life's routine.

HWD: *But I can't think of you as defeatist. Won't what you've called the 'transcendent' power of drama, and of art generally, by* *transcending, in the end also change the scene and the system? Or was Auden right: 'poetry makes nothing happen'?*

DE: I am indeed sometimes ashamed of myself for fooling myself – for thinking, not so much that I might make a difference to the world with my plays, but that I might make a difference to Theatre! I do really think that at the heart of this whole thing is the fact that our culture doesn't understand Art. Either we dismiss it as a word that ponces use or it is a word that ponces use. And I say ponces because ponces are the regulators of prostitution – which is what the world of 'art' is about. The whole deal about going with a prostitute is that orgasm is superficial. Nothing transcendent happens because she's not going to let it happen. Economic screwing is, at best a craft but there's no art in it. The art comes when your lover lets you transcend by giving you as much or more than you can give her or him. The experience of most people visiting the theatre is the experience of visiting a whore.

Someone recently stole Munch's painting 'The Scream'. This is considered a great tragedy but all that's gone is one physical manifestation of the creativity – of the thought and vision. We have limitless reproductions of the painting.

HWD: *I see what you mean, and clearly the survival of creativity itself is more important than the survival of one manifestation of it. But wouldn't the equivalent in drama be the permanent loss of a script, and the only comfort thereafter the satisfaction that 'creativity' had occurred, and that we still have somebody's paraphrase?*

DE: Except that in our world the object, the thing that can be made a commodity of, is consistently more important than the vision. Our theatre mimics this reality.

True theatre exists in a timeless present. It's not the world of those who populate the policy-making offices, those behind the curtains in the back-stage darkness, those lurking behind the arras and the Machiavellian Artistic Directors. Think about that title for a moment. Who *directs* art? Or who directs the art of the play? Or what director is so arrogant as to think he's artistic? Most (I do want to keep saying 'most', not 'all') ADs are uncreative, self-serving, cultureless parasites who have no concept of art's timelessness or transcendent power but only their quotidian petty preoccupations. While these who know nothing about the ownership of Art, the democracy of Art, play politics with theatre, we, like Socrates and Shakespeare will make theatre of politics and not the day-to-day party politics but a politics that Lincoln let us catch a glimpse of, a politics which resides in the deepest motives and relationships between human beings with all their flaws and glories and betrayals, their needs and desires: those human goals that are not particular to any one culture or any one country or any one language. Theatre is life just as life is theatre, and when all this dust settles it may be seen, if there's anyone left to see it, that there was this practice engendered by man's natural desire for goodness and virtue and justice, and by his quest to understand why, for example, we ever indulge in the horrors of war.

Too much of our theatre today measures everything by the evening's profit; they are petty war zones and made absurd by that fact. This theatre belongs in *Gulliver's Travels*. Artistic Directors seem bent on destroying their theatres (if audiences diminish, it's never because of what's *not* on!) but they cannot destroy Theatre.

HWD: *So why so much animus against today's theatre?*

DE: Surprisingly, it's got nothing to do with me living in Wales but everything to do with it (by which I mean the abstract generality) being run by cultural enemies who would rather lock me up in a real prison than a real theatre.

Wittgenstein's Daughter by Dic Edwards

Charles Way

Interview One
March 1996

HWD: *You were brought up in Devon, educated at Rose Bruford, and worked with the Leeds Theatre, the Theatre Royal, Stratford East and the Theatre Centre, London. A very English background in rural as well as metropolitan locations: so what brought you to Wales?*

CW: Marriage – in the sense that my wife spent a lot of her childhood in Aberystwyth. In the late seventies we were living in London and one day my wife had a telephone call from Gwent Theatre. I, by then, had just come to the end of my contract with the Theatre Centre in London where I had been resident writer for a year. That year was a very important one in terms of my training as a writer, but I knew I didn't want to live in London, and neither did my wife. So we landed in Crickhowell. That was in 1980.

HWD: *I asked what brought you to Wales, but of course, Crickhowell places you in an area that is more accurately called 'border country', a term that carries its own complexity. You wrote* Border Town *for Monmouth and did a stage adaptation of Bruce Chatwin's* On The Black Hill. *Did your own sense of 'border-country' lie behind your choices?*

CW: Yes, but that interest in border country took a long time to gather momentum. I didn't know anyone in Crickhowell and I didn't know the history of the Welsh. I was in a new country. But during that period I walked hills and took an interest in the history of the area. I suppose you do that when you move to a new place. I now live in Abergavenny and I enjoy living in a market town which is about the same size as the town in Devon where I come from, with similar social values, but not as conservatively led in the same way as the small Devonian town where I grew up. So a mixture of walking the hills and talking to people led to my interest in the Border, and it has become a very interesting metaphor for me.

HWD: *I used the word 'complexity', but your own word 'metaphor' of course conveys that – and is better. Can you tell me something about what the metaphor means for you?*

CW: It's to do with not belonging to one state or the other. I'm an Englishman, but being a Devonian I'm not the same as an Englishman from the Home Counties. I understood early on that there was a difference and that I did not identify fully with the culture of the Home Counties. But I also knew that I couldn't associate fully with the culture of the West Country with its landed classes. In coming to Wales I could in a sense be independent, and attach myself to and take nourishment from a new set of ideas, literature, people and places.

HWD: *You'd had two years' experience of writing for theatre before you came to Wales. What was the nature of that experience? What part of it did you bring with you?*

CW: My experience of writing for the theatre in the late seventies was one which I still keep pursuing. From the beginning I have sought to work with actors in a predetermined space, and to place myself within the theatrical process. When I left college, I got a job as an actor with Leeds Theatre and we toured schools with plays which we ourselves had made, so I was involved with a group of people who asked questions such as 'Why should we make this play now?', 'Who are we going to make it *for*?', and 'In *what* theatrical context?' We went into a school hall, got the kids to come round in a circle, performed the play in front of them, and then had the time to examine what we had made and what effect we had achieved. We examined the entire process. Making that kind of theatre was an act of collaboration, and that is essentially what I still do. The act of making theatre with actors remains important to me, combined of course with a growing responsibility for the writing part of it.

HWD: *In the Introduction to your published volume* 3 Plays *you refer to the 'invigorating partnership' you developed with Hijinx Theatre in Cardiff and the fact that you offered two of the published plays,* In the Bleak Midwinter *and* Paradise Drive *to the actors in scenario form, in order to stimulate improvisation. When working so closely with actors and directors – or whoever – isn't there a danger that the finished work will appear like 'a devised play' or a 'group effort'?*

CW: Improvisation can fail if the writer does not have already – ahead of time – a clear enough idea about how to benefit from the skills of the actors. When I was learning my craft I used to try to include all the ideas the actors themselves had given me, not with a view to the strength of the play, but because I felt a responsibility towards the actors' own input. But with Hijinx in particular, as the working method became more mature we were able to do our own individual jobs, and do them individually. So the design was able to be as good as any one designer could make it, with input (as opposed to interference) from other people as well as myself. The actors were also mature enough to do very silly things in front of the director, the writer and, of course, one another, and to create raw material which I could then bend, use and mould into what I like to think of as my own 'individual voice'. So it didn't seem like a 'devised play'. It didn't appear to be a 'group effort', but a play written by one person. After all, the skills of the writer were still apparent. The individual voice wasn't lost within the process.

HWD: *The relationship with Hijinx has obviously been a creative one. How was it first established?*

CW: The connection was established through a long process of belonging to a theatre movement with its roots in community theatre and young people's theatre, in which there is a strong network which allows you to meet companies like Hijinx. They had seen the work I'd done with Gwent and other companies and in due course they invited me to participate in their projects. I like to think that the combination of my writing and their technical skills has resulted in stronger and more individual work and indeed in better theatre.

HWD: *I would imagine, however, that working in community theatre could mean that you're not in control of the situation in the way you are when working with a company performing in main-line, large-scale venues. So what does control things? Is it 'community' or 'theatre'?*

CW: There is no doubt that working in the field of community theatre is very risky, but the rewards are also greater because audience, actor and play are in closer contact. One of the first pieces of community theatre I did was *She Scored for Wales* with Gwent Theatre. It was written for a specific community but I now feel confirmed in my feeling that it was a work that had universal application. It was a piece of theatre that the audience responded to in a completely vocal way. It was a play based on *Lysistrata*, and I used the metaphor of the Welsh Rugby Club in which the women went on a sex strike in order to stop their men from ruling their lives. They wanted their *own* leisure activities. We went into Pontypool Rugby Club with this and the result from the audience was total engagement. The play obviously worked on a humorous level, but at the same time it hit a note which was quite electric, and amplified. We got a sense of great enjoyment where a whole community was relishing, and realising, a play. We felt the audience were fully aware that something was being challenged. And there were indeed quite a few arguments and questions after the performance.

Community theatre takes drama to people who don't normally go to see actual performances of plays. That doesn't mean to say that such people aren't educated in how to respond to, or interpret what is going on. In Wales the collapse of the traditional big industries had led to a collapse also in the sense of community, and it follows that there is a change in the nature of community audience. But that audience still appreciates the fact that you are performing in their space – invited in, as it were. The relationship between the audience and the actors is therefore different, because there is communication *before* and *after* performances. There is a whole ethos there which has its own awareness of communication and its own values.

At the same time, I would like now to develop my skills as a writer, and ask the audience to watch a moment with greater intensity. Sometimes in community theatre you cannot get the complete intensity of the moment. This is because, as you rightly say, you can't 'control' community theatre. The light, the sound, the action, the nature of the audience itself, are beyond the dramatist's control. So you have to work harder, because you can get only the basics *absolutely* right. In community theatre you always work with something beyond your characters or your story.

HWD: *You clearly have firm faith in this kind of theatre, and I gather that the play you're working on at present is a community play. Can you tell us a little about the new play?*

CW: It's called *The Dove Maiden* and it's based on a Russian folk tale. This is an access point for me which is based on story-telling. It's a play about Evil. There has been so much happening, from the James Bulger case to Bosnia to Dunblane, to make us all so aware of this word 'Evil' and its significance that it has made me question whether any of us, in a different situation, or if our world were to collapse economically, would be so above other countries and structures that we couldn't descend into barbarism. And if we did, would it be possible to live a normal life afterwards? This is really what is at stake in my new play. The form of the Russian folk tale means, as I said, that this new community play has an access point which is story-telling and therefore universal.

It's about a soldier who has done terrible things. Although he has committed atrocities, he tried to lead a new life after the war. His past chases him in the form of Death, in the way that Death appears as a character in Russian folk tales.

HWD: *That prompts me to ask whether there is any background research called for before you start scripting?*

CW: It depends what the subject is. Obviously being a writer is a solitary activity, and for me, in order to get intellectual stimulation, I need to get the *opposite* idea to the one I've got in my mind. I go out and look for that, and I try to get it through talking to people or through reading. You've got to recognise the opposition. You've got to recognise – or at least imagine – that it's worthy of respect. There's a great deal of truth in the old saying 'Give the devil the best lines.' My plays are now more about asking questions than making statements. Which is not, I hope, to say that they don't embody 'answers'. When I began writing I was trying to *state* something and my research focused on finding out the facts. That has changed but I still have to know the world in which my characters are moving, but at the same time I need to develop my own attitude towards that world. I've recently completed *Somebody Loves You*, a play about a family who go on a Country and Western weekend. So I attended that kind of event – in Scotland, with ten thousand Scots people, in Butlins, a hugely alcoholic affair with Country music – and it was great. I even dressed up as a cowboy, and I'm convinced that I would not have been able to write the play had I not done it in terms of this particular social experience. That particular experience didn't change the 'meaning' of the play. I knew what I wanted to get at before I went to Scotland, but that research was important. I do a great deal of work before I start writing. The writing comes later on in the process.

HWD: *But whatever the background or the social experience of the play, you have frequently said that what you seem to do in your plays is 'tell a story', and you've emphasised the importance of harnessing and relaying the energy and power of story-telling.*

CW: Story-telling goes back to childhood when one heard those magic words 'Once upon a time'. So there's an element of escape in it, but at the same time an element of engagement.

If you can combine those two things for an audience then I think you're on fertile ground. Stories are 'deconstructed' so much at the moment because that's the fashionable thing to do, but I tend to try to harness their power as *narrative*. I find that stories are the best way of engaging with immediate social problems without necessarily writing socially realistic plays. I enjoy flights of fancy. But that need not be a matter of fleeing from anything.

HWD: *Social realism and a flight of fancy. Are both descriptions true of, say, your domestic play* Paradise Drive?

CW: Ah, that's a one-off. I've written only two 'socially realistic' plays. One was *Witness*, a play about Julius and Ethel Rosenberg, executed for allegedly selling the secret of the atom bomb to the Soviets. The other was *Paradise Drive*, and a newspaper article was the source of inspiration for that play. It's about an artist who was trying to survive the 1980s and also about what was happening to the Arts under Thatcher's government. Although *Paradise Drive* has its roots in realism it is not naturalistic; every now and then the characters burst into song which transcends the action in a spectacular way. The music was by Philip Thomas who writes very expansive music which took the play out of the box of the ordinary. We had quite difficult responses to that play and the company were very brave to give it another production. The second time around we made the first three acts before the boy commits suicide quite light and opened it up, and this made the final act more 'allowable'. We'd earned the right to make that suicide happen. But in *Paradise Drive*, as in my other plays, I was still telling a story.

HWD: *But at the same time you've also said that there is 'in any good play, the story* behind *the story'. What do you mean by that?*

CW: I mean that the writer needs to struggle to find clarity of purpose. For me, a piece never works unless there has been a struggle to find this clarity. I always need to answer the question 'Why do I need to write this play?' and once I know the answer I can make it clear to the audience what exactly I seek to examine. I can then be sharp rather than woolly or obscure, and for me, the art of playwriting is to give a clear vision, a particular insight to the audience through the characters and through the action. Sometimes when I see a play that doesn't work I feel that a writer has an *instinct* about what he seeks to write about but hasn't really discovered the driving force behind the work. It has to do with emotional and intellectual rigour. A writer has really to test himself and ask 'Is this what I *really* want to show?' and, if so, 'How may this be interpreted?' Very often a story, a metaphor can convey what I really want to show, while helping me also to tell a particular tale.

HWD: *This is very much the case, isn't it, with your psychological Western,* Dead Man's Hat, *where it seems you've turned the premise of the film* Shane *on its head. But, first of all, a general point about America. It appears that, as for many other dramatists in Wales, America has been a powerful magnetic force. You've said, for example, that, for you as a child, America and its culture was 'a good deal closer than the North of England'.*

CW: Indeed. When I was a kid all the programmes on television I remember were American – Rin Tin Tin, Bronco Lane and a whole series of Westerns. And then through the 1960s you got the powerful image of *The Man from U.N.C.L.E.* American culture was very strong. Everything seemed lively and bright over there. In terms of watching films, America was also an important part of my politicisation. I'd been fed all this stuff about Westerns and adventure movies, and then suddenly, in the late 1960s and early 1970s, along came several films like *Soldier Blue*, where that world was reversed. As a young student of course I'd read books like Dee Brown's *Bury My Heart at Wounded Knee*, and all at once there was a collision of the old world, which I'd imagined to have a certain moral certainty, with this new uncertain world.

HWD: *It's that dichotomy that's interesting. Against the background of early attraction, there is by no means on your part an unquestioning allegiance to 'old' American values. On the contrary,* Dead Man's Hat *is all questioning.*

CW: The situation of *Dead Man's Hat* is indeed a reversal of the film *Shane* where the lonely gun-slinger who is trying to go straight – although that's a huge lie in itself – saves the homestead from the evil cattle barons. By turning it round I was trying to look at the image of the outsider and at the image of the family who trusted this man to save them. The outsider, Clay, in my play represents America but he also is the one bent on destroying it. It's important to see that Jim Averill, the character in the play who is the liberal, misreads Clay's character completely. He thinks that Clay represents the West and freedom, but Jim Averill, from his idealistic standpoint, can't see the dark underside of Clay and what he stands for.

HWD: *That's particularly interesting because, after all these years of 'viewing' America from a distance, I understand that you'll be coming face-to-face with the country this summer. Where will you be based, and what is the occasion of your going?*

CW: I've been invited over to the Sundance Institute in Utah near Salt Lake City in the Rocky Mountains. The Institute was set up by the film star Robert Redford to develop theatre and film scripts, and it also has a children's theatre section. I'll be there for three weeks, working on *The Dove Maiden*, the play I'm currently writing for Hijinx

Theatre. There'll be twelve other writers there from all around the world, and we'll be working with twenty-four actors. This is a rare opportunity. I'll also be realising a long held ambition simply to go to America.

HWD: *How did the invitation come about?*

CW: David Kirk Chambers, the Director of the Sundance Institute, was asked over to a festival of young people's theatre at Aberystwyth recently, and Yvette Vaughan Jones, the International Officer of the Arts Council, gave him a copy of my plays. He read them, and three weeks later I received an invitation to Utah.

HWD: *You've also received this year a Writer's Bursary from the Literature Committee of the Arts Council of Wales. Why from the Literature, rather than the Drama Committee?*

CW: I applied specifically to the Literature Committee because I felt I wanted to write something that wasn't strictly a play and because I wanted to find an individual voice outside the 'practical needs' of the theatre. I wanted to be able to concentrate simply on the *word* for a change and on my own development as a writer. I work very much by commission, responding to the demands of theatre – and, under those conditions, you have to work quickly. You have to get the play in – and on – in time. There's always this very finite period. Suddenly you've got to stop writing even though you feel the script could be improved if you were only given a little more time to work at it.

I think the Literature Committee saw in my work a lyrical and poetic voice which could find a meaningful form outside the parameters of theatre.

HWD: *In* Oh Journeyman, *your play about the poet Alun Lewis, you brought an actual playwright and poetry itself within the* *parameters of theatre. What drew you to write* Oh Journeyman? *Was it, as Yeats would have asked, the life or the work?*

CW: Oh, the poems definitely. As the father of young children I found I didn't have time to read long prose works, but I read a great deal of poetry. It seemed to me that in Alun Lewis's poems there was a wonderful journey from Wales and the closed world of church and chapel and valleys to the world of mystical experience in India. But his discovery was hampered by being in the Army and his central concerns with being a pacifist. Alun Lewis's own religious and spiritual journey seemed to me to be things worth talking about in our time. He had found ways in his poems of talking about his concern with a lyrical sureness of touch which I found fascinating. I tried to use these themes and tried also to create a love story which was about Alun and his wife Gwenno. I wasn't mature enough at that time. I was too much in awe of the material. I wasn't sufficiently relaxed as a writer to write the play freely, so I never found my own voice. It was always a pale shadow of Alun Lewis's voice. I may come back to the play one day.

HWD: *Is it significant that we've moved from your delight in story-telling to your fascination also with the rhythm of poetry and with the expressiveness of lyrics and songs? The latter forms are apparent in nearly all your plays. Frequently characters burst into song, and dialogue is interspersed by song and haunting refrains. Why?*

CW: Time, or a sense of time – music – is always dynamic in the theatre. You can't provide landscapes in the theatre as you can in a film – say of Bruce Chatwin's *On the Black Hill* – where you can pan about, zoom in on, and look over the border country and have two little people look like ants in such a context. In my stage adaptation of *On the Black Hill* I used music throughout to conjure the missing landscape. Music has that function – no, that power. Music in the theatre has also the power of being able to move you from place to place, without employing the mechanics, the trappings of theatre. That is to say, you can *move* through song. You can also reach an emotional place which is not attainable just through words. Music allows a release in the audience, and the use of music, song, physical theatre and text is one of the most important mixtures that theatre has to offer these days. Anyway, I've always liked music and song – it's a richer experience than the one you get within 'naturalism'.

HWD: *'Naturalism' in the strict sense wouldn't of course work within your particular kind of theatre, certainly not in the venues where many of your community plays are performed. How do you think your audiences would react to a really 'naturalistic' play?*

CW: If you go into a small village hall it's very hard to do a play naturalistically. You can't these days go through the pretence of the existence of a 'fourth wall' and do a play as if the audience weren't there. So you immediately enter a much more lively theatre zone. Also naturalism seems to be associated with a particular set of playwrights we've moved away from.

HWD: *Your play* In the Bleak Midwinter *defies questions about realism of any kind. Here, you've adopted the convention of the medieval miracle play, where the Wakefield Second Shepherds' Pageant is relocated in the Abergavenny border country. The Hijinx production of* In the Bleak Midwinter *received lyrical reviews, and rightly so. What do you yourself think accounted for the success of this production?*

CW: The Second Shepherds' Pageant was a great source of inspiration. I had previously done a whole set of miracle plays in the Devonshire dialect and knew that in terms of richness of language and rhythms they would adapt equally well to the border accents around Abergavenny. Although

In the Bleak Midwinter is very contemporary and comic, it was wonderful to see audiences, about a third of the way through the performance, realising that they knew the story, that it was that of Mary and Joseph, and that the shepherds in the play were the shepherds of the Christian story. I tried to harness the inherent energy and fun of the miracle play nativity story, and to use them as points of reference.

HWD: *You have in your work used several other sources as points of reference. What are the advantages of using, for example, established texts, or films, as starting points?*

CW: As I've mentioned, *She Scored for Wales* was based on the *Lysistrata*, *Dead Man's Hat* on *Shane*, while *Ill Met by Moonlight* took *A Midsummer Night's Dream* as its inspiration. I find that these points of reference give me an invisible person to argue with! I question the values embodied in the original. They also provide a form I can mould and use to my own ends. So, for instance, even if people weren't fully aware when they were watching *Ill Met By Moonlight* of the nature of *A Midsummer Night's Dream* they would recognise Puck in the character in my play and they would soon be aware of the fact that several of his speeches half-referred to Shakespeare's play, thereby providing a ripple effect. There is a kind of safety in the form. The relationship between the fairy world and the world of mortals in my play is allowable because there is a 'history' to this relationship in Shakespeare's *Dream*.

In the first movement of *Ill Met by Moonlight* the different desires of the four central characters are established and from then on the play goes through a journey that either obstructs those desires or complicates them. The audience enjoys watching the way in which the characters react to these obstructions, and is also prompted to ask 'Will they get what they want?' Underneath all that is the further question, 'What does it mean?' If they don't get what they want, it's a tragedy; if they get what they want, it's in Chekhovian terms a comedy. What I like to do is to show how different characters get different things and how all their emotions are rubbing up against one another so that a very rich human experience is provided at the end. In writing that play I think the story went its full length, which I believe is another important thing for a dramatist: you don't cop out half way through. You actually take the story as far as it can go, and force the characters through as many difficulties as you can, so that the release at the end is emotionally worthwhile and thought-provoking.

HWD: *We've talked about backgrounds – your own and that of the theatre for which you write – and we've talked about theatre as both escape and engagement. I have a strong sense of a moral force in everything you write. I'm pretty sure you wouldn't think of a play as a medium for moralising, but does theatre have, for you, a moral intent that can be described at all?*

CW: I'm very keen not to be seen as moralistic in terms of trying to teach 'lessons' about something in particular. I prefer to see my plays as a journey of exploration, including self-exploration. The more you acknowledge your own weaknesses, the keener you are to look at your own life, and ask how you should live it in a way that gives meaning, purpose and ultimate fulfilment. I think theatre has an important role to play in that debate, because religion doesn't do that in the same way that it used to. I'm not saying that theatre should take the place of religion. It's just another arena in which we can think seriously about life, while at the same time having a wonderfully enjoyable experience of it.

However, plays do come down to moral dilemmas, so you put a person in a situation where he or she can ask 'Is it right to do this or that?' and of course a mature play will show that, in different situations, whatever choice the character makes can at least be understandable, even if it is wrong. That's part of the point of *In the Bleak Midwinter* where you have three absolutes: 'You shall not kill', 'You shall not commit adultery', 'You shall not steal'. We see an episode where each one of these becomes understandable. The poor man steals, the main character has such an agonising time with his marriage that he is forced to ask whether it would be so dreadful to go with this young girl. And then finally, when someone has been involved in something so awful as the Slaughter of the Innocents, is it wrong to take revenge on such a person? Even if these things are not right, at least within the play they are understandable, if seen in a human context.

HWD: *So far, we've discussed your theatre writing. You have, during your career, also diversified. You have recently completed a script for animation. What exactly was that?*

CW: This was something I particularly enjoyed doing. I scripted a ten-minute animation of a Russian folk-tale for the same company that did the animated Shakespeare. The tale is called *The Two Brothers* and it continues my interest in writing for young people and my interest in stories. So I suppose in that sense it was familiar ground. But the form is completely different. I think, for me, surviving as a playwright over the past twenty years already had to do with diversifying, with creating different markets for myself – community theatre, young people's theatre, adaptation, radio, television, and moving slowly into each one in order to keep fresh – indeed, to keep going at all. There isn't that much theatre work to be had in Wales.

HWD: *You talk of 'surviving'. And, as you say, the amount of theatre work available in Wales is limited. These facts raise the question of financial survival. Why is it, since you have moved at least momentarily into television, that you haven't as yet been tempted to script for a 'soap' – where, of course, the big money lies?*

CW: I think I would feel tempted to write for television in that sense, if I could be in control of the characters and of what happens to them. Obviously in a soap you are part of a team, often working or developing somebody else's ideas, and at the moment I don't feel the urge to do that, because in theatre as in the radio work that I do I can be in control of the lives of the characters, and in control also of the central meaning. I regard myself as being 'in progress' as a writer and I don't want to halt that, or hinder it by scripting for a soap when I don't really financially *have* to do it. There might come a time, of course, – perhaps when I begin to think about my pension! I might very well then feel that I should write for *EastEnders*. But I don't know whether I'd be any good at it. It demands a certain skill, I suppose. But yes, I'd be interested if I could control the stories and the plot.

But then there's the whole issue of television and how important or otherwise television is vis-à-vis theatre. Television is important in terms of numbers. When I did a play for BBC2 called *A Figure of Eight*, the producer phoned me up to tell me that 120,000 people watched it in Wales. Well, that's more people than will ever see a single play, but, for me, theatre is an act of working in a space *with* people. It's a completely different poetical and social experience. It's to do with human relationships in a very important way. You have to get on with people, whereas you don't have to get on with people on the box, because you can just switch them off. Inasmuch as it's not playing to a vast number of people and, given that it's not making a vast amount of money, the theatre experience has been marginalised. But I firmly believe that theatre is set to return as a vital force in people's lives.

HWD: *In the meantime, do you think that there is in Wales an 'enabling' culture for theatre writing?*

CW: Over the years the network of small companies with five or seven actors which toured England and Wales had declined – particularly so in England. There is not any more an investment in such companies. It doesn't seem to be a priority. In Wales the theatre context of having eight companies who do the work still exists, and I would fight very hard for their maintenance and their growth – not just this endless existence on a shoe-string. That is a theatre context in which a writer should be able to flourish – as long as the companies have the money to commission them, have an open-door policy to writers, so that writers feel that they are part of the theatre context, not just a service industry whereby they are given a commission, write a play and then go away again. I want to *belong* to the theatre. The companies I've worked with – Hijinx, Gwent, Made in Wales and the Sherman – have all been 'enabling' in that sense.

HWD: *These are relatively small companies, of course. What do you feel about the establishment of larger units in Wales – a National Theatre for example?*

CW: I have friends who have had plays put on at the English National Theatre and it seems a very different scene. In any discussion concerned with establishing a National Theatre in Wales we've got to bear in mind the nature and geography of the country. What we have here is a great number of small market towns, which make up the body of Wales, and they need and desire theatre to go to them and to be part of their lives. They would not necessarily benefit from a big stage somewhere else.

At the same time, as the theatre tradition in Wales grows and develops and we have a body of published plays, we've got to recognise that these will need to find a home somewhere, a place which gives us a recurrent sense of belonging to something that gives status and has importance. I used to argue against the establishment of a National Theatre in

Wales, but I think I would now argue for it. We need to be able to write for a big stage that would attract a bigger audience. I'm confident that playwrights would rise to the challenge. But you would have to have an infrastructure that allows training as well as experience. We'd *have* to keep the smaller companies, because, in a sense, they have been the National Theatre of Wales. But certainly, a larger, more visible venue could also be 'enabling' for a writer, and for Wales.

HWD: *Is the Welsh Playwrights Company an 'enabling' body?*

CW: Its purpose has changed. When we first got together as a group it was to make theatre happen. We've changed, the group is very much in flux, and I don't know whether it will survive. I hope it will, because it has allowed us to meet, share ideas, sit down and talk about plays. Through the group I've got to know Dic Edwards, Ed Thomas, Lucy Gough and Alan Osborne, playwrights I didn't really know before. The Welsh Playwrights Company is important and I think we now need to open up and encourage dialogue with younger playwrights.

HWD: *Which younger playwrights exactly?*

CW: There must be some. The new Made in Wales organisation under Jeff Teare is looking for them.

HWD: *But can you name some?*

CW: No, I can't, but they must be out there.

HWD: *The theatre critic Benedict Nightingale drew up a list recently of the best new young UK playwrights who'd had their plays performed at the Royal Court in 1995-96. There wasn't a playwright from Wales amongst them, though Scotland and Ireland were represented. Are you surprised at that?*

CW: No, I'm not surprised at all. If you live and work in Wales, and your work is toured in Wales, it's got to be judged and evaluated within Wales. Why do we need the appreciation and success granted by people and theatres from *outside* Wales? There's a particular London axis which does exist – it's where the money, the jobs, the actors and the theatres are – the Royal Court, the National Theatre, Hampstead and the Bush. That's where a great deal of 'new writing' is bound to be seen. But it's very city, very urban, and it's often very aggressive theatre. Here in Wales I see myself and my work in a very different way and I don't even bother to send my plays to those places because I'm involved in something quite different, and write for audiences that don't share the same concerns as the audiences that frequent the Royal Court and Hampstead. I have now come to terms with that difference and I have decided that I won't choose that, that I'll take the long way round and do what I want to do. If my plays are any good they'll survive without the Royal Court's seal of approval.

HWD: *Even so, we've got to come back to the fact that perhaps Wales isn't fertile ground for young playwrights, or not as fertile as it might be. There's a cluster of good playwrights of your own generation, but no one seems to be coming up. Can you account for this?*

CW: Perhaps. There has been considerable emphasis in Wales on 'physical' theatre, the kind of theatre represented by, say, Volcano which just doesn't primarily use the skills of the playwright because the nature of 'plays' is being challenged in their work. I think that the predominance of the playwright will return. Physical theatre can, of course, be helpful to writers and exciting for audiences, as long as it's not seen as the only theatre, as opposed to being yet another way of challenging the notion of what theatre is. I don't understand when groups, in any walk of life, choose a particular form, and then parade it as *the* truth. We live in a society where variety is itself a rich source for exploring meaning. Theatre is various. Music, performance, art may be the vogue, but ironically, the skills of writing will always be needed, and we therefore need to provide a theatre context in which writers can grow. Writers are not going to come out of the ether. Unless you have a theatre network which attracts writers, and a network that allows them to put on even a bad play, that gives them the right to fail, then you are never going to nurture and develop new writing for the theatre. There must also be a network that allows play-wrights to experiment with different forms and with different audiences.

HWD: *Of course, in that sense, you yourself have been extremely fortunate. Your association with different companies, ranging from opera companies to those in small venues, has given you, presumably, the opportunity to experiment.*

CW: Yes, and I've enjoyed in particular the opportunity to work on large-scale community plays where I've been able to explore the ways of scripting for a large number of actors. In the professional theatre now you have to script for a small number of actors, because of the expense, of course. When I did *On the Black Hill* I was allowed thirteen actors, but now I count myself lucky if I'm allowed five. But with a community play you are given free range. For example, in *Border Town*, the play I did for Monmouth, there were fifty speaking parts. Writing a big play demands a different skill, and if we in Wales will have one day a large professional stage, then we'll also need the skills to cope with it. The community play gives a writer the opportunity to think on a larger scale. I've written plays where whole towns can feel part of the performance and those plays and performances have been some of the richest experiences I've had as a writer. I've had a sense of complete belonging, of involvement with a large group, of understanding people who seek to 'put something on'.

HWD: *Talking of involvement, you have of course sought to be intimately involved with the production of your plays. You have several times co-directed your own work. Have you found that your presence at rehearsals has intimidated the actors, or curbed the freedom of the main director? Are they inhibited?*

CW: They can be, yes. I do believe very strongly in the role of the director and in his freedom to challenge the ideas of the writer in a positive way in order to release those ideas. Sometimes the playwright needs a fresh mind to do that. I have made mistakes in the past with directors where I've been too intrusive – though with the best intentions. But I think it's wrong, particularly for me, to be excluded from the rehearsal space, and it's natural to feel, especially at the beginning of the process, that I know more about the play than anyone else. I've got, of course, to allow the actors their journey, because they've got to go through the same struggle, to understand the meaning and release it, otherwise it won't be a properly felt experience; it will be just a shadow, an imitation performance. But I can give a lot to it; the more I've been involved in rehearsals, the more I've learnt about the theatre, and then this rolls on into the writing. But you've got to know when to hold back and, yes, I'm sure that some directors would say that I've put in at the wrong time.

HWD: *Your adaptation of* On the Black Hill *was extremely successful. You've also adapted* Frankenstein *and the* Odyssey. *What attracted you to adaptations in the first place?*

CW: Part of the attraction is that it is a way of getting a large play onto a main stage. The need to achieve that end in this way is simply a fact of life in our time. It gives the audience a 'name' that is recognisable, or a title that is immediately saleable – Sweeney Todd, for example, or Frankenstein.

But let me say that I've enjoyed the work of adaptation. The one I enjoyed most, and got most out of, was the adaptation of *On the Black Hill*. I could see in Bruce Chatwin's book concerns that attracted me – the rural context, certainly, but also the look at a whole century and the particularly dramatic metaphor of the twin boys as a way of looking at the opposition of male/female, church/chapel, English/Welsh – in a sense our duality as expressed again through the metaphor of the Border. I saw that that central metaphor would transpose very well from book to stage. And, yes, it did work well. The twins became marvellous symbols.

For me, therefore, the attraction of adapting *On the Black Hill* was very specific. But I have to say that there was at one time in such adaptations a disease (I think it is changing now) whereby a novel, in reaching the stage, was simply filleted. Only the best dialogue was chosen, and, of course, the adapter's name given prominence. I don't think adaptation is about that. You have to find a way of arguing with the original author or authors, and of challenging their values. But you can't completely dislodge or dismantle their words. When I did *The Search for Odysseus*, I looked at the *Odyssey* through the eyes of the son, searching for this man who was thought to be a hero, and finding out in the end that he wasn't so grand or heroic after all. In that way, I was arguing with the values that Homer brought to the *Odyssey*, particularly in Odysseus's treatment of Penelope and the creatures he met and killed along the way. So what you get in terms of this adaptation is a critique of The Imperial War Machine, as represented by Odysseus.

In adapting, you've got to ask, 'Why is it worth doing this, now?', and 'Is it worth adapting at all?' You've in any case got to find a form that removes it from the page and makes it suitable for a group experience. The form of *Frankenstein* is a series of letters, and in reading those letters you have the vicarious experience of entering someone else's world. That form wouldn't work within a play in the theatre, so you have to find another one. With *Frankenstein*, what I did was create a chorus of people who were the ghosts of all the victims of the doctor, and it is they who tell the story. As they went through the story, each one died – Justine, the maid, the boy – but they never go off stage, and at the end they are all there in white and form the ice-cap on which the last scene takes place. It was a 'theatre' technique, and I enjoyed playing with the form in that way.

HWD: *As we've mentioned before, you work with several companies in Wales, but you also continue to have a close working relationship with the Orchard Theatre in Devon. Is that part of your continuing association with the West Country where you grew up?*

CW: Yes indeed it is, and working with the Orchard Theatre allows me to write in a theatre context that continues to support my own voice, as reflected in *Border Plays*. It's a rural voice, and it is interesting that the arguments that you – we – get in Welsh theatre about being ignored by London, about not getting reviewed, or about the necessary changes from text-based theatre to physical theatre, are exactly the same. The one thing they haven't got to struggle with, or benefit from in Devon is being bilingual, because the old Devonshire dialect died out at the turn of the century. I enjoy working with Orchard Theatre, and I have every intention of maintaining the link.

HWD: *Finally, in your Introduction to the Seren edition of your plays, you say that 'an act of theatre is an act of society'. What exactly does that mean?*

CW: It reflects my own optimistic nature about life. Plays, for me, are about problems, and about overcoming problems, not about looking downwards. I don't believe – and this doesn't mean that I don't believe in tragedy – in writing plays that are so bleak as to give an audience no purpose in coming to the theatre. I like to feel that it adds something to somebody's life to see a play of mine. The 'act of society' is embodied by coming to the theatre in the first place. It is a social act, and a contract that the audience makes with the actors – to sit and watch, listen and respond, and have respect for the actor. It is a civilising act that transcends our ordinary lives, and which in the end takes us out of merely individual lives. It puts us in a situation where we can talk *as a society* about 'meaning', about the roles of others in our lives. Theatre runs contrary to the ethos that says that only the individual, Number One, is important. The act of putting on a play defies that; and the very act of going to a play, and responding to it as a group, also defies it.

Interview Two
July 2004

HWD: *It's nearly eight years since I last interviewed you, and during that period you have worked mainly outside Wales, notably with Orchard Theatre, New Perspectives Theatre Company and Polka Theatre, London. What initiated this partnership with English theatre companies?*

CW: It's hard to remember where I was eight years ago. I was certainly working with Hijinx and was involved with community theatre in Wales. My partnership with Hijinx came to an end as a result of the demoralising drama strategy of the Arts Council of Wales in the late 1990s. That strategy effectively led to the collapse of English-language theatre in Wales and to community touring in particular. That kind of touring had been my link to new writing and to audiences in Wales. Since there's been so very few opportunities to work in Wales I have indeed been working a great deal in England and abroad. I've just done two plays in Lincolnshire with New Perspectives theatre. One of the plays is set in Iceland, the other in Greece, and taking those European tales around the village halls of Lincolnshire was an exciting and energizing experience. The point is that those plays weren't inward looking and I'd like to see that kind of theatre flourishing here in Wales, particularly on the rural circuit.

What I'm interested in is the way community theatre can be reinvented now that the communities themselves have changed. Our rural community theatre doesn't always have to be about what it's like to a hill farmer. I've written about that in my time, but hill farming isn't what it was when I wrote *On the Black Hill*. That story is waiting to be retold by somebody, but certainly not by me. I've been identified in Wales with that work because it was what brought me to the attention of a wider audience and a wider circle of critics. I now wish to be identified with the newer and fresher work I've done since you last interviewed me. But it's interesting that *On the Black Hill* was a play, not for two or four actors, but for twelve or thirteen. It was a sophisticated play with songs that was written for an unsophisticated form, namely community theatre. Now that the opportunity for writing for larger casts no longer exists in Wales, I don't necessarily want to go back to the old form of 'a play with songs', but I do think that playwrights in Wales should have the opportunity to develop and cultivate the skills that writing for a large cast demands.

HWD: On the Black Hill, *is therefore, a play very much of its time?*

CW: It may very well be that. It has a universal quality in its story. That was provided by Bruce Chatwin's novel, but the way I told that story for the stage links my play with the 1980s and with the RSC *Nicholas Nickleby* mode. Now the nature of the stage has changed and it is being used in a very different way. Although *On the Black Hill* might now appear a little old-fashioned, probably all it needs is a good director to re-invent it. I'd love to see Michael Bogdanov do it, who might have access to a larger cast.

Charles Way

HWD: *Shouldn't a good play be able to travel well whatever its material or the temper of the times?*

CW: There are particular times for particular plays. I remember what Arthur Miller said of *The Crucible* in his autobiography *Timebends*. He noted that whenever and wherever there is repression *The Crucible* comes into focus and is performed and re-performed. That play will always be a great play but there will be times and places where it will really come into its own. I think that powerful plays have a strong narrative. I'm a firm believer in narrative theatre, and in my own work I haven't moved away from the fundamental aim of telling a good story. I am now telling the story in more complex ways, particularly in the play *Red Red Shoes*. In that play the audience didn't always know where they were, but as with every good story, all became clear in the end.

HWD: *I can appreciate the fact that children look for a strong narrative. Do you think an adult audience requires a narrative to the same degree?*

CW: I'm in the middle of reading *War and Peace* at the moment, a novel which has an exceptionally strong narrative and one which allows you to follow several characters on this huge journey. In terms of the attraction of narrative I don't think there's a great difference between children and adults. A story satisfies a deep psychological need to go on the full journey and to come to its end because that journey mirrors all our lives. It even mirrors our progress during a single day. The Hollywood notion of how to tell a film story takes you down a blind alley. It's sentimental, slick and unsatisfying. But that doesn't mean narrative is dead.

HWD: *In the late 1980s and early1990s the typical audience for a Charles Way play would be a mixture of children and adults. Would you say that in the past few years you've concentrated more on children's theatre?*

CW: Yes, and it was a conscious decision. I felt that in England the same thing was happening with children's theatre as was happening in children's literature in the works of Philip Pullman and Michael Morpurgo. A new, imaginative art form was being created and I wanted to be part of it. I've worked a great deal with Polka and the Unicorn in London and the two companies have a very expansive idea of theatre which wasn't merely audience-led. They were basically saying to me, 'You can write on any subject that pleases you and we will have to find the appropriate way of presenting it.' They believed in the primacy of the artist. I found that immensely liberating, and it allowed me to write a number of plays which pushed and extended my idea of total theatre in terms of the combination of text, dance, music and image.

HWD: *In his introduction to* The Classic Fairytales, *an edition of three of your plays for children, the director Roger Haines states that all three plays 'have contained much humour, but haven't fought shy of the darker side.' One of the 'darker elements' you've explored in several of the plays is the damaging effects of war on society and on children. What are the difficulties you face with dramatising, within the framework of a play for children, the horror of war and its damaging aftermath?*

CW: It's all to do with good storytelling. I often adapt fairytales and all those tales contain the darker elements. Children can cope with that. A sensitively dramatised fairytale allows them the space to explore, through characters and images, their own journeys and conflicts. Recently I spoke on the subject of war in my plays at a conference for 'Action for Childrens' Arts' which was held at the University of Roehampton, Surrey. My fellow-speakers, Phillip Pullman and Michael Morpurgo, the current Children's Laureate for England, talked about their personal experience of war as well as how war was reflected in their works. I am slightly younger than they are and, unlike them, I have no first-hand recollection of the second world war. I'd experienced the war vicariously through my parents and grandparents. Indeed, I was the first male in the family not to have confronted war first-hand. And yet, when I look at my work, war and conflict is given a considerable amount of space. For example in *The Search for Odysseus*, the young boy goes in search of the war hero, and finally finds him in the halls of the dead.

I can't really tell you how the war images in my plays affect the children who watch, but I do know that I bring my own values to whatever I write. Mine are liberal values. What I try to do is explore and understand what happens to a human being within a conflict situation and also in the aftermath of the conflict. After the end of the second world war I was reading those comics where the Germans were always portrayed as ugly and shouted 'Achtung Englander', and Tommy in his turn was shouting 'Go on, give 'em 'ell!' That kind of war propaganda continued right through the 1950s and 1960s. It took me some time to unravel all the threads and come to my own response to the war.

The Search for Odysseus is a play about fallen heroes, and that was a theme that preoccupied me when I stood some years ago in the centre of Dresden and contemplated the destruction of that historic and beautiful city by the British. As a child I was given tales of bad guys and good guys, but standing in Dresden made me question any preconceived notions of goodness and badness.

HWD: Red Red Shoes, *commissioned by Unicorn Theatre, and a play which was nominated Best Play for Young People for the TMA/Barclay award in 2002, certainly didn't soft-pedal the realities of war.*

CW: Soft-pedalling has never been a temptation. *Red Red Shoes* doesn't lie to children about any aspect of war and conflict. In that play I took a risk – it was a serious thing to do in the world of children's theatre – and killed off the child protagonist at the end of the play. The play has, as its central character, a girl from Kosovo, and in the final moments of the play she sacrifices her life when she tries to save someone else. That act of self-sacrifice stops, momentarily, the cruel cycle of revenge. But all does not end well in that play. It seems to me that there is in the UK a trap that children's theatre falls into too readily. Theatre here takes children through an emotional experience to an ending that is always cathartic, one that always ends comfortably, that doesn't reflect things as they are. In Sweden, Denmark and Holland children's theatre allows the dramatist to present the harsher as well as the comfortable aspects of life, to present life as it really is. In those countries the power of the art form is recognized and respected and practitioners are not afraid of the fact that the stage presentation could possibly upset the audience.

HWD: *In 2003 two American academics, a sociologist and an professor of women's studies condemned the inimical effects of fairytales on children, particularly girls. They drew attention in particular to the association of ugliness with evil in the stories and they 'strongly recommend parent or adult interaction while children read or view fairytales.' What is your response to Liz Graverholz and Lori Baker-Sperry's view and recommendation?*

CW: These academics see only what they themselves are specifically looking for in these tales. Yes, you do get beautiful princes and princesses in the tales of the brothers Grimm, but I've always taken these to be psychological representative notions of self, rather than real princes and princesses. Children are well aware that these roles are not literal ones, but even so they like to make believe that they themselves are the hero or heroine of a particular story. Children go along for a while with the myth; it helps them face their hopes and fears, but at a safe distance from the story. I agree with A S Byatt, who has written in her introduction to Maria Tartar's Norton edition of Grimm that she despairs of 'sociologists

134

who want everyone to tell realistic stories about people living in tenement blocks and being abused'. She believes, quite rightly, that it's vital for children in the first instance to 'explore a world that is full of imagination and magic.'

I'm interested also in looking at fairy tales from the point of view of their adult content. Take *Sleeping Beauty* for instance. The tale confronts serious adult concerns such as change and the killing of parents. In the original tale the princess is actually, while sleeping, penetrated by the prince, and wakes up pregnant. The mother-in-law, jealous of her right to succeed to the throne, kills the prince and princess's children and bakes them in a pie. The prince then arranges the killing of his mother in order to recreate a better world. How do you stage that for children?

HWD: *Most children are extremely resilient and optimistic. Many of the DVDs specifically for children contain fairly frightening images, but I've seen small children watching these videos in the complete confidence that the baddies will be overcome. Theatre, however is a different and more dangerous medium. To what extent can a dramatist portray violence on stage for a young audience?*

CW: Theatre is dynamite. One simple act of violence on stage is worth a thousand images of terror in a film such as *Harry Potter*. On stage if a person is shot and actually falls down, that one image is worth a thousand images of terror in a *Harry Potter* film. If on stage a person falls down 'dead', for a child that is actually happening. It's not at a distance as on a DVD or cinema screen. On television now there are so many goodies and baddies that I feel children themselves must be confused. The time has come to entice children back to the theatre.

HWD: *Your plays have drawn huge audiences to the theatre in England. Is there any hope that the children of Wales will be given the opportunity to enjoy these plays?*

CW: I hope so. But we'll have to wait and see. A Swiss Company wants to put on performances of *Red Red Shoes* in Bern and I know that when Unicorn move into their new theatre on the South Bank the play will be produced by them again.

HWD: *The production of* Red Red Shoes *was an inspired fusion between a theatre company, a dance company and a playwright. Shouldn't we in Wales encourage that kind of creative partnership?*

CW: There's no reason why here in Wales the Diversions dance company shouldn't do a show with Hijinx theatre company. One of the ways in which English-language theatre in Wales will progress and challenge and explore the different ways of telling stories will be by collaboration, co-operation and co-production, so that companies can benefit from larger casts and audiences can benefit from seeing different forms of theatre. However, that needs investment, and there is ultimately no way of improving English-language theatre in Wales except by increased funding provision for the theatre sector.

HWD: *Where in 2004 do you stand on the question of establishing an English-medium National Theatre Company for Wales?*

CW: That debate has been going on for so long and, no doubt, will continue. The fact is that there is no major European country that doesn't have a main theatre stage for the language that the majority of people speak within that country. The title 'national' however seems to conjure up notions of grandeur. Right now the whole ecology of theatre in Wales needs to be investigated, and artists need to be encouraged to return to Wales to perform, direct and write. There are two arguments here. One is that you need to establish a national theatre in order to draw people back to Wales, and the other is that you don't need to establish a national theatre at all since we have it in the companies that exist already, and that when those companies work effectively, with proper funding, they will create the need for a building which will showcase their work to the world. It's a chicken and egg situation.

HWD: *Now that we've got the Millennium Centre in the Bay I can't see that the Welsh Assembly Government can be persuaded to invest in another huge capital project. What hope is there therefore for a worthy theatre space to showcase Welsh theatre talent?*

CW: What about creating a 'theatre factory' in Cardiff? Recently I went to such a space in Sweden where practitioners, artists and playwrights come together to produce work that could be sold to the venues. Such a space challenges artists. One of the products of that theatre factory was a play for children. In it, children were literally packed into cardboard boxes in a huge warehouse, and this became a metaphor about the way human beings treat one another. The play caused enormous controversy in Sweden, but it also drew large audiences. It was a participating experience for the children, too – they just weren't part of an audience sitting quietly, and watching a play. That kind of theatre could not have been created, however, by adhering to the way we in Wales create theatre. Why not expand our notion of theatre here and allow artists more time and space and freedom to develop new, exciting kinds of theatre? That work could then go into a variety of spaces and also fill a gap in middle-scale touring. The sad thing is that in these times a radical company like Volcano can work only with two-handers. It should receive as much funding as Complicité. Volcano and other companies must be allowed to expand the art form.

HWD: *The fact is that the impoverishment of theatre in Wales had led dramatists and actors to work elsewhere, and Wales has been all the poorer for their enforced absence. Your work has been performed far more regularly in Europe and America than in Wales. Is that frustrating?*

CW: Yes and no. If you work in children's theatre you are part of a worldwide theatre family. In two weeks' time, I've got a play opening in America. It's called *Merlin and the Cave of Dreams* and it's set in Wales. It's a play about adoption and about the use and misuse of power. This theatre in Washington performed my play *A Spell of Cold Weather* ten years ago. Then they commissioned *Merlin* and now I've been asked to write yet another play for them. The challenge for Wales is to get their artists back home again by giving them the same enthusiasm and facilities that they get elsewhere. There's no reason, of course, why playwrights should stay in Wales. People in film and television don't stay in one place. Right now Wales and the facilities it offers to artists are just not attractive enough. I am now, however, having meetings with Sgript Cymru, Hijinx, Gwent Theatre and Spectacle. I am hoping, with the Peter Boyden report into English-medium theatre in Wales, that there will be a rebirth. We need, of course, first of all, to persuade the politicians to invest in that rebirth.

HWD: *'Ay, there's the rub.' What hope do you hold of persuading our elected politicians to fund anything that has to do with process?*

CW: Politicians don't recognize process. What they want is product. What they want to see is a building where they can say 'Look, we saw to that, and to prove it, our name is carved on that Welsh slate on the wall.' But there has to be process before product. Jumping through political hoops isn't my particular skill. But I would like to persuade them to invest in a European style 'theatre factory' space where the process of creating new and inspiring work will eventually result in a worthwhile product. That theatre factory could also be part of a theatre institute that would serve the artist. The playwright Ed Thomas has championed the role of a talented creative producer who can link artists with venues, inspire and instigate projects and create links between theatre, television and film. Maybe that creative producer could be part of a theatre institute as well, an institute which would be pro-active in creating work and international links for theatre artists.

HWD: *From my experience of theatre in Europe and America I'm convinced that, abroad, the artist is shown considerably more respect than is given to him or her in Wales. Has that been your impression?*

CW: In most of the European countries I've visited as a playwright the role of the artist in society is primary rather than secondary. In Britain there's an assumption that you're lucky to be involved in the Arts, and since you're lucky, it's okay to be paid next to nothing for what you do. In other countries I get the strong impression that art is central to their understanding of themselves, and theatre is central to that process of understanding. I don't think the Welsh public see that relationship between the artist and society, and certainly theatre isn't seen as central to any process. There was a brief moment in Wales when theatre was becoming part of a lifestyle, but that moment quickly vanished. What I get when I go abroad is confidence. People say over and over again, 'Yes, what you're doing is worthwhile and theatre is a valuable form.'

HWD: *Couldn't it be argued that the establishment of a Welsh-language National Theatre Company is proof that theatre is recognized here in Wales as a valuable form?*

CW: I think it's sad that a National Theatre for Wales exists only in the Welsh language. Wales now is about bilingualism and internationalism. I feel we have jumped the gun and that we should have established a theatre where an English-speaking Welsh person could also be identified nationally through its theatre. I'm very pleased that so much money has been invested in the theatre, but I wonder what the future holds. Will it retain its Welsh-language-only status?

HWD: *In the last six years, not only have you worked mainly in England and abroad, but you've also taken your plays to English publishing houses. Indeed,* The Classic Fairytales *(2002) was published by Aurora Metro Press with, strangely enough, a grant from the Arts Council of Wales.*

CW: After Seren published three of my plays in 1994 I wrote to them about the possibility of further publications. Essentially, I had the message back that Seren would no longer be publishing plays because they didn't sell. I was then approached by Aurora Metro, a small press that is rapidly making a name for itself. They have now published nine of my plays. It was wonderful to be working with a press interested in publishing plays and in marketing them. Ideas and money needn't stay within borders and there's no reason why an English publisher shouldn't invest in Wales. We want money from film to come into Wales from abroad. Why shouldn't we, especially since most publishers in Wales are not enthusiastic about plays, invest a little money in having the work of writers from Wales published elsewhere? The alternative is to have those plays die the death. Anyway, I don't see Wales as an insular place where everything has to be self-referential.

HWD: *I agree, but don't you find it strange that theatre in Wales is featured in drama courses in some English universities while the WJEC and many institutions of higher education here at home, effectively ignore our indigenous dramatists?*

CW: I would argue that the theatre ecology here has a piece missing when the academic world isn't taking any note of it. I know that in Sweden you can enter a University to take a three-year course exclusively in Children's Theatre, and that Swedish Childrens' Theatre is given due academic attention. I'm not aware of the existence at the moment of even one module in Wales's higher education institutions that gives students the opportunity of concentrating solely on the works of playwrights from Wales. I think it's vital that universities and colleges here should take the country's theatre seriously. Another important part of the ecology that is missing here is the existence of theatre criticism that deserves respect and serious attention. Playwrights, companies and artists would all benefit from informed critical reviews of plays and performances.

HWD: *How about the future? Is it possible to re-energise the theatre scene in Wales?*

CW: A few years ago Peter Boyden did a report on the state of theatre in England. He emphasized the vital importance of theatre in society. The recommendations and underlying philosophy of the report led to a high level of funding for regional theatre in particular. The resulting invigoration of regional theatre meant that London wasn't necessarily seen as the heart and soul of English theatre. Places such as Nottingham, Leeds and Derby are now creating their own work and the regional theatres are providing opportunities for co-production. The venues also are more accessible to touring companies such as Paines Plough and to other companies that provide more radical work. The result is that audiences are being offered different kinds of theatre, rather than only the staple diet of regional repertoire with its three-week run. It's not worthwhile investing in an end-stopped three-week run any more. Now Derby is producing work that can tour to York, and Nottingham can take its productions to Birmingham and on to Exeter and Plymouth.

The Peter Boyden report on theatre in England had a whole raft of proposals that were made attractive to the politicians. It led to the rebirth of theatre in England. I have faith that the Boyden report on English-language theatre in Wales will lead to proposals that, if adopted, should encourage, at last, a vibrant and vigorous Welsh theatre scene.

The Search for Odysseus by Charles Way

Gareth Miles

HWD: *You've declared that it was the establishment of the Welsh Fourth Channel, S4C in 1982 that enabled you to become a full-time writer. Where creative writing is concerned, one hears of television more often as the poaching competitor than as an enabler. What exactly did you have in mind when you made the link?*

GM: I had, of course, always been a writer, but the Fourth Channel enabled me to become a *professional* writer. Indeed, it was the Channel that made it possible, for the first time since the end of the nineteenth century, for a Welsh writer actually to earn his living as a full-time writer. But it goes beyond simple remuneration. It involves the question of attitude. I think that being able at all to write professionally

143

changes your attitude towards writing itself. As a full-time writer you've got to admit that you are now engaged in writing for a living, and that adds a bit of 'dirt' to the composition; it makes it slightly disreputable. Paradoxically, it makes it a bit more like 'real life'.

HWD: *Your commitment to writing began early. You had already translated a play – Ionesco's* Victimes du Devoir *– before you became a professional writer, and your translation brings in another medium: it was broadcast on BBC radio in 1963.*

GM: Yes, that was when I was still a student. I was interested in European plays. But I should add that, in the 1960s and 1970s, I was also writing articles on politics and current events nearer home for *Y Faner* and *Tafod y Ddraig*, the newsletter of *Cymdeithas yr Iaith Gymraeg* (The Welsh Language Society), and writing two collections of short stories. So I was from the beginning interested in different genres as well as different media, at home as well as abroad, and experimented with them as far as my other employments would allow me. But I should also like to bring in a different aspect to this point about 'starting early'. There is a tremendous difference between beginning to write at nine in the morning and starting to write at nine o'clock at night, after a full day of teaching or organizing. People say that, if you are a writer, you must have tremendous willpower, because I think they imagine that a writer spends his daytime hours on the pop or whatever, and then starts writing around midnight. The reality is quite different. If you're a full-time writer, you get down to work (rather than 'going to work' – though I actually do go to my office in Pontypridd) at nine in the morning, or earlier. Some writers find that their creative juices flow much earlier, but I'm not quite that much of a masochist.

Gareth Miles

HWD: *What were your first stage plays after becoming a professional writer, and how did they emerge from, or tie in with, the theatre opportunities of that period?*

GM: The first play I wrote was *Diwedd y Saithdegau* (The End of the Seventies) in 1982. It was a one-acter developed from a short story. I showed it to the actress Sharon Morgan who, after working in London, had come back to Wales and was anxious to do some work here. She had got David Lynn interested in directing the play and had enlisted a couple of actors. David helped me develop it into a two-act play, and then, working with Gruff Jones and with the actors, we developed it into a stage play that was in the event of production quite well received. It was on radio recently, and it was very heartening to hear something you'd written (and had been well received) in the early 1980s also working well, and in another medium as you say, over fourteen years later.

My next play was *Unwaith Eto 'Nghymru Annwyl* (Once Again In Dear Wales) in 1984. I was a founder member of Hwyl a Fflag, the company that encouraged and performed new writing. I always worked with writers and directors who helped me shape the work I was engaged on.

HWD: *Let's bring this idea of working closely with specific companies up to date. You are now collaborating – happily? well? to what effect? – with Bethan Jones of Dalier Sylw.*

GM: Initially, my background was literary, and I did need the help of experienced theatre people to teach me the language of the theatre, because it is a different language, a different *deployment* of language from the expectations of a more purely 'literary' work. Now we have come to a different stage. Since I now earn my main living writing for television, and since the two media are so different – however similar they may superficially appear to be – I still need the advice of a director who thinks solely, but creatively, in terms of the theatre. This is what helps me eliminate, or control, writing that is merely televisual or too specifically cinematic, and to concentrate on what is possible or challenging in the theatre, *as theatre*.

HWD: *We mentioned earlier your translation of the Ionesco play, and your interest in European drama generally. In fact you have often been referred to as 'the most cosmopolitan' of Welsh writers. What accounts for the 'cosmopolitanism'? Was there a 'political' base to it?*

GM: I'd prefer to be thought of as 'internationalist' rather than 'cosmopolitan'. I think it was probably due first to my father's influence. He was a miner's son from Pontrhydyfen and had an internationalist outlook on life. It was a period when the politics of the 'local' embraced the 'international'. Saunders Lewis and his Francophilia was certainly another influence, but possibly in a different, even opposite, direction. He wanted of course a monoglot Wales, but I myself consider that to be unobtainable. The only way to avoid the compromise of bilingualism is to be trilingual or polylingual. I do think it is so important for writers in a small country like Wales, which is so close to England, to have at least one other world language beyond English. I went to France after taking a degree in Bangor in English and Philosophy, and became fluent in French. I have ever since worked to maintain close contact with many friends in France and in Brittany and have kept up my interest in French culture and literature.

HWD: *That would certainly help to account for the highly successful translation into Welsh of Marivaux's* Le Triomphe de l'amour, *directed by Ceri Sherlock. Do you have any further thoughts on what made that translation work so well?*

GM: I have a theory that French translates very badly into English. Of course, I am here speaking instinctively rather than as an expert in linguistics. But, certainly, French 'theatre' in particular (a dimension beyond just language) does not translate well into English. I think that English has such a large vocabulary, such a wide choice of words, that – a paradox – translators cannot find the exact word for the French original. Welsh and French also have to use the syntax much more. I also think that English has lost touch with the vernacular. Anybody who speaks in dialect – Liverpudlian, say, or Scouse – is assumed to be comic or stupid, and as a result English has lost the muscularity of the vernacular. I myself much prefer to read American English. It's so energetic, so vigorous and inclusive, rather than refined and set apart. In Wales we are still in league with the vernacular even while writing a literary language, and I feel this to be a unifying factor as between Welsh and French.

HWD: *And yet I imagine it was a particular kind of energy and vigour in John Webster's language – the language above all else – that drew you to adapt Webster's* The Duchess of Malfi. *The devil described as a 'rusty watch', for example, the general word-play, or the amazing simplicity of 'Cover her face; mine eyes dazzle: she died young'.*

GM: I translated – and as you rightly emphasise, adapted – that play because I was so impressed by it when I studied it for my 'A' level examination in English. I did enjoy it so much more than the Shakespeare text we were studying. And when I studied English at university in Bangor, where the Shakespearean scholar Professor John Danby was head of department and a very great friend, even there I reacted against what I saw as 'Shakespeare idolatory', this English nationalism that elevates Shakespeare into a prophet, an icon. I also reacted against his medieval world-view which has been imbided so much by the ruling class's consciousness and given new life by the Englishness of later writers like Wordsworth and poets of that kind, and made, not only 'English', but reactionary and rural and so on. I found that Webster and Jonson lived in the world we live in, where there isn't a natural justice that will overcome everything. You take things as they are.

Webster is a tremendous poet, with a sharp knowledge also of the political society of his time. On the other hand, I think he's a dreadful dramatist. Instead of telling the story of the original novella, where Antonio is brutally assassinated in church by the Cardinal's men, he has turned his play into a melodramatic Jacobean Hammer Horror. And with the character of Bosola he gets sidetracked into, not morality, but moralizing, where characters become instruments. In my version, therefore, I stuck to the original story. Webster didn't quite know what he wanted to do, whether he wanted to be a dramatist or a poet, or a moral preacher. I was arrogant enough to feel that I could improve the structure of the play, although, naturally, I could never hope to achieve the vision of the poetry. But I did my best.

HWD: *You say that you reacted against what you term a 'Shakespeare idolatory'. But I take it that I am not going to the defence of the impregnable by saying that you can't possibly mean that you wanted neither to read nor see Shakespeare's plays.*

GM: No, absolutely, I admire him as a practitioner. It's his world-view that I have to reject. When I became a full-time writer, and was working with actors on my third play, *Ffatri Serch* (The Love Factory), which is very much a satirical play, I introduced a great many jokes into the long speeches because I'd been writing a lot of satirical stuff which contained jokes in publications such as *Tafod y Ddraig*. This really was what I was used to doing. The actors, however, kept cutting out these terrific jokes. I asked them 'Why? Shakespeare has long speeches, so why are you cutting out lines from *my* play?' And Clive Roberts answered, 'Well, with Shakespeare, it doesn't matter how long the speech is, the story, the action keeps flowing through the speech. A good joke can sometimes hold back the action, and in the theatre the action is paramount.' That was a very important lesson.

I did, I admit, react very strongly against Shakespeare for several reasons, including the tedious examination work on him. He appeared to be 'pious Shakespeare'. The turning point came when I read the article 'Why I Stopped Hating Shakespeare' by the black American writer James Baldwin. He seemed to have suffered the same problem with Shakespeare as I had. Then when I became a writer for the theatre I saw that what he really was was a practitioner, a writer *for* the theatre, trying his best to avoid censorship while also getting subversive bits into the plays. I see him as a dramatist, not as a great moral prophet or poet.

HWD: *Shakespeare, of course, based so many of his plays on previous sources. You too seem to do this. Is it true to say that you prefer to create your version of established myths, and adapt established texts, rather than start from scratch with an invented plot or fresh story – whatever 'invented' or 'fresh' might mean in this sense?*

GM: Several of the plays I've written have in any case been commissions. For example, the *Bacchai* was commissioned by Dalier Sylw, and I was also asked to adapt the Marivaux play. But *Hunllef yng Nghymru Fydd* (Welsh Nightmare, 2030 AD) was an original reworking of the *Antigone* myth. In a sense, it is a wholly original play. I've always been interested in Greek theatre, and I reacted again against the spurious hand-me-down I received as a young person: that the great Greek writers were above politics and – you know – 'universal'. The fact is, of course, that they were intensely steeped in the politics of their time. Also, my interest in the Greek classical theatre coincided with my investigation of the *Mabinogion* and other Welsh classical myths. It is not because dramatists like Aeschylus and Sophocles have any greater understanding of human nature that their works have survived, but because their works are the cultural manifestations of social contradictions which existed then and which exist now. I think that the Athenian states of Classical Greece very much resembled Victorian England. They had problems of industrial development, of the creation of the proletariat and of imperialsm. It is as if Victorian England had jumped from pre-conquest England into Victorian England in about two or three centuries. I also think that part of the background to Greek mythology, as to the Mabinogion, is the reduction, the lowering, of the status of women. The emancipation of women has been one of the major themes of theatre since *Antigone* – from Roman theatre, through Shakespeare, Molière and Ibsen.

HWD: *What has emerged from your answers is your interest in the 'political' aspects of the plays you've mentioned, and the same is true of your account of the attitudes and factors in the background of your own writing. You are generally thought of as being a 'political' writer, but do you see yourself as intensely 'political'?*

GM: Yes, and perhaps too much so. Who knows? But I do really think that political is personal. I believe that the role of the theatre is political in the Greek sense of the word. What are the important matters for theatre to discuss? For example, in *Hunllef yng Nghymru Fydd* I ask questions about the nature of Welsh nationalism. I used to be a Nationalist, but I would now regard myself as a patriot. That is an important distinction. For the Nationalist, the nation is the essential unit of social organization, and every individual's first allegiance is to his or her nation. If he or she rejects that, he or she is a traitor. The survival of the nation is the *sine qua non*, which means that anything can be justified – any kind of violence, for example. But when I was writing *Hunllef* I wanted to create a play in which a woman choosing to be loyal to the memory of her brother thereby chooses a path that leads to her own death. In Latin America, at least in the recent past, as in Argentina and El Salvador, it was possible for a woman to be killed for that loyalty. That situation was the beginning of my play. And then I was interested in liberation theology and in the question of nationalism. As a writer, you put all these things into the creative pot and boil and stir them and hope that you get a nuclear reaction, or whatever is the literary equivalent.

HWD: *Do you regret then that, with such powerful things to show in this play, it was decided to limit the number of tickets available for the performance of* Hunllef yng Nghymru Fydd *because of the 'promenade' nature of the production? Only a very few people got to see the play.*

GM: That's the problem of writing in Welsh. If you write in the Welsh language you've got a restricted audience anyway. The 'promenade' production of *Hunllef* at the manor house of Llancaiach Fawr was very effective. I find proscenium arch theatre stifling and I liked the inventiveness of Dalier Sylw's presentation of the play. *Hunllef yng Nghymru Fydd* has been published and let's hope it gets done again. At Llancaiach Fawr I had the exact response to the play that I'd hoped for when writing it. In the play, the Fascist dictator quotes from Saunders Lewis and from Emrys ap Iwan, and Welsh Nationalist friends of mine who saw the production, and initially sympathised with the liberation theology pastor, found themselves in due course aghast that they were sympathizing with, and supporting, the words of the Fascist. Now, that's what a dramatist hopes his play will do.

In *Unwaith Eto 'Nghymru Annwyl* the main character has left Wales for South Africa in disgust at the failure of Welsh Nationalism. In South Africa he works undercover for the African National Congress, but when he comes back he claims that he has been working for the Afrikaners. He baits his wife and his friends by claiming that Afrikaners and Welsh nationalists are the same in the sense that both are a small people fighting for their language. Dafydd Iwan told me that he was disturbed when he saw the play and that he found himself identifying with the Afrikaners. But at the last moment, of course, the main character reveals his true colours.

I do think that theatre has an important democratic role to play in society. The bar is an important place in a theatre because it is very often there that you can see whether the play has been a success or not, if people stay on to talk after the performance. It's not that important whether they talk about the play itself as such. The important thing is that they have been charged and excited, and that has so much to do with the actual performance. Going to the theatre, unlike going to see a film, is a collective experience, and in that sense theatre is a democratic form. My plays raise questions of sexual politics, class and nationalism. The theatre is not only a lively but a vitalizing forum for such questions, unique and therefore important.

HWD: *Such questions come up again in the* Bacchai.

GM: It was a way of investigating classical Greek drama. In a play like the *Bacchae* of Euripedes so many of the themes that have run through theatre down to the modern period are already there: the suppression, as I said, of women's rights and the liberalism of the nineteenth century reacting against conservatism, taking a drink, becoming alcoholic, and reacting against it. The contradictions that exist today are there in the original play. In turn I'm very grateful to Ceri Sherlock and Dalier Sylw in 1991 for their help in making my own theatre more visual. As I say, I come from a literary background which has made me conservative on the importance of dialogue, and the overriding importance of language in Wales hasn't aided a theatre that is visual.

A great many of the verbal felicities – if I may be so presumptuous – indeed, a great deal of the good things I've written have been missed; but, on the other hand, I know I have gained and that the audience gained from the visuality of the performance of *Bacchai*.

For me, it was instructive to see how political theatre can be visual. And it was good too to break from Naturalism. I do think Naturalism is the enemy of Art. The *Bacchai* production by Dalier Sylw was a much needed reaction against Naturalism. And they wouldn't have been able to do it had they not had the text. Theatre needs a text and a story. I do not have a high opinion of Brith Gof. Theatre is a text interpreted by an actor for an audience. Non-textual theatre is not theatre; it is exhibitionism and indulgence.

HWD: *You've described your theatre as one that makes use of myths, ancient and modern. Your play and film involving the story of Branwen makes use again of the* Mabinogion. *Did it translate or adapt well?*

GM: I first wrote *Branwen* as a story and I asked Wyn Williams of Hwyl a Fflag if it could be read at a drama festival. He suggested I develop it into a play. I did that, and sold the television rights to Teliesyn to get some money to go to Belfast for a week. I was very surprised when S4C decided to make a film of it. As a play, it is the one I'm least satisfied with. I think the play suffered again from having filmic elements in it, and the work on the original film script suffered in turn because of the influence of the theatre. The final screen play is a collaboration between Ceri Sherlock, Angela Graham and myself. Though Ceri and Angela injected elements into the film that were not mine, I'm quite happy, given the tiny budget, with the end result.

HWD: *Do you think you will venture into film again soon?*

GM: No. In the digital age, no. I was commissioned to write a scenario for a ninety-minute film which had been accepted by the S4C commissioner of drama, but because of the tardiness of S4C in formulating acceptable agreements and contracts for the digital age, the initiator of that project has withdrawn. It's disappointing.

HWD: *The current production of your most recent translation, however, is by no means disappointing.*

GM: It was certainly very well received at the Sherman Theatre in Cardiff in February. *Lludw'r Garreg* is a straight translation of *Cendres de Caillou* by Daniel Danis. By the way, I found the fax machine extremely useful during the process of translation because I could send my queries over to Canada and receive a reply on the same day. The style of the writing in Danis's *Cendres de Caillou* corresponds to my own. It's a synthesis of poetic and vernacular, sometimes very coarse, very vigorous, very aggressive. It was a pleasure to translate. It's not an overtly political play but the social milieu described has close Welsh equivalents. You have a father and a daughter from a large city – Montreal/Cardiff – the mother is raped by a madman, so the father takes his daughter to live in the back of beyond, the *cefn gwlad* of Dyffryn Conwy, say, or the backwoods of Quebec. The same kind of situation is there – a rural area urbanized but without any of the advantages of living in the city, young people unemployed, messing about with drugs, drinking, fighting.

We have a similar social situation in Wales; alienated young people with a feeling of belonging to a nation that isn't a nation; people who have all the disadvantages of belonging to a stateless nation without the cultural advantages of the middle class. It was a play that was amenable to translation, and I feel it is important for us in Wales to make contact with regions like Quebec and Catalonia, not for any small sentimental nationalism, but because their experience of not being quite a nation state is similar to our own. It's almost universal these days because there are only about four or five nation states, so everybody's marginal. I was saying to people from Quebec, '*Tout le monde est gallois!*' – 'Everybody's Welsh!' Everybody's got to live with the English language, as we have done here in Wales for so many hundreds of years. In the past the Celtic writers in Wales, Scotland, Ireland and Brittany were very introspective, parochial and petty. I think that's finished, the 'Celtic twilight' syndrome is over. We have a similar cultural experience and as peoples we want to move forward to a full expression of our cultural heritage without being chauvinistic, without being xenophobic. It's a patriotism which is inclusive, which is universal and democratic and based on aims of social equality and justice at the same time. I think that is very exciting and the way forward.

HWD: *You've lived in Pontypridd for twenty years. You haven't been impelled to root any of your work in the South Wales valleys.*

GM: If there were more opportunities to write for Welsh language theatre I would like to write a play drawing on my experiences of living in the area. I did write a couple of scripts for the recent series *Iechyd Da*. But a project I have currently in mind is a novel based in south-east Wales, the areas of Pontypridd and the Rhondda Valleys. It's a historical Welsh experience, that of a person who comes from North Wales to South Wales. It's one of the great themes of modern Welsh literature, and it's certainly something I intend doing. I do feel the need to use the experience I've gained here in Pontypridd. When I came here there was great hostility towards the Welsh language, but there's been a change in the attitude to the language. In fact, there's a very strong feeling in favour of the language because it's about the only badge of nationality we have left. Starting next year, I shall be gathering material for the novel. The main character will be a person suffering from post-traumatic stress disorder, part of the Welsh experience of militarism and so on.

HWD: *From that strong sense of place, and a continuing engagement with it, it seems natural to move to a factor common to many of the other dramatists I've interviewed in this series – the fact that they have written plays about America. You are now, in your new play about John Evans, Waunfawr, also writing about a journey from Wales to America. Have you been to America?*

GM: No, but America's been in me since I was about five years old. We're not living in America, but America's living in us. I'd love to go to the Americas. I don't know whether I'd enjoy visiting the US of A. HTV once considered sending me out to interview Howard Marks, whom I corresponded with while he was in prison. Whatever one thinks of his misdemeanours, he was certainly courageous and intelligent, and acted according to Eirwyn Pontshan's advice '*Os wyt ti mewn trwbwl, rhaid iti ddod mâs o fe*' (If you're in trouble, you've got to get out of it). But I didn't get to go over. The last play I wrote, *Byd y Banc* (The Life of the Bank), was set in a Latin American country, and *Hunllef yng Nghymru Fydd* was really 1989 El Salvador.

And this new play, as you say, is about John Evans, my fellow-villager from Waunfawr, who in 1792 went to look for the Welsh-speaking Indians. He claimed he was going out as a Methodist evangelist to convert the Indians to Christianity. He was doubtless sincere, but it was also a way of justifying his going to America. He wanted to get out of Waunfawr! Some people have stayed there, some people haven't! He did meet Iolo Morganwg and the Gwyneddigion Society who had Jacobin and Republican motives for looking for the lost brethren. I do think John Evans was helped by the American government and that he was working for them. He promised to let them know what he discovered. He was employed by the Spanish government who owned Louisiana at the time and he went up the Mississippi and the Missouri, pulled down the Union Jack, and expelled the English from Louisiana. He did intend to return with guns to help the Mandans (the supposed Welsh Indians) defend themselves from their enemies, but by the time he got back to St Louis the Spanish Empire in America had collapsed. What he did achieve was to keep Louisiana Spanish, until the Spaniards transferred it to France who in turn sold it to Thomas Jefferson – 'the greatest land deal in history'. Had Evans not done that, it is quite possible that the English would have come down from Canada, British North America would have expanded, and North American politics would have been very, very different. He did serve the interests of the United States and Spain very well. He was a very heroic figure.

HWD: *My final question will come oddly in the wake or slipstream of the heroic theme you've just outlined, but I'm sure many will be interested in seeing how you steer it. Theatre in Wales at the moment, certainly Welsh-medium theatre, seems very much in the doldrums. How do you view it?*

GM: I think, with regard to Welsh-language theatre, that for a people who pride themselves in the Arts, the Welsh are not much interested in aesthetic values, and they are interested in poetry only as long as it promotes the Welsh language politically. In a country like England or France, where you have a real ruling class instead of the professional media bourgeoisie that we have here, there are people who want to know what is happening in the world. They want left-wing plays as well as right-wing plays. They need the Arts to understand the world.

A couple of decades ago we had a pseudo ruling class that was fundamentally an academic one. Now the balance of power has shifted to the media, and that has not been a great advantage to Wales. I do think that people engaged in education have at least certain cultural, philosophical and moral values, but I think that the media have sunk more and more to mere populism. Our present media ruling class has embraced American globalism, and all we're going to get from them is Anglo-American rubbish in Welsh. Just now and then we're given a few squirts of high culture, just to keep up pretences. I don't think these people need culture or theatre. Alan Plater, a member of the Writers' Guild, a writer I much respect, has pointed out the difference between what people need and what people want. Television gives people what they want. We all want to be happy. On the other hand, what we need is to understand ourselves and what is happening in the world. This is what the real writer wants, and it isn't arrogant or élitist to want it. I think theatre, as the Greeks knew, is extremely important for a democratic society.

It's a way of debating, in a non-overtly political mode, the deeply political elements of society. I do think there are possibilities. In the past we've had contradictions between the Welsh language and the English language, between Nationalism and Socialism, and between British nationalism and Welsh nationalism. We're in a situation now where both British nationalism and Welsh nationalism are redundant. A society that believes in a Welsh patriotism that is universal, based on social justice and a view of Wales's place and role in the world, is one that needs theatre. We do face the possibility of a world dominated by Rupert Murdoch and his kind. Theatre provides, not an antidote, but a point of reaction, a platform for the rejection of that culture.

Gareth Miles

**Interview Two
October 2004**

HWD: *Since our interview for* New Welsh Review *in 1997 you've continued to be extremely productive as a novelist, critic, journalist and television script-writer, but am I right in thinking that theatre has failed to attract you during the last seven years?*

GM: My last piece of work for the theatre was performed in 1999. It was *Madogwys*, a play about John Evans's epic journey up the Mississippi and Missouri rivers in search of the native people reputed to be descended from Prince Madog and his followers. This had a cast of eleven, including three native American actors. It used up one and a half years' budget for Dalier Sylw and was that excellent company's last production before being subsumed by Sgript Cymru. The following five years were very lean ones for theatre in Wales in both languages as a consequence of the well-documented failings of WAC's Drama Department at the time. Since the sort of play I wanted to write had a social and political dimension, it required a large cast at a time when budgets allowed only monologues and small-cast domestic or abstract dramas to be performed. These blighted years have left their mark on Welsh-language theatre.

The new, resuscitated companies now commissioning work appear to be imbued with petty-bourgeois pessimism, resulting in plays which reflect the despair of a privileged but politically impotent middle-class which fears that the language which sustains it both spiritually and economically is sliding inexorably, albeit comfortably, to extinction. The writers whose plays are performed regard themselves, I'm sure, as being politically left-of-centre, but their works reflect the Thatcherite, neo-liberal view that there's no such thing as society, only competing individuals and, though they're nationalists to a man and woman, they appear to have no interest in the history of Wales. To this school of writers, 'politics' is a dirty word; but 'I'm not interested in politics!' is itself a political statement. It disappoints me that the present generation of young theatre critics inhabit the same well-upholstered cocoon and lack the intellectual and ideological tools which would enable them to analyse productions with rigour and precision. They have nothing but kind words for any Welsh-language play that is fairly well performed and has a worthy subject.

HWD: *Your latest undertaking – a translation of* Hamlet *into Welsh – cannot have failed to be challenging. It also brought you into association with Michael Bogdanov.*

GM: Michael and I get on well together (like minds), and working with him has finally cured me of the Shakespear-ophobia which infected me when I studied English Literature at the University College of North Wales Bangor (as it was then) many years ago. In translating *Hamlet* I realised how much I and 99% of most audiences have been missing. The English language has changed so much in the past 400 years that for most of us the performance of a Shakespearean play is a quasi-operatic experience; we let the dialogue flow over us until the big speeches come along and we can do a karaoke. These treasured purple patches, however, don't mean precisely what we think they do. The Anglo-Saxons will have to bite the bullet sooner or later and commission translations into contemporary English so that they can enjoy Shakespearean theatre again.

HWD: *You are a member of the Board of Theatr Genedlaethol Cymru. What are your thoughts on the achievement of the company to date?*

GM: In its brief history so far, Theatr Genedlaethol Cymru has done much to distance Welsh language drama from the bitter company sectarianism and parochialism of the past seven years. Our aim must be to develop a National Theatre which gains European and world-wide respect. There remains much to be done.

Bacchai by Gareth Miles

Claes Hartelius in *Frida and Diego* by Greg Cullen

Greg Cullen

Interview One
October 1997

HWD: *How did you, 'a Cockney lad', come to work in Theatr Powys? Where exactly did you come from, and why to Wales?*

GC: I came to Theatr Powys from London in September 1983 on an Arts Council Writers Attachment Scheme which involved writing two plays in six months. The first play was *The Snow Queen*, an adaptation of the Hans Christian Andersen story. Theatr Powys at that time toured a Christmas production and *The Snow Queen* filled that slot. The second play was to be more open and, theoretically at least, more writer-led. I had come to Wales from Chats Palace which was a Community Arts Centre in Hackney. We had squatted in what was then a disused library and had persuaded Hackney Council to let us have the building, and so with the help of Free Form Arts Trust and members of the local community we rebuilt the library. This was a very radical time when people were reclaiming possession of their communities. I had my first professional job as an actor there, but at the same time I also ran a youth theatre and an adult devising company. We put on huge shows. I also worked as an actor with The East End Theatre Group, and with Harlow Theatre Van – that was my day job!

So I came to Powys from a radical, revolutionary background and serious involvement in the arts and in politics. Powys, I must say, came as a bit of a shock to me at the time. For a start, everybody was white and there were more sheep than people. I didn't know where I'd landed. I was an East-End London lad with a completely urban agenda. But I'd had a strong association with Wales through my teachers at school all of whom seemed to be Welsh and Welsh-speaking. As a kid I used to hitch-hike to Wales as often as I could, so the idea of spending six months in the Welsh hills writing two plays seemed like heaven. Fifteen years later I'm still here.

HWD: *But how was it that this Attachment, advertised by the Arts Council of Wales to be held in mid-Powys, went to a radical revolutionary London artist?*

GC: I wouldn't have known of the vacancy if my girlfriend, who was an actress, had not told me about it. And when I came for my interview at Theatr Powys there weren't any Welsh-born writers up for interview. There was Carl Tighe, a Cardiff-based writer but I don't think he's an indigenous Welshman. Now, fifteen years later, I wouldn't as a Londoner get the job, because we have now twenty or thirty dramatists in Wales who were born here and who work here, and they would be applying for the post. In those fifteen years something positive has happened in terms of writing for the theatre here in Wales. To some extent this has happened in spite of funding patterns and in spite of the fact that the infrastructure of the Welsh theatre is based on Community and Theatre in Education companies. But those companies, as with Theatr Powys in my case and Gwent Theatre with Charles Way, gave us an apprenticeship and an introduction to the kind of resources that were unavailable in fringe or youth and community theatres elsewhere.

HWD: *It's good to know that indigenous Welsh candidates have increased since then, but good also to hear you say, looking back, that "we have now twenty or thirty dramatists in Wales". The inclusiveness of that 'we', that inclusion of yourself in the situation in Wales, is what is welcome. But you must have impressed the interviewing committee with your playscripts and so on. How many plays had you written before applying for the post? Were you fairly experienced as a writer?*

GC: No, not at all. I'd only had four or five of my plays produced. The first play I wrote, *The Flyboys*, which still remains in first draft, was based on actual experience. While I was at St Mary's University College in London I got a job with an American airline company flying cargo to fairly unlikely locations. We were flying Hercules transport planes which could land anywhere and when I left college I went to work for the company full-time. I spent about eighteen months in Angola because I wanted to see what a revolutionary country was like. As a student, I had supported the Anti-Apartheid Movement and other South African liberation movements. So being actually in a revolutionary country, instead of having a theoretical construct in my head, was very important to me. The experience of those eighteen months formed the basis of *The Flyboys*, which follows the lives of an American and British aircrew flying cargo into heavily disputed diamond country. The clash of cultures and values within the group is sparked by their interface with a newly independent black population. I really didn't know how to write a play and it ended up being a very long piece of work. Four months ago I found it under the stairs, and when I read the opening scene I thought it was superb. I find writing the opening scene of a play a tremendous chore, but there I was, in 1979, writing my first play and devising an opening scene which was like a piece of Chekhov!

HWD: *You refer to 'transport planes', to the 'clash of cultures and values', to 'an independent population' and 'a revolutionary country'. In Referendum Wales these seem relevant to Wales itself. You mentioned earlier that your first show for Theatr Powys played to capacity audiences, but that your second play was more writer-led. Was it?*

GC: As it turned out, no. The second play was *The Bride of Baron Duprav*, a Gothic Horror comedy. It was to be hosted by the Young Farmers' Clubs throughout Powys and they were to be responsible for rustling-up an audience. They were paid a percentage of the box-office takings as an incentive to do this. When asked, the young farmers said that they wanted something funny, which is pretty much the standard response you get if you ask people what they want. However, that was not what I wanted. As part of my application package to Theatr Powys I had submitted a poem about the bombing of the Sir Galahad during the Falklands war and the subsequent death of about fifty Welsh Guardsmen who were on board. I had been listening avidly in my house in Hackney to the debate where Dafydd Elis-Thomas had tried to force through a public inquiry into what exactly took place and why those men were left on the Sir Galahad in broad daylight in full view of the Argentinians and why ammunition had been off-loaded from the ship in preference to the men.

It just so happened that one of the young actresses in Theatr Powys when I arrived there was in a long-term relationship with a Captain of the Welsh Guards who was the second in command on the Sir Galahad on that fateful day. She showed him my poem and he was so moved by it that he agreed to talk to me. I interviewed him in London on numerous occasions and I ended up with over twenty hours of tape which was gold-dust. I approached Theatr Powys with the idea of a play about this Captain and the Falklands war. Theatr Powys had previously approached issues such as nuclear disarmament and the Greenham Common protest in a very gentle way, and here I was coming forward with an idea for a play that was deeply controversial.

The head of the management of Theatr Powys then was a Colonel Stephenson whose son was a major in the Welsh Guards, and he himself, of course, had had a long association with the military. People in Theatr Powys were a little wary of treading on his toes. I was asked to present three options for my second play. I chose to speak most forcibly in favour of *Taken Out*, the proposed Falklands play. The Company abstained from voting in its favour and I found myself trying to get the go-ahead to write a controversial play on the strength of an abstention. So I wrote *The Bride of Baron Duprav*, a play dealing with Fascist ideas about gender. Despite the fact that the central character, the Baron, was based on Nietzsche, it was, I feel, an extremely funny play in which a man and a woman get their brains switched round, with this leading to a whole set of complications.

HWD: *Even though Theatr Powys did not allow you to do* Taken Out, *a politically-committed play, did the experience of working there contribute to your development as a playwright? Was there, for example, a clash between the commitment of what is 'writer-led' and the requirements of a devising company of actors?*

GC: A clash certainly, but also a wonderful creative tension. Those first six months in Theatr Powys were very important to me in terms of learning my craft. I was working with people who knew more about structure than I did. Before I came to Theatr Powys I was writing from instinct most of the time and trying to avoid the discipline of structure. I wanted a wonderful explosion on the page. But writing a play doesn't work like that. The dramatist has to have a cool head when structuring and a passionate heart when scripting. But one can also look at it in another way. At the end of those six months with Theatr Powys I had learnt a great deal about craft but hadn't satisfied any of the questions as to why I was writing in the first place. My job at the theatre came to an end, but I accepted an invitation to stay on to devise a Theatre in Education project. I was happy to do this since I'd been involved with the Harlow Theatre Van who were members of the Standing Conference of Young People's Theatre, which was a radical talking shop and a theoretical body seeking to develop the processes, techniques and concepts of Theatre in Education work. I devised *Past Caring* for Theatr Powys, a Theatre in Education project for six to seven year olds which sought to fuse the drama-based ideas of Dorothy Heathcote with theatre. In *Past Caring* we came up with a synthesis of drama and theatre.

HWD: *In fact,* Past Caring *was featured by ASSITEJ as an outstanding play for young audiences and was performed as far afield as Malaysia. Theatr Powys, from the pattern set by the play, became of course famous internationally for its innovative work with young people. How was it that a small, rural mid-Wales theatre became the focus for Theatre in Education throughout the world?*

GC: With *Past Caring* I used techniques whereby we could simulate children's play patterns. I looked at the ways children use to enrich and improve their experience of a story. For example, children at play will say 'No, no, I tell you what. I'll do this and then you'll come in and do that'. They'll replay their game until they get it right and feel a thrill of excitement at the end of it. We applied that to theatre. These methods of course relate to the theories of Augusto Boal, Paulo Friere and Gavin Bolton as well as to the theories of Dorothy Heathcote. In *Past Caring* we had a huge map marked with such things as a river, a bridge and roads, and the children would be asked to design the kind of house they'd imagine living in, in the 1930s. Parents and people from the community would be brought into the schools to acquaint the children with another time and almost another space beneath the one they were living in. The children would then place their houses on the map and talk about their neighbours and friends. By deepening their sense of community we were then able to launch a drama where the children felt they had an investment in the future of that community and the changes that were taking place within it. We used theatrical processes such as mime because children are acquainted with such processes. If a child wants a gun he or she can just lift an arm and point and there is the gun! In *Past Caring* we were also seeking to convey to six and seven-year olds the fact that action leads to repercussions. Children of that age are beginning to realise that if they take action there are consequences.

In *Past Caring* we were dealing with social interaction which showed the child that he or she had a degree of power and that actions and responses had an effect. The child can change things. Theatr Powys after *Past Caring* continued to develop these processes under the direction of Louise Osborne and the company went on to do some really superb work, in particular *Grandmother's Footsteps* and *Careless Talk*. Indeed you're right to say that theatre Powys was recognised as one of the leading companies in Theatre in Education. It was a golden era in its history. Now I'm very glad that after several years of warfare within the company, it's returned to a more drama-based and child-active methodology.

HWD: *I can't imagine that, where children are involved, 'methodology' is the only driving force or abstract 'education' the only result. What are your memories of the work you did in schools in Powys and the practicalities involved?*

GC: Being at Theatr Powys was one of the most creative and exciting times of my life because we were as a company developing theatre that interacted, not just with a community, but with a vivid and a particular one. We had at the time a huge and unreliable blue removal lorry which we used not so much to drive as to drag around the country with an AA man permanently attached to the rear bumper. Non-actors such as the technicians and set designers would go with me into a school for up to a month at a time, devising and designing a play and involving parents in the realisation of their children's imaginative work. We would take all the furniture out of the school and re-build each classroom as a different location in the story. The audience would then progress around the school following the development of the story. It would end with a *Noson Lawen* where members of the community would contribute to the entertainment. At Llanfihangel Rhydithon we had so many members of the community coming to the performances that the poor children had to do two a night. Those were radical and adventurous times. It was multi-art and multi-media and it involved the local community in Powys in such a way that everyone could see the positive benefits of theatre as a palpable learning medium.

HWD: *You have always used theatre as a learning and debating form. In 1984 during the Miners' Strike your Christmas show* Aladdin *mirrored the concerns of the South Wales coalfields. Can you say something about that joining?*

GC: It was something I couldn't ignore. What interested me about the character of Aladdin – and this is almost a glitch in the original story – was that when he asked the genie to build him a palace that would make him worthy of the princess he actually had the palace built on top of the community where he had previously lived. I wondered what had happened to the people and the dwellings that were already there. It became a metaphor for individualism versus the community, something I felt was part of the struggle of the Miners' Strike. That strike was a very important part of my consciousness at the time. I knew that if we lost that strike the power of Thatcher and the Tories would know no bounds and many peoples' lives would be ruined. Also our ability to monitor and control the excesses of government would be severely weakened. I used theatre as a way of engaging the ideas that were being debated in 1984 and I used them even in a Christmas show. When we toured *Aladdin* in Wales people enjoyed it as a ripping yarn with great music and visuals and some very funny performances, but at the same time we were reflecting serious concepts. And at that time Theatr Powys was touring to ten thousand people. That is, ten per cent of the people of Powys were coming to the theatre. If ten per cent of Cardiff went to the theatre we'd be looking at a very different capital, and a very different Wales.

HWD: *So there was room and occasion for* Aladdin, *where* Taken Out *had been itself taken out. How did things develop from* Aladdin *onwards?*

GC: After *Aladdin* I had had enough of churning out work for the Company. A writer-in-residence for a company like Theatr Powys has problems. The actors are used to either doing extant scripts or devising their own work. The actors at Theatr Powys are very good at devising their own work and they like having ownership of that material. I found that they lived uneasily with the idea that there was a playwright within the company with his own agenda. They couldn't see that when they employ a writer they have a responsibility to ask what exactly it is that makes that dramatist write. I think some people in Theatr Powys saw me as just a servant to the company, a scribe for their ideas. I'm quite happy to serve in that way; I'm happy to use my craft and any skill I have with words and my innate sense of drama to improve, enrich and frame the ideas of others. But I came to feel that Theatr Powys's ability to meet the responsibility of encouraging and nourishing the writer himself was completely lacking. This sense of frustration caused me once again to try to win support for the Falklands play *Taken Out*. This time the company backed me unanimously. I felt passionately for those involved in the Sir Galahad disaster and I had talked a great deal with the families of the Welsh Guards. Because of this, *Taken Out* was one of the easiest plays I've ever written.

HWD: *And yet, in T S Eliot's words, 'ease is cause of wonder'. You've explained why such an unconscionable military act should have been accessible to you through the strength of your own feelings, and through your contacts with the families of those most intimately involved. But wasn't there also the difficulty of working the theme in two mediums at one and the same time?* Taken Out *was broadcast as a radio play and performed as a stage play by Theatr Powys in the same week. So you were working – how? – simultaneously in two mediums....*

GC: Yes, that is often my practice and it's an exciting experience. In 1985 Adrian Mourby, then newly appointed drama producer with the BBC, was keen to discover new voices in Wales and so *Taken Out* was one of the plays in a season which introduced to radio playwrights such as Charles Way, Robert Gittings, Alan Osborne, Robert Peart, Herbert Williams and Carl Tighe. This first series won a Sony Award. It was an exciting period and I felt in my case that one medium was feeding into the other. This set up a process which I've followed ever since. I've often written a stage play and adapted it for radio and then fused both together months later to form the definitive theatre play.

HWD: *What else were you doing at this time?*

GC: *Taken Out* toured Wales during the summer of 1985 when I was writing *Spoiled Papers*, a play about the Miners' Strike. I had been the local organiser of a Miners' Support Group and we were sending money and giving aid to the Neath, Swansea and Dulais Valleys Miners' Support Group. I became very involved with the people down there and greatly admired women like Hefina Headon from Seven Sisters whose lives were transformed by the strike. They became politicised. Although we came to realise that it was almost impossible to win the strike we had witnessed the need for Socialism. It was a heady time. We saw the power of working people to form organisations and we saw that people across Europe could identify with us. But we underestimated the enemy.

HWD: *It seems to me that the filaments that reach through that period were still those that came from* Taken Out, *and what that meant for you.*

GC: Yes. That autumn *Taken Out* was performed at the Standing Conference of Young People's Theatre. Now I can't think of anywhere I would least like a play of mine to be performed than at the Standing Conference because it's one to which people come with knives unsheathed. It's a critical audience where everybody is looking to make a clever political point. The Standing Conference at that time was influenced by a small group of people who were members of, or associated with, the Workers Revolutionary Party and they talked WRP gibberish. They had miraculously turned Trotskyism into a religion and anyone who lacked faith was a traitor. I found at the Standing Conference that Marxism in the mouths of some of the delegates could provide an answer to everything. And everything fitted into certain relationships where it was easy to deduce answers. Marvellous! But I couldn't go along with that.

Around this time I really began to question and re-examine the ideas that I had taken on board when I was a student as part of the package of being a Socialist. And so I also had, as a dramatist, to re-think the way I approached my audience. The mental image I conjured up for myself was that of a spider's web which has points of contact all the way around to draw one into the web. I placed the characters in my plays at those points of contact and I tried to get each one of them to draw the audience into the centre. When I wrote *Taken Out* I didn't do what a good Socialist Realist would have done which was to place people in roles which would then interact to produce some Socialist truth. That had been the tradition I'd been working in but that post-Brechtian stuff wasn't for me any more. I was sick of seeing socialist plays with characters that had started out as Marxists or had miraculously become them and plays with plots that explained everything. I was finding myself in a world where I couldn't explain things and I was bemused by the confusion.

In *Taken Out*, therefore, I wrote characters as they occurred, as they seemed natural. In writing the play, I tried to take into account the range and scope of my audience so that they could identify with the different characters and classes. I had a captain in the Welsh Guards, a middle-class woman, a bereaved mother and father, a pregnant young wife and two dead soldiers whose ghosts appear in the play. Through all these characters I tried to provide points of contact for the multifacted audience. And I was dealing, not only with the political aftermath of the Falklands war, but also with the nature of bereavement and asking fundamental questions about the nature of our civilisation.

HWD: *The response of the Standing Conference clearly goes deep.*

GC: *Taken Out* was like a red rag to a bull to certain members of the Standing Conference of Young People's Theatre. At the end of the performance everybody sat in stunned silence, deeply moved. And then the analysis groups convened.

Indeed the director, Sue Glanville, was assaulted by WRP newspaper sellers who insisted that the play was highly reactionary because we didn't support Galtieri and the Argentinians. In their opinion, in the world overview of things, it was better that an imperial power such as Britain was defeated. Were they seriously therefore at this Conference asking me to support a drunken fascist who was responsible for the torture and imprisonment of thousands of people like me and members of the WRP? We saw what the Falklands war did for Thatcher; it made her unimpeachable. I dread to think what would have happened to the Argentine had Galtieri won that war because I think his retribution on the radicals in his society would have been far greater than anything we experienced in Britain. But as was often the case with the British Revolutionary Left certain members were always willing to fight to the last drop – of someone else's blood.

That Conference was a breaking point for me. Not because of the criticism. A dramatist expects that, but because of the *nature* of the criticism. I was accused of breaking with Marxism as a doctrine that can explain everything from your toe-nail clippings to the prospect of blood. At that Conference, too, I encountered criticism from ethnic minorities who felt that the racism displayed by the Welsh Guards should not have gone unchallenged by some other character in the play. My point was that the racism of the Welsh guards was part of their fighting mentality. If we as playwrights counterpoint everything negative then we are making our theatre idealistic. In an attempt to be *absolutely* moral we are bound to lie. It was the confusions and the contradictions that I wanted to deal with. Here were Welsh Guards fighting for a piece of land on the other side of the world to which they had no affinity or relationship, and there they were being racist, not towards the Argentinians or the English but towards the people who were working for them – the Chinese crewmen, for example. One of the contradictions is embodied in the scene where the English-speaking Welsh Guards Captain is introduced by a Welsh-speaking Welsh Guards Sergeant to an Argentinian prisoner-of-war who is Welsh-speaking.

In writing that play I was more concerned with the confusion in people's minds than with the clarity of my own thinking. I'd been reading about Chaos Theory and the universe seemed to me to have rhythms which people mistook for certainties whereas in fact everything that happened was new, spontaneous and distinctly different. I was also laughing hugely at myself because of the things I'd taken on board because I wanted to see myself as a revolutionary radical – the newspaper seller, the guy who was always out on the picket lines: mind you, I'm still angry today and I still rail against colonialism in Wales, medievalism in Wales, feudalism in Wales. I still rail against the class system, prejudice, narrow-mindedness and the inability to engage positively with change. I therefore find mid-Wales incredibly frustrating because, in many aspects of its life, it contains several of the things I abhor.

HWD: *But in a sense, Thatcher wasn't 'unimpeachable'. In the end, a certain kind of democracy got her out. And 'analysis groups' of any faction, right or left, cannot finally dictate the language of what a poem or a play, of whatever wisdom, wants to say.*

GC: I reworked *Taken Out* in 1987, and the definitive version was performed in London by Spark Theatre and directed by Sue Glanville at the Drill Hall, Cheyne Street. The Drill Hall, of course, is a venue more associated with the Women and Lesbian Movement and I was very flattered that they felt that *Taken Out* was a play they had to do because the women characters had, in all their contradictions, been captured with compassion, understanding and dignity. The play did extraordinarily good business in London.

HWD: *And I feel I ought to rejoin, to one who has just described himself as 'a revolutionary radical – the newspaper seller, the guy who was always out on the picket lines', that this was at the height of the tube strike and a rail strike.*

GC: Bloody Unions!

HWD: *Depending on whom I talk to in Wales, people have different opinions of what your theatre interests are or of what kind of writer you are. People categorise you according to the kind of work by you they have seen.*

GC: I know that I have several different personae as a writer. Because I have been the Artistic Director of Mid-Powys Youth Theatre for eleven years and have written so many plays for young people I am labelled as a Youth Theatre writer. Others perhaps would see me as a writer in the David Hare mould, one who goes away and researches a subject and then writes a play about it, such as the play about the Tower Colliery, the miners' strike, the Sea Empress disaster and the Falklands war. A third persona would be the adapter and the craftsman. People ask me to do a play, say the adaptation of *Silas Marner* which I did in 1996 for Theatr Clwyd, because they know I'll do it in a given time and get good results.

HWD: *So now will the real Greg Cullen please stand up.*

GC: The real Greg Cullen is in the plays I write for myself. Those plays have a more fantastical quality to them. I enjoy metaphor more than gritty social reality, although I do deal with that reality in everything I do. I'm a story-teller in a very naïve way. The film *Birdbrain* which won the Wales Film Council/BBC competition to celebrate fifty years of cinema is a story about a disabled boy on a remote farm who has the power to free himself through his relationship with a buzzard. Right now I'm working on another story, *Cherubs*, in which

177

the dysfunctional relationships of three sisters and their father on a remote, barren mid-Wales farm are transformed when the corpse of a beautiful man washes up in the river. His astonishing beauty changes everything.

The piece contains the more poetic side of my work. Poetry does feature a great deal in my plays, certainly in the language, and I'll turn to poetry even when I'm using documentary material. That's the lyrical persona. I use language in a poetic form because it frees me, as does the soliloquy, to be able to penetrate into the soul of a character. Also, it's important to me as an entertainer that I give people words which are a pleasure to listen to or are exacting or provocative. I can write Pinteresque dialogue on the one hand and something more abundant on the other. But to me, theatrical language is more than words. It is also a visual language and one that has to embrace music. As a dramatist I'm dealing with a mixture of human sounds and movement. I like to see a play in three dimensions and hear my play in a series of roller coaster rides. And sometimes the language of a play has to be freed from naturalism in order to make the audience aware of what it is really like to be in a particular situation or at a particular emotional stage.

HWD: *Many of your plays, especially the more 'poetic' works are rooted in mid-Wales. Is a sense of place important to you?*

GC: It's very important to me. Mid-Wales is where I've lived for the largest part of my life and it is absolutely natural for me to write about this area. I'm working at the moment on a play called *Whispers in the Woods* which I've been devising with Mid-Powys Youth Theatre. It's a story about a tailor and his daughter and it's drawn from the world of folk and fairy stories, and we're using that vocabulary to describe the rites of passage of a young woman into maturity and independence. Alongside that go many themes that arise from living in mid-Wales: prejudice, a closed attitude, a meanness of spirit, the love and warmth of community, the need to be different. Here in mid-Wales the great and the good are at war against the culture of young people, an alternative culture as they see it. But in my view it's an extremely creative youth culture. It seemed natural to devise a play about it.

HWD: *Do you think that expecting a 'Welsh context' from dramatists writing from Wales leads to the stereotypical? Or was William Carlos Williams right to claim 'The local is universal'? Is the BBC drama department, say, or Made in Wales, realistic in looking for plays with a Welsh experience, or set in Wales? Does a play have to be localised so firmly?*

GC: Even *Waiting for Godot* is localised. There's a landscape there. The play is set by a tree, and people are operating within that landscape. Setting my plays in a Welsh landscape seems a perfectly natural thing for me to do. For me the invisibility of Wales and the lack of recognition for Welsh artists seems absolutely bizarre. So I need to say in my plays what aspects of living in Wales are like. But I don't own that debate. I'm not going to go around trying to be some Anglo-Welsh composite. I'm not playing that game. I'm a Cockney living in mid-Wales. And an Irish Cockney at that. I'm a mongrel. Welsh people in America, Australia and Canada are mongrels. We are the immigrants, and the feeling of immigration and of not belonging is one I share with millions of people around the world. It's a feeling of landlessness.

I live in Wales because I like it. My son was born here and goes to school here and I get work here. I write about mid-Wales because that is where I am. I have no romantic or political ideals when I set my plays in Wales and I write with a consciousness that what I write is invisible to the rest of the UK. I write for my immediate community, and from that specific I hope something universal will arise. It doesn't always, and doesn't always have to. Sometimes you have a piece of theatre that has an immediate impact and is gone.

Take *Taken Out*, for example. Who now wants a play about the Sir Galahad? But it served the bereaved families at the time, and the soldiers whose stories were suppressed by the Ministry of Defence.

HWD: *You mentioned the 'invisibility' of Wales. Does that mean that you as an artist feel isolated in mid-Wales? Do Welsh audiences get to see your plays? For example, how many theatre critics saw the powerful productions of* Mary Morgan, An Informer's Duty *or* Tarzanne?

GC: The sad thing is that those pieces of theatre have been seen only in mid-Wales. People in Cardiff talk resentfully about everything being London-centric. Here in mid-Wales people talk of things as being Cardiff-centric. You try and get a journalist or critic to drive the one-and-a-quarter hour journey from Cardiff to mid-Wales and you soon realise that this area just doesn't exist. I have concentrated on providing theatre of excellence, not only in its presentation but also in its process, but, yes, I and the practitioners feel that we are isolated here. Furthermore, the ability to project Wales into the wider world is hampered by the constitution of the Arts Council of Wales which restricts the Council to give money to theatre companies to tour outside Wales. The Arts Council of Wales should be looking to provide funding to allow companies to tour outside Wales, to act as cultural ambassadors with all the economic spin-offs that cultural envoys in other fields can develop.

When my play *Frida and Diego* won the Fringe First Award at the Edinburgh Festival in 1989 I was astonished that people outside Wales considered it to be so good. I thought they should come to Powys to see how excellent our work was here. But nothing has changed in almost ten years. In that time Welsh dramatists and practitioners have achieved excellence and an edgy grasp of the way the world is shaping, and they are blessed with an 'otherness' and 'outsideness' that helps them to write incisively and be like poets that see Wales and the world afresh. But nobody across the length and breadth of Wales sees what we are doing. Until that happens dramatists in Wales can guarantee their success only beyond the borders of Wales. That has been my experience. My greatest recognition has been in the United States, Europe and England. In Wales I am invisible.

HWD: *And that despite the fact that you are recognized as one of the most talented writers working in Wales and that many of your plays have won international awards.* Mary Morgan, *for example, a play set in Powys, won the City Limits Award for New Expressionism.*

GC: It's a pity that not more people in Wales saw *Mary Morgan*. It's a powerful story. Mary was a servant girl who in 1803 worked for the Wilkins family near Glasbury. Wilkins senior, a wealthy Member of Parliament, had made his money in India with the East India Company. He destroyed the mixed-farming method in and around Chittagong by converting to a cash-crop system and when the international wheat prices fell it is said that three million Indian people died of starvation because of his high prices. He returned to open a merchant bank in Aberhonddu which later became Lloyds Bank. Mary Morgan was hanged for murdering her baby, the illegitimate child of Walter Wilkins junior. The judge in the case was George Hardinge MP, a cousin of the Wilkins family, and the foreman of the jury who condemned Mary was Wilkins junior, the father of the child. Mary's sentence caused a riot in Presteigne and a rider was sent to the King to plead for clemency. Judge Hardinge brought the execution forward but the local carter refused to carry Mary to the place of execution, the hangman refused to hang her and the people of Presteigne did not turn out for the hanging. Her body, ordered by Hardinge to be taken to London for medical research, was stolen by the local people and the vicar buried her within his garden walls. A nice little touch is that the wall has long since gone and the churchyard now includes the garden. Mary's grave is now in consecrated ground.

HWD: *It is certainly a powerful and moving story, especially to someone who has had the Wordsworthian experience of visiting Mary Morgan's grave at Presteigne. But it also returns us, in terms of your play, from the human message to the medium, because your production of* Mary Morgan *was acclaimed particularly for its striking staging. Looking back, how would you analyse that?*

GC: I wanted, you see, to show how class struggles can change society and how our morality does not correspond with humanity and human needs but with an artificial culture based on wealth. And this was reflected in the play's staging. The play looked at how classes interact and how that interaction has both global and personal consequences. Therefore the staging of *Mary Morgan*, a play about democracy, was set on three levels. The king was aloft a moving tower whereas the Wilkins family were beneath him on a raised stage. The audience were milling about on ground level with the working-class and the dispossessed in a promenade situation. The one powerful thing about promenade is that the quality of voyeurism associated with theatre is often greatly enhanced because the audience form part of the acting. They are not locked into their seats. In *Mary Morgan* I got the audience where I wanted them so that during her trial they find themselves, to their surprise, in the middle of the scene. The emotional impact was strong and the old cliché of 'grown men wept' became fresh again.

HWD: *And audiences from Stockholm to San Francisco were enthralled again by your play* Frida and Diego *which captured several prestigious awards. And yet, when Red Shift Company brought a production to the Sherman Theatre in Cardiff in 1989 the audience was so sparse that the run had to be curtailed. Does this tell us something about Welsh audiences?*

GC: It may tell us something about the nature of the administration at the Sherman Theatre at that particular time. The tour of *Frida and Diego* in the UK had been doing 90% business but in Cardiff hardly anyone came to see it. But at that time the Sherman couldn't sell carrots in a market.

HWD: *Peter Mortimer in* The Guardian *described* Frida and Diego *as 'theatre as intended, dangerous and exhilarating and irresistible', and as 'a play resonating long after it's finished, singing in your head'. The story of these two Mexican revolutionaries and painters is certainly another brimming and volatile one. How did you come across it in the first place?*

GC: Over a cup of coffee in my house in Hackney! I was idly flicking over Hayden Herrera's biography of Frida Kahlo which a friend had brought back from Mexico. In it were pictures of Frida and Diego with Nelson Rockefeller, Henry Ford, Leon Trotsky and André and Jacqueline Breton. Then I saw pictures of Frida's powerful paintings and I knew there and then that there was a play here somewhere, and a play for Theatr Powys. I saw the potential of engaging Powys County Council who were just completing their new County Hall to put some money into public works of art which depicted, as Frida and Rivera's paintings did, the history and culture of their area. The two painters, as a result of the Mexican revolution, had thrown out all things European and had discovered their true history as Mexicans, not just from the arrival of Cortez but reaching into their pre-history as well. Suddenly in Mexico the depiction of pre-Colombian society was mixed in with images of modern times, and Frida and Rivera were clearly attempting to carve a post-colonial culture for an emerging nation which had an unique and fascinating history.

Although the core of the play was the story of the two Mexican painters I felt very strongly that, to me, the play was also talking about Wales. Theatr Powys, however, rejected the proposal for the play because, once again, there was a clash between the needs of the writer and the collective culture of the company. I then approached Made in Wales with the proposal, but I got very short shrift there, because the play wasn't actually based in Wales and it wasn't about Welsh people. At that time *Mary Morgan* had won the City Limits Award for New Expressionism and we reworked the production for the Riverside Studios in London and performed it with Red Shift Theatre Company and Mid-Powys Youth Theatre. At the Riverside Jonathan Holloway, the Artistic Director of Red Shift, asked me if I had another idea for a play and when I mentioned *Frida and Diego* he signed me up there and then without hesitation.

HWD: *Having previously mentioned the importance of 'place' with respect to Wales, I suspect that this particular Mexican theme involved an even more dramatic sense of place, and of the people who give places meanings. How did that aspect of the story's potential come into focus?*

GC: I went to Mexico to research the play and met friends and pupils of Frida and Diego, remarkable people like Lucienne Bloch, Stephen Dimitrov and Martha Zomora. In San Francisco I met Marylin Sodie Smith who, with Martha Zomora, had written a biography of Frida and another extraordinary woman called Ella Wolfe whose husband, Bertrand Wolfe, Diego's biographer, had been the US representative of the International Comintern after the revolution in Russia. Before that time they had been stationed in Mexico to train Russian agents to speak English. Ella then in the dead of night would take them over the border to the United States where they would take bogus posts within the American administration and Trade Union movement. The two broke with Stalin at a time when Diego Rivera was beginning to embrace Trotskyism.

All these people were an inspiration for *Frida and Diego* and the other great inspiration was the whole culture of Mexico. The Mexicans have a dialectical way of seeing things. They accept that one's death is always with one, otherwise life is not worth living. From death comes life. Frida in one of her paintings depicts herself lying on the riven, volcanic landscape just outside Mexico City and from her body roots are growing down into this barren soil. The Mexicans are preoccupied with blood, death, flowers, music and place and with identity within that place. Frida's self-portraits could be either Frida Kahlo or it could be Mexico, and when she's painting these self-portraits she's depicting, not only her external appearance but also her internal condition. That placing of oneself within one's art was such a relief to me to witness because of what I'd done in *Taken Out*. That play was so full of myself and full of poetry. That is why devising actors found it very hard to chew. Frida and Diego's painting liberated me from any guilt that I felt as a Socialist that I should put myself at the centre of my art. And so the play came at a time when I was redefining myself and discovering my theatrical landscape.

HWD: *In* Frida and Diego *you reworked biography into vibrant and powerful theatre. The Swedish production at the Stads-teatr ran for a year, the San Francisco production played to full houses and at the Mid-Powys Youth Theatre's version at the Cottesloe in London people were crowding the aisles and standing four-deep round the galleries. What is your response to that kind of, well, response?*

GC: That Cottesloe production with the young people from Wales summed up everything I've been trying to do with theatre. It was, as a good Irish Catholic would say, 'a blessed experience'. The young actors performed with passion and ferocity even in the dress rehearsal. Ken Campbell who was to introduce the company on stage that night, saw the rehearsal and, when Richard Eyre walked into the auditorium, shouted to him 'Oi, you've got to get every fucker in the building to see this'. Word went round that something special was happening in the building and, yes, it was an absolutely packed audience. Nick Evans, one of the most talented actors of his generation, played Diego Rivera and when he said the opening lines 'We shall walk in the Alameida Park and dream a little' it was as if I'd never heard them before in my life. The audience stopped shifting, stifled every noise. At the end of the performance they erupted like a football crowd, and when Ken Campbell came onto the stage he couldn't stop the cheering for a full ten minutes. It was a rare moment of triumph. The other great production was the Stockholm one because there they understood that this was a dream play, that it had a psychic flow, and that it didn't move in chronological sequence. The American production got it wrong because they thought the play was a documentary, a pity since it played at the City College theatre, the home of Diego Rivera's 'World Fair' mural. Ella Wolfe, Marylin Sodie Smith and Emmy Lou Packard came to see one of the performances, and so the wheel came full circle.

HWD: *I want to ask you specifically about the* form *of* Frida and Diego, *a form that cannot be disentangled from the tempestuous life and powerful paintings of the protagonists.*

GC: In form the play attempted to mirror the paintings of Frida and Diego. Some of the scenes are writ large in mural form, others are soliloquies which mirror the self-portraits. Sometimes the play is broadly comic, almost agit-prop as some of Diego's paintings are. Some of the scenes reveal the distances between people, the silences, the things unsaid. Others are as noisy as the Mexicans themselves. I use direct address and dance. I use a great deal of music and movement in my writing. As a dramatist I'm a collaborator because I have enjoyed working with composers, designers and choreographers to create a whole. *Frida and Diego*, despite winning numerous awards, has been criticised for being about too many things, but then Mexico and Frida and Diego's lives are a rich jumble of images, of contradictions, a mix of apparently unrelated things which nevertheless suddenly spark off meaning.

HWD: *This was clearly a visually stunning performance. Many critics shouted 'Don't miss it'.*

GC: But not everybody liked it. I remember at a performance at Croydon Warehouse a man getting up, walking across the stage and shouting, 'What a load of bloody rubbish'. But, yes, in Scotland, England, Sweden and America most audiences were enthusiastic. It came in 1989 at a time when Britain was at a cynical zenith. But as a dramatist I wasn't cynical and neither were Frida and Diego. They fought for a meaningful, creative life for everybody. The play went out there and said 'There's life and there's death and we exist in a precarious relationship within that contradiction'. Some of us call the end forward because we can't deal with the shifting, confusing nature of existence. I love confusion in plays, and maybe that is why at times I play around with farce, in order to make sense of absolute absurdity. I find life rich and humorous. I spend a great deal of my life laughing at myself and I suppose that gets into my plays. In the mural 'A Dream of a Sunday Afternoon in the Alameida Park' the two painters are in the middle of the painting and Frida is holding hands with the figure of Death. Their life and their work contain strong vibrant images that sing of life and the determination to live fully in the face of death. These images have informed my work ever since. I also believe passionately that if we are truly to engage with life we have to be creative because human beings can transform themselves and their lives through creativity. In our technological society many people perform mechanical, abstract tasks all day and *make* nothing. Everybody can create, and creativity is necessary not only for the health of the individual but also for the health of the whole of society. As a dramatist here in mid-Wales I can participate in meaningful creative activity with young people and theatre workers.

HWD: *It is clear that you take your force from many sources, many of them having to do with the available, the suddenly discovered, the local. Do you at all wish you could work more often with a professional – say, a national – company with all the full resources that that would make available?*

GC: I've been concerned in my professional life with the whole ecology of theatre in Wales. I've worked here in every sphere of theatre activity and I'm convinced that if we are going to aim for a National Theatre in Wales we must see to it that we're feeding the roots at the same time. I see it as part of my responsibility as an artist to work with young people to allow them to be creative and fulfil their potential. I've worked with B/Tech students, with youth theatres, with universities, with the Welsh College of Music and Drama and with the BBC. I have seen the potential here in Wales. Those who plead for a National Theatre and do nothing to feed the roots are just self-serving individuals. Wales is such a small country that we need theatre artists who are able to leap from the school playground onto the national stage and back again. We need to have a flexibility, a guerrilla warfare mentality, in the creation of theatre. Role models for Welsh theatre and Welsh playwrights do not exist. We have the responsibility to create them. Too many actors and theatre workers are interested only in self-promotion. They are wankers who belly-ache about the profession in Wales only when they themselves are out of work. We have to stop complaining and start building a National Theatre, brick by brick. People in Wales want multi-storeys but they don't care about the foundations. I wish those people within Wales who fail to nurture the roots would bugger off to London.

HWD: *You spoke earlier about the experience of coming to a completed play of your own, or to its performance, as if for the first time. Keats once wrote that, whenever he read a poem of his, it always struck him as if it had been written by somebody else. To some degree, there must be a comparison possible between a poet experiencing his own finished work and a playwright directing his own plays.*

GC: As a director I'm dealing with something live happening in rehearsals. Often when I'm directing a piece I've written I'll talk quite objectively about 'the playwright'. I'll tell the actor 'I think what the playwright is getting at here is...', but I forget that the playwright is me. When I'm directing my work there is a level at which I'm uncovering the meaning of my own plays. That's very enjoyable. Actors, designers, musicians, choreographers, musical directors, all throw meanings at me. As a director you're actually shaping this now living thing. A local drama teacher in mid-Wales once told her class to look at my production file because the notes the director made alongside the script would be all-important. I showed them my script and there were no notes at all. I don't have the staging blocked out on paper. I'm not looking at the script but at the actors.

Theatre is a three-dimensional art form and I see myself as a sculptor and a painter as much as a writer. Directing a play is for me a living, organic and manipulative process. Until the actors have learnt their lines they are not acting, they are just looking at a piece of paper or remembering dialogue. When they begin to act 'in the moment' the script becomes a spontaneous living thing. So I would urge playwrights who get precious about their dots and commas, and throw tantrums about the sacrosanct nature of their script, to think of their work as clay that can be moulded. Very often it's the very speech or the best joke that the playwright wants to *preserve* that actually stops the play from working. That joke, that speech or that moment is jarring maybe because it is trying to say what the play is 'about' instead of letting the play speak for itself. And, yes, as you say, very often you only see that from the outside.

HWD: *Much of what you've spoken about and evaluated suggests an interest in the national and international face of theatre. From a previous answer, you would seem very much in favour of a national theatre, would you like to make a stab at that question before we end?*

GC: Yes, I am in favour of a national theatre. We in Wales need somewhere to go, otherwise we are ducks paddling around the same little pond all the time and bumping into each other occasionally along the way, and only able to have the concentration-span of a duck. We need to have something to aspire to. We need a stage on which we can experiment. I myself got tired of writing plays for a bunch of people who jump into a transit van with their set. What I have enjoyed whilst working with the Youth Theatre in Powys is the scale of the productions we can mount. I'm good at doing ensemble plays, but why should our work in theatre be shaped by poverty all the time? We have in Wales to be able to expand and to learn new skills. I would like to write for a National stage and be able to control big themes, a large cast and a grand staging. I have learned the craft of grand staging here but I haven't got anywhere near a large main stage in Wales. Indeed, very few dramatists have. The Welsh Theatre establishment in its panic to appease the Welsh middle-class has done an enormous disservice to the development of the theatre tradition in Wales. By thinking short-term they have virtually destroyed this tradition in the 1990s. We now have less theatre than when I came here at the beginning of the 1980s. Everybody who has been associated with any of the leading theatres in Wales should be sacked immediately and I should be put in charge!

Greg Cullen

Interview Two
February 2004

HWD: *You moved from London to Powys in 1983 and worked there as writer and director for nearly fifteen years before moving to Cardiff. What prompted the move from country to city?*

GC: I realized that staying in mid-Wales was, career-wise, not advantageous as I was stagnating in the same pool of work. I felt I'd done everything I could with Mid-Powys Youth Theatre. I also realized I wasn't getting any younger and that my son was getting older and would soon be going to college. I felt it was important to move him into a city to give him another experience of life. And I myself needed to earn some money. These are the real concerns that impel people to move. My partner was studying at the Royal Welsh College of Music and Drama, so Cardiff seemed the right place to move to at that point.

I left for Cardiff with only two projects in the offing. One of those was to write a play for Hijinx. That play, *Paul Robeson Knew my Father*, had been rattling around in my head for years. I knew it was going to be a good piece, and to be honest, I didn't want to sell it to Hijinx. I knew, with their level of funding, that they'd be able to give it only limited exposure. But beggars can't be choosers and I sold the play for a knock-down price.

The other job was to write a play for Mid-Powys Youth Theatre. The idea for that play had also been rattling around in my head for some years. Ostensibly it was a play about the introduction of wind-power to the landscapes of mid-Wales, but actually it was about something that had happened in Rhayader where a wind-turbine site had been located. Initially the local people were hostile towards the project, but after being led up the garden path by developers and others, they fell over themselves to welcome the wind farm without realizing that all the promises they'd been given had been given with a handful of dust. It was a great story, because while the town had been tearing itself apart over the issue of the wind-turbine site, they'd also been trying to put on a community play. And so my play involved a group of people who were writing and producing a community play, and as the central situation develops the play they're writing becomes totally corrupted and they tear one another apart.

I had only these two projects when I went to Cardiff, but I felt I had to close one door behind me in order for another to open, and I thought this would take several years. I braced myself to be poorer than I'd been for a while.

HWD: *But in fact you needn't have worried, because the situation turned around within a very short time. Your first commission in Cardiff however came, not from a theatre company, but from the BBC.*

GC: The BBC had just launched a radio soap series called *Station Road*, and I argued I should be included as a script writer. They gave me a trial run and I must have done well because I was a regular writer for the programme for two and a half years. I'd always thought that I'd never be able to do that kind of work and that I'd rather hang up my hat than script for a soap. But in fact I really enjoyed it. I also enjoyed the social environment, away from the loneliness of the long distance writer. The people involved with the series were great colleagues and, of course, I was well paid. It was good to work within the tight little paradigm you have in a soap and making its universe mean something. I didn't feel I was betraying anything by scripting a soap because I was addressing the same human issues I would address while writing an original play. I remember a Cardiff novelist saying that he'd rather stack shelves in Sainsburys than work with *Station Road*. I pointed out to him that, unlike me, he had never had the experience of stacking shelves in Sainsburys, and that he had no idea what he was talking about.

When I first started to work with *Station Road* it was like trying to unlock a Chinese puzzle. You had a certain number of actors you could call, a certain number of actors who could appear in an episode, a certain number of scenes, and you had to have certain scenes that could be cut from the omnibus at the end of the week. Trying to work all this out was mind-boggling, but I soon mastered it – as you do. The series was commissioned by Dai Smith, and when he left the BBC and new people came to power they looked at the £650,000 budget of *Station Road* and decided to cut the series as a way of stamping their personalities on Radio Wales. It was ironic that, at the same time they were cutting *Station Road*, the series had a growing and loyal audience. By the time they finished with the programme, the series had an audience of 90,000 a day. That's a full Millennium Stadium audience with another 20,000 people standing outside, day after day.

As I was driving the other day from mid Wales to Cardiff I tuned in to Radio Wales and listened for the best part of quarter of an hour to a conversation between the DJ and someone from Llanelli, on the subject of rhubarb, and I thought, 'Here we have it, the new Radio Wales!' The new people also cut music programmes for young people, particularly on Friday evenings. Radio Wales has settled itself very comfortably into that grey-haired niche and failed abysmally to see itself as a national radio station. They argued at the time they were cutting *Station Road* that somehow, having a soap set in the Valleys was denying the rest of the country of expression. That's laughable. It's like arguing that we can't watch *Fiddler on the Roof* in the Valleys because we can't identify with Jews. The new powers also cut down mercilessly the number of hours allocated to radio drama. Meanwhile Radio Cymru can afford to support its soap series for a very tiny audience. So many of the decisions made by the new Radio Wales team have been philistine, executive decisions. The woman who decided to cut the number of hours allocated to drama said, 'There's no place in the new Radio Wales for 'recorded dialogue'. That's a remarkable statement, especially since we've known it as 'drama' since the days of the Greeks. Now apparently it's 'recorded dialogue'!

HWD: *You mentioned earlier the two projects you were engaged on when you left for Cardiff. You've outlined one of them, the Mid-Powys community play project. What about the other project, the play* Paul Robeson Knew my Father?

GC: I was extremely proud of that piece. I directed the production for Hijinx and I managed to assemble a super cast with Paula Gardiner as musical director. The show re-toured the following year and we took it to Croydon Warehouse where we had excellent London reviews. But, as I originally feared, Hijinx wasn't really in a position to elevate the piece to the stature it deserved. It remains unpublished, and yet it is one of the most poignant, well-made plays in terms of craft to come out of Wales in the last twenty years. I say that without hubris and in the sure knowledge of having seen most of those plays, and written some of them myself. The sad thing is that there is still no avenue, after twenty years of writing in Wales, to get the play published. There is no avenue for exploiting a good Welsh play. There is nowhere for it to go. Hijinx is going to do a re-run of *Paul Robeson Knew my Father* this year. Same company, same play. It's as good as you can get in Wales.

HWD: *'Same company, same play'. Are you saying that, despite Sgript Cymru's programme and Theatr Clwyd's remit to stage the work of writers from Wales, there is no real outlet for new writing here, that there is, in your words, 'nowhere for it to go'?*

GC: I don't believe in Sgript Cymru any more than I believed in Made in Wales. I think the idea that you can have only one dedicated new writing company in Wales is laughable, and sad. That is no reflection on the excellent work Simon Harris and his team are able to achieve. As for Theatr Clwyd, I think it hasn't honoured its remit. In the past it's had literary managers whose job it's been to generate new writing. These people came from outside Wales and knew nothing of what was happening here. They therefore assumed they 'had to get something going' and that writers in Wales 'had to be sub-standard, otherwise they would have made it by now'. They thought the best thing would be to dig up new young writers and start afresh. These people came into Wales, had their little flurry of activity and then thankfully disappeared and left us alone.

The point is that there are some very good playwrights in Wales who are not given the opportunity to put on their plays on main stages. Playwrights here are not going to gain credibility by putting on plays that go in the back of Ford Transits. We need more main stages. I've been saying that for the last twenty years, and it's still not happening. The only writer who has got anywhere near a main stage recently is Ed Thomas who is just finishing a commission for Clwyd, a commission which he received about five years ago. Other than that, the only other main-stage production I can quote is my play, *Frida and Diego* which was shown at the main stage in Theatr Gwynedd, the Sherman and Theatr y Werin, Aberystwyth.

HWD: *It's often argued however, that there isn't an audience for new writing in Wales.*

GC: I can well imagine that someone like Terry Hands would be in trouble with his comfortable standard audience if he were to stage a radical, new and adventurous play. However, there's new writing and new writing. Should he commission Brian Friel, then Friel would come up with something that would suit Hands's traditional audience beautifully. We have a ridiculous attitude towards new writing. We tend to associate it with something very radical, with bright flashing lights and with pvc tights wrapped around the leading male actor while he's being rogered from behind by his father. But there are writers in Wales who are able to present beautifully told stories without resorting to that kind of infantile sensationalism.

If you put on a particular kind of theatre, you find a particular kind of audience for it. Last year I directed, for the first time, the National Youth Theatre of Wales and succeeded in trebling the audience within six months. I intend to double that next year by having a strategy of contacting people and pulling them in. It's often argued that with a youth theatre company it doesn't matter what you put on. You could do Super Ted and parents and relations would still come to see their kids perform. But, if you look at the cast of a youth theatre production and give them each a mum, dad, brother and sister, that accounts for about a hundred and fifty audience members. From where, then, on the tour of *Frida and Diego* did the other three thousand come? They were there because of professional outreach, good marketing, calling in favours. It's all about the way you appeal to people, how you hustle.

HWD: *Your* Frida and Diego *YouthTheatre production was certainly not a Ford Transit van production. It had a large canvas and a large cast. Was it the play's potential to work splendidly on main stages that made you opt for it as your debut production with the Youth Theatre of Wales?*

GC: Yes, but in some ways *Paul Robeson Knew my Father* is also a very 'large' play although it has only four characters in it. It speaks of large communities in America, in Guyana and in South Wales. It also speaks of a political landscape that unites those three very disparate countries. It's a tiny play with a huge canvas. You therefore don't have to go big in terms of cast in order to make a big play. But also working with so many young actors on *Frida and Diego* gave me the opportunity of working with incredible human imagery and variety. With so many actors you don't really need an elaborate set and it's really interesting that the production won the Theatre in Wales design award when, in fact, the design was very simple. It consisted of three screens, gauzes which flew in and out, a bandstand, a park bench and two trucks which looked like a painter's scaffold. That was it.

HWD: *And yet, throughout the performance, the audience were given the impression of ever-changing scenery and scenes. How did you manage that?*

GC: I've always been a lover of paintings and I'm fascinated by the way Renaissance painters grouped a large number of people. When I'm directing a play and grouping actors I concentrate on making the human eye follow a certain path across the stage to the exact spot where the action is. In the images in *Frida and Diego* I worked from the artists' canvases. At the opening of the play the actors became characters from Diego's *A Dream of a Sunday Afternoon in the Alameida Park*. There were other images in the play inspired by Frida's self-portraits and by paintings such as *The Trench*. That Diego painting has about eight figures in it, but I had about fifteen or twenty guys in the scene and we created something quite new about the Spanish Civil War. What the audience saw on the stage of *Frida and Diego*, what elevated it, was the sense of detail. Wherever your eye looked, every actor was giving his or her soul to what he or she was doing, and that was because their souls had been elevated through the act of creating a piece of theatre. It wasn't just about having fun, which is crucial, or thinking or moving on stage, which again is crucial; it was about the conviction of being elevated by a sense of belief in the very art of theatre. That elevation should, in turn, reach the audience. That is what art is about.

HWD: *I'm struck by your emphasis here in that it seems to link your own writing to a concern for the wider social value of drama per se, beyond the provision simply of a particular play for a particular performance in a particular place.*

GC: Yes indeed, I speak regularly and unashamedly to young people of the significance of art and of the role of theatre in ordinary people's lives. While rehearsing *Frida and Diego* I got quite annoyed with one young student who said, 'What we do is no more important than cutting the grass for the local council.' I regarded this comment as some kind of inverted socialist egalitarianism that belongs to the era of Chairman Mao or to some cultural revolution where we deny the fact that art has a key role, and that acting has a significance beyond the act of cutting grass or filling a petrol tank. Of course actors are special. When did you last open a newspaper and see photographs of people who had just finished laying the M1 or repaired Mr Smith's plumbing? Artists, beyond the curiosity of personality, hold a special place in our society. We have to accept that with it comes an enormous responsibility to be true and honest and to put your heart and soul on the line while you're performing. If you say that to young actors and design artists they respond in a way that elevates the entire enterprise.

HWD: *You are therefore, as current director of the National Youth Theatre of Wales, training and nurturing young people who have taken your message on board. What do you think will happen career-wise to these young, talented actors. Are there opportunities for them in Wales?*

GC: I think there are opportunities here, but not anything like the opportunities that there could or should be. I'm aware that a great deal of the frustration we feel about the situation in Wales cannot be resolved. It's a small country and can't have the resources available in countries with a larger population base. But I'd like the Arts Council of Wales to ask itself this question, 'Has the Council, over the last twenty years, presided over the survival or the demise of theatre in Wales?' I would really like to know the Council's answer to that particular question.

When I came to Wales in the early 1980s there was an abundance of good theatre here and real liveliness. There were experimental companies and traditional companies. There were companies which specialised in story-telling and others which sought to marry the textures of poetry, music, the spoken word and dance. It was a time of radical re-thinking of what was possible. I could go and enjoy all that diversity twenty years ago. What do we have now? Nothing.

HWD: *Here we are then with, as you claim, 'nothing', and building this huge and hugely costly Millennium Centre in Cardiff Bay. To house and showcase what then? Nothing?*

GC: Well, it's going to house Diversions and the WNO. Some time ago I had a circular from the Millennium Centre admin office asking me what I'd like to be kept informed about and I had to tick various boxes – dance, opera and so forth. But there was no box for theatre! I returned the card with the statement, 'I want to see theatre' and the question, 'Why is there no box for theatre?' Now I hear that theatre will not be included as an item for the main stage but that several other smaller spaces in the building will be more suitable for theatre. And there you have it! Immediately people are coupling 'small' with 'theatre'. That's a slimming down, a lack of ambition. One of the things that has to be tackled in Wales is this fundamental lack of belief in the ability of dramatists and theatre practitioners here to produce anything worthwhile, given that we have in Wales something that the rest of the world might want to see. It's an attitude that has permeated the theatre policy, or rather the absence of a theatre policy, of the Arts Council of Wales.

It is also present in the attitude of the artistic leadership of some of the main houses in Wales.

HWD: *Therefore, for 'large-scale theatre productions' in the Millennium Centre read 'musicals'?*

GC: Yes, I think so. That's what the 'bums on seats' brigade is looking for, and let me add that I don't have any problem with musicals. Everyone has the right to be entertained; everyone has the right to read the *Beano* and the *Dandy*. I myself am now working on a musical which I hope will be produced in the United States. I'm also writing for the WNO. I never considered myself much of a musical man, but I'm currently working in the field, and enjoying it. And why shouldn't new musicals be written in the so-called 'land of song'? We've got great stories to tell, talented composers and fine playwrights. I'd love to see the creation of a Welsh musical theatre.

People who enjoy light musical theatre have paid their taxes and made a financial contribution to the Cardiff Millennium Centre. I myself wouldn't want to go to see, say, *Oklahoma* in the Millennium Centre but there are plenty of people in Wales who would jump at the opportunity. It probably wouldn't need to be subsidised. Subsidy is there, ideally, to protect and nurture what is fragile in the arts, what is new, and what will have minority appeal.

It's a pity that the Millennium Centre isn't located, like the Rugby Stadium, in the heart of the city. The Bay itself is an inhuman place in which to walk around. Already you've got that 'Craft in the Bay' building stuck right in the middle of an island. You're not quite sure what it is. Is it open? Is it closed? What's in it? How do you get to it?

HWD: *You mentioned there your 'work in progress', an American musical and a WNO project. How did the American commission come about?*

GC: Three years ago I sent *Paul Robeson Knew My Father* to a London agent who was working with Tom Polum, a New York composer. Polum was looking for someone with no preconceived ideas about what a musical should be. They'd been to Don Black and to the guy who had written the lyrics for *Fiddler on the Roof*, but no one had really come up with what Polum was looking for. They wanted someone who could throw the rule book out of the window, and someone who could write with a real sense of period. Through the London agent, Tom Polum contacted me and I was sent the script of an opera entitled *Abelard and Heloise* and a CD of some of the music, which I hated. I was very reluctant to get involved but Polum came from the States to meet me and was very persuasive in that particular American way.

I turned up to the London meeting in my usual gear of trainers, hooded top and denim jacket, and Tom Polum sat there in his Armani suit, black shiny shoes, perfect skin and perfect hair. We took one look at each other and thought 'This is never going to work.' After two and a half hours of ripping the script apart I returned gratefully to Cardiff thinking, with relief, that I wouldn't have to be involved in the project any more.

But that night Polum telephoned to say he'd be in Cardiff in the morning to work on the script. And so we spent five days re-writing and restructuring the script of *Abelard and Heloise*. I was then given a day and a half to write the lyrics for an opening song for Abelard and for Heloise. I handed them over to him, and what happened next was quite fortuitous. He said, 'These lyrics are real pretty. Now I need to get to that piano.' At that point I started rummaging in my briefcase, unaware that he was really asking me to leave the room. Then he said, 'I don't normally compose with someone else in the room.' But nevertheless he made a start, and I was there to chop, change and suggest alternative words. If I'd left that room the lyrics would have taken weeks of negotiation. Despite the fact that we're chalk and cheese we worked well together and completed half a dozen songs in a very short time. When he returned to the States his partner Bert asked him 'What's he like, this Greg?' and Tom Polum replied, 'Well, if you were at a party, he'd be the last person in the room you'd want to talk to.' I want that on my gravestone, 'The last person you'd want to talk to at a party'!

We've had two rehearsed readings of *Abelard and Heloise* with about twenty-eight Broadway singers, a little orchestra, a conductor and director. We've now got a producer and money to put on the show. We're talking here in the region of eight million dollars already pledged. It could be that in 2005 it goes on an American tour that would lead us into Broadway. It's all very exciting, risky and expensive, and for me it's been a steep learning curve in terms of how a Broadway musical gets done and of the whole production process. I feel as if I've gone from playing for Merthyr to playing for Real Madrid. I thought I had a huge budget when I was allocated a hundred and twenty-five thousand pounds for the National Youth Theatre last year but, as I said, for *Abelard and Heloise* it's eight million dollars.

HWD: *And now back to the world of Wales and the WNO commission. From what I know of what they pay dramatists such as yourself, working for the WNO is certainly not like playing for Real Madrid.*

GC: What I'm doing for the WNO is a youth opera for WNO MAX, their education and outreach work. I was absolutely delighted to get the job. I whooped for joy when they telephoned me to say that they were commissioning me. But what I'm getting for the work is outrageously low. They're paying me only £5,000 for a full-length piece of work. That's not even ITC rate. For one of the best-funded arts organizations in the United Kingdom to be paying a mere £5,000 for the kind of work I've been commissioned to do just shows that we have a long way to go in acknowledging that work for young people is as valid as work for any other audience. The WNO cannot expect to be able to tick their community and outreach box by short-changing artists. What they allocate now to outreach is just crumbs off their table. It's insulting to the audience, it's insulting to the young people who perform the opera and it's insulting to the professionals who do the work for them. It denigrates the WNO. They fall flat on their faces and right into the pockets of anyone who claims that they are a fat, bloated organization that sees itself in relation to the great opera houses of the world rather than to the people of Wales.

I've been working with some wonderful artists in the WNO who are great musicians, voice coaches and so on. These are people in their forties and fifties, with priceless expertise, and yet they are paid far less than they'd be paid if they worked for the National Youth Theatre of Wales. I know what I'm saying now won't endear me to the WNO moguls and that I may be jeopardising my chance of ever working for them again. But somebody has to say something and it might as well be me.

The opera I'm doing for them is based on *Whispers in the Woods*, the play I devised for Mid-Powys Youth Theatre. I'm taking the core narrative from that. It's about a tailor whose daughter falls in love with a wolf and it deals with parenthood, about becoming an adult and a sexual animal, about parents needing to let go of their children and not being able to, and about falling in love. It's dressed up as a kind of fairy-story and is going to work beautifully as an opera. I'm working with Brian Irvine, a Northern Ireland composer, and we move between the Grand Opera House in Belfast and the young opera group in Cardiff. We're having a ball. The young people and the staff at the WNO are wonderful.

I'm thinking of pretty much the same project for the National Youth Theatre. I'd prefer not to talk about that project at this stage because it's not even cast yet.

HWD: *Seren published three of your plays in 1998. Is* Whispers in the Woods *available in published form? And* Paul Robeson Knew my Father?

GC: No, publishers in Wales don't know what to do with a volume of plays. In the 1990s Seren published plays by Charlie Way, Ed Thomas, Dic Edwards and myself. But the volumes continued to sit on shelves. I had meetings with people at the press and suggested possible markets and reviewers. Did they do anything to activate my suggestions? No, they didn't.

HWD: *You went last night to see a production at Henry VIII School in Abergavenny of your new play* Ice-Cream, *a play you were asked to write for the Wales Playwrights Commissioning Group. What exactly is the 'commissioning group' and how does it operate?*

GC: *Ice-Cream* was commissioned by five South Wales schools under the auspices of the Wales Playwrights Commissioning Group, an organization formed by the schools themselves. Each school put in £3,000 towards the scheme and the Arts Council of Wales provided additional funding. With some of the money, they commissioned me to write a play and Paula Gardiner to compose the music. Each school then put on a production of the play and there is a sixth production for a cast coming together from all five schools. I'd like to direct that final production, which the schools hope will go into the Millennium Centre.

The wonderful thing about the project was that I could work with twenty young people from each school on a completely blank sheet of paper. I had no idea what the play would be about and I asked each group to come up with characters from their communities whom they found odd, obsessed, eccentric or interesting. I ended up with about one hundred characters. I placed some of these characters in family relationships and came up with the play, the central character of which is an ice-cream man. It was a boy from Bryncelynog School who improvised this character. When I hot-seated the boy he revealed that his mother had died giving birth to him and that his siblings had rejected him. To complicate matters, his father was a serious drinker. The ice-cream man was lonely and isolated, and when I asked him what he wanted to do with his life, he said, 'Travel'. I asked him where he'd like to go and he replied, 'I don't really mind as long as it's got this beautiful sunset.'

This gave me the idea for the play, which is about a loner who has the very public job of being an ice-cream man. He's had an unhappy childhood, but as a seller of ice-cream he can now give pleasure to children. When I started to think about the destination to which the ice-cream man could travel my mother said, 'Well maybe he doesn't have to travel as far as all that for a beautiful sunset. You can get some very nice ones in Pembrokeshire.' So that was settled.

This sixteen-year old boy from Bryncelynog had such a poetic soul that it prompted me to think, 'What if, in the process of dying, the mother had passed on her life-force to her son, and that transference had carried with it a heightened sense of anguish?' I endowed the ice-cream man in my play with this sense of anguish that made him able, in the act of handing out the ice-cream to the children, to glimpse their inner lives and see the unhappiness they were suffering. And so I constructed a whole series of mini stories and sub-plots in which the ice-cream man affects the lives of the characters and makes them better and happier. Three quarters of the way through the play everything the ice-cream man does goes wrong, and, thinking that his entire life has been wasted, he goes to Pembrokeshire with the intention of ending his life by driving his van off the cliff. In this long musical journey towards his death, the audience keep seeing the satisfactory resolution of each story and they see that the ice-cream man has been a force for good. Unfortunately the ice-cream man himself is unaware of his good influence, but when he arrives in Pembrokeshire he sees the most blindingly beautiful sunset, and he cannot bring himself to end his life.

I've been very impressed by the great job the different schools have made of this play. The kids and staff of all five schools have responded with enormous imagination in the different ways they have realized the piece.

HWD: *It seems to me as if the last year for you has been about getting out of series scripting and returning to writing plays.*

GC: There was a period when I was doing *Nuts and Bolts* for HTV and was in that farming drama mode. I also directed for the Royal Welsh College of Music and Drama. But the last year has been about the return to writing plays. During the year I wrote *Mud Crawlers* for the BBC for the Voices Project. For that play I went to Pill in Newport and worked with the local community researching their history. We came up with an extraordinary set of stories.

The starting image for the play was that Pill a hundred and fifty years ago was just a land of bog and marsh. When it started trading with coal, iron and slate, ships would come up the Usk empty, but they would have to have ballast to keep an even keel. When they got to Newport they would offload this ballast and so gradually, Pill, which as I say had been a bog marsh, was filled in with soil and stone from all over the world. Along with the ships came also people. There's one part of Pill where shamrock grows because of the Irish soil that was offloaded.

My play was based on that poetic idea of sand, soil and stone coming from all over the world to Pill, and also people arriving there to look for a better life. While researching for the play I met some Iraqi Kurds who had been tortured, an Irish priest who could date his family's arrival in Wales to the period of the Irish Famine, and a wonderful woman called Cissy whose father had been a Nigerian sailor who'd married a local woman. I also interviewed the West Indian population who came over in the 1950s and 1960s. The play got to be about that immigration and migration. So, yes, I have been writing plays and returning to the stage.

HWD: *'Returning to the stage.' This is the appropriate point in this interview to ask you if you are still in favour, as you were in my 1997 interview with you, of the establishment of an English-medium National Theatre in Wales.*

GC: Yes, I definitely am. We shouldn't get stuck in that parochial myopia of 'Should we go for a rugby stadium, an opera house, national touring companies or a national theatre?' These should not be in competition, shouldn't be pitted against one another. I'm not being naïve in saying that we need all of them. What we've seen here in Wales is the decimation of the theatre ecology. I'm in there with youth theatre because it's a crucial part of that ecology. What I've learned from my experience with the National Youth Theatre of Wales is that there is a huge audience out there, and enormous enthusiasm for theatre. We need a national theatre for several reasons. We need it because we need excellence and we need to be able to present our particular perspective on a large, national stage. That doesn't mean that we shouldn't be looking constantly to regenerating radical, new ideas through project funding. We need revenue-funded companies to create new work. Money should also be put into publishing to make absolutely sure that the plays that have been produced in Wales over the last twenty years are available so that Welsh students and theatre companies can reinterpret and re-stage texts. We need to have our excellence on record.

HWD: *Doesn't that also mean that we need a follow-through in terms of quality reviews of plays and performances here in Wales?*

GC: I remember well a conversation I had with Alan Osborne, Dic Edwards, Ed Thomas and Charlie Way about the standard of criticism of Welsh productions. We despaired at the fact that it seemed as if the pinnacle of our achievement was to have a review by David Adams in *The Guardian*. We asked ourselves, 'Is *that* the best we can hope for as dramatists here in Wales?' Now of course, since *The Guardian* no longer commissions David Adams, we are more marginalised than ever. The standard of criticism in the few Welsh newspapers that carry theatre reviews is appalling. Very often the review tells you more about the reviewer than the production itself. Many of the reviews of the National Youth Theatre production of *Frida and Diego* last year were egotistical, with the reviewers more anxious to reveal their own prowess than discuss the performance. They also concentrated too much on me and the play. I wanted to ask, 'Did you not notice the forty-five brilliant young actors on stage, and did you not notice the set and costumes that the team of young designers had created?' They dismissed the achievement of talented individual actors with the sentence, 'It would be unjust to mention any one person in particular.' The low level of theatre criticism here in Wales is unacceptable. I would say to some reviewers that they should quit immediately, and to others, 'Go and wave your academic knickers elsewhere. Not in my face please!'

Alan Osborne

Interview One
May 1998

HWD: *You told me once that music was your first love, then visual art followed, and a little later music theatre and then theatre itself. In what sense was there music at the beginning?*

AO: It all started when I was eight or nine years old. My grandfather had taught himself to play the piano when he was sixty and he, in turn, gave me lessons. The first song I ever played was 'The Song of the Volga Boatmen'. It was like playing the song of international socialism, and to me and to others at that time, the rest of the world, in endorsing international socialism, was merely being an ally to Merthyr! Merthyr was the centre of the world. The second song I mastered was 'The Marseillaise'. So the first song was influenced by Russia, the second by the French Revolution, and the third had a personal resonance. Gladys, my grandmother, had bought a second-hand dress with a motif of the Star of David on it. She had no idea what the motif represented, but she thought it was absolutely beautiful. I told her, 'It's Jewish', and she replied 'I don't care. It's still beautiful, and anyway, they're the same as us.' And when she was wearing that dress my grandfather went round the house singing 'When Israel was in Egypt's land, Let my people go – Gladys'. That was almost a little piece of music theatre, combining humour and song and I provided the piano accompaniment. So that early influence of music was pretty strong.

HWD: *And this early influence led you to apply for a place at the Welsh College of Music and Drama.*

AO: I was offered a place there when I was fifteen. But I didn't take it up because I became really obsessed with sport. I also got interested in painting and drawing after Colin Jones, the portrait painter, joined the staff of the Quaker's Yard Grammar School. What a change he effected; he brought the world into the school, and it was then that I began to be influenced, not by Welsh culture as such, but by universal and European traditions in painting. That influence affected my work. Colin Jones also introduced me to a piece of poetry written by Rilke. I've still got a copy on my desk and I look at it virtually every day. It's this: 'If your everyday life gets you down, do not accuse it. Excuse yourself and say to yourself that you are not poet enough to summon up its riches. For the creator there is no poor or unimportant place.' That idea has, to me, been the driving force underlying everything. Colin Jones's inspiration was a major influence.

HWD: *So it was that influence that led you to apply for a place at Newport College of Art.*

AO: Yes, and I enjoyed Newport because you had there young people from south-east Wales, and they were talented and energised people. They had come from rough, tough and poor homes, but how they could paint! The standard of painting there was probably the highest in the country. I don't suppose I learned anything from the lecturers at Newport College of Art, although they were good painters in their own right. I was learning from the other students during my college course; in fact we were all learning from one another. It was there that I met Christine Kinsey, Bryan Jones, Dave Peterson and Ozi Osmond. The highly inventive Bryan Jones gave me supportive roles in scores of films and plays he had concocted – on the spot! But I hadn't written a thing at that stage.

HWD: *But you'd written poetry at school....*

AO: Yes, but it was a very odd kind of poetry. It was very much influenced by events in Merthyr history, and naturally so. Merthyr in my time was a very strange place in which to grow up. If you spend most of your early life with 'Martyr' written over your heart, it's inevitably going to influence the rest of your life. When I was at school there was a button factory and ICI in Merthyr, and sometimes the dyes from these industries were tipped into the Morlais river and it would change colour. One day it would be a bright red river, and a yellow one the next. That fascinated me and in my poems I was responding to these changes and seeing the extraordinary in the ordinary. My work was 'almost poetry' and very surrealistic. I entered the poems for the School Eisteddfod competitions and I used to come last every year! The adjudicators thought I was bonkers. The poems were influenced by paintings and in them I sought to create visual images. I had read an essay by Eliot on the visual culture from Dante onwards and I was fascinated by the fact that poems don't have to be exclusively 'literary'. Good poems can often be very visual.

HWD: *So there was this relay of creative forces from different arts, each obviously feeding the other. But after Newport you decided to become a teacher rather than a professional artist.*

AO: I fell in love with teaching and saw it as a means to give to lots of kids the opportunities I myself hadn't had. I also wanted to be a bit like my art teacher, Colin Jones. In fact, after a period of teaching at London and Faringdon I came back as art teacher to Afon Taf which was the old Quaker's Yard Grammar School. I was appointed as the art teacher there and I felt that the wheel had come full circle, and that I could try to do the kind of work that Colin had done at the school when I was a pupil. It was a kind of nemesis. It was important for me to identify and encourage the children's ideas, hopes and dreams, and I liked the creative output of the pupils and staff at Afon Taf. When I was teaching at Faringdon I felt very guilty that I wasn't helping out in Wales with Bryan Jones and Christine Kinsey at their new concept – 'Chapter, Arts for the Community'. Karl Francis was helping out – he was tidying the toilets upstairs and laying tiles! I too wanted to make a contribution and that was one of the reasons for returning to Wales.

HWD: Terraces, *'an atmospheric piece', was your first contribution. It was certainly in 1979 one of the most ambitious performances to be launched at Chapter Arts Centre in Cardiff.*

AO: *Terraces* was a set of thirty poems and I wrote the lyrics based on the poems, and composed the tunes. I also did a number of large paintings to accompany the work. *Terraces* attempted to show my general impressions of Merthyr, of the mountains, the people and the character of the town. After reading the script, Mick Flood, one of the directors, said to me 'You don't really need the paintings, your script is graphic enough. In *Terraces* you're writing for the stage.' I was gratified, but surprised to hear that I was writing for the stage. You see, I came to theatre writing from a different direction from the other dramatists you've interviewed. I came to it from the direction of art and music. The eleven canvases I'd painted for *Terraces* were not incorporated into the set, but they were on view in the foyer.

HWD: *So the various art forms as such were beginning to separate out.* Terraces *received an enthusiastic response from audience and reviewers alike. Indeed the reviewer for* The Stage *called it 'a memorable theatrical event'. What exactly did that success mean to* you?

AO: I was naturally delighted that the queue for the performances was fifty yards long every single night. For me, writing *Terraces* was an act of homage and an act of exorcism of all the things I'd been through. When I wrote it, all members of my close family had died and I was back in my old home in Abermorlais Terrace in a house that had been built in 1820 on iron-ore from the Cyfarthfa tips. I enjoyed my work as a teacher, but I was feeling exhausted from the sheer amount of the work, and I was slowly running out of love, and I knew it. I needed to do something for myself, something creative. And so I wrote *Terraces* which had characters straight off the streets of Merthyr. My home in Abermorlais Terrace was a rich source of inspiration in terms of stories, characters and music. I remember as a child being awe-struck when the pianist from the electric theatre came to our front room to thump classical and popular melodies on the piano. In *Terraces* I wanted to record the images of Merthyr I'd had as a child, images which had become much clearer and more focused because I'd been away. And so I wrote about the people I'd known, the events I'd encountered, and the influence of Hollywood, and I did cheeky and unpredictable things such as having members of the Dowlais Male Voice Choir sing rock and roll and Hollywood songs. In *Terraces* I was as cheeky as the boy who wrote poems for the School Eisteddfod about the Morlais river changing its colour. But this time round the surrealism of my writing was acceptable.

HWD: *Your next piece, which you co-arranged with Bob Jones was the 'jazz musical of the night',* Johnny Darkie. *The character Johnny Darkie was in* Terraces *of course, but only in a small way. What drew you to him, and what made you enlarge him?*

AO: *Johnny Darkie* was based on a real person, a rag-time character called John Dark. He was a shady character, a huckster of the night. In our stage musical we needed a jazz player, a musician of the night. And so we came up with this catalytic, mystical figure, a saxophonist who represented the spirit of place, in this case the spirit of Cardiff Docks. I used to go to the Docks in the early 1960s and it was an amazing place with musicians coming over from Colston Hall, Bristol. They came to the Ghana Club at the top of Bute Street. The Club was run by Johnny Silver. In the front room you'd have a curry on a gingham plastic tablecloth. Down there in the Docks it felt more like the city than the city itself. I loved the architecture, but I also loved the community. They should never have knocked down the houses in the Bay. They were beautiful. There was also a wonderful bar down in the Docks known as The House of Blazes and the whole area felt like some mysterious other world. I wanted to capture the spirit of that place in *Johnny Darkie* and Bob Jones and I got it. We kept coming at that spirit from different angles and the performance was multi-media and celebrated colourful characters and places that have vanished or been destroyed.

HWD: *You helped finance the highly successful 'café' production of* Johnny Darkie *with your prize money from the Academi Gymreig's 'Play for Wales' Competition in 1982. Was the production as ambitious and as expensive as* Terraces?

Alan Osborne

AO: *Terraces* was a special case. Mick Flood had for a long time had several American productions in Chapter, *Highway Shoes* was one of them. *Terraces* was a Welsh idea, it was indigenous while still being American or international. Because of this local firms, organisations and businesses took an interest in it and gave generous financial sponsorship. Seventeen firms contributed money because they were excited by the fact that this was indigenous and that it had all the armoury and energy of Chapter behind it.

HWD: *In her Introduction to your recently published volume of plays* The Merthyr Trilogy, *Gilly Adams says that 'other writers have emerged with similar preoccupations, and a feel for the rich poetic idiom of English-speaking, urban South Wales, but Alan was the first. He can be said to have pioneered a genre of dramatic writing....' Were you aware that you were pioneering?*

AO: Gilly Adams was always an enabler and constantly encouraged me to create something indigenous. And there was Dic Edwards showing, again in 1981, that a city idiom worked excellently with his *Late City Echo*. Mick Flood at Chapter had suggested that I do something universal that dovetailed into the familiar. But in both *Terraces* and *Johnny Darkie* the familiar became the Big One. America became too small for Wales. There was rich humour in that. When I wrote *Terraces* it was a very strange time. Thatcher had just got in and artists felt that they should squeeze some things into their art before they themselves were squeezed out. Geoff Moore, Peter Mumford, Mick Flood all said, 'Let's get things done now because we're not going to get grants for much longer.' There was a sense of urgency to write and to perform because of the cuts in funding. And Gilly Adams was there encouraging and providing opportunities with, for example, *Johnny Darkie* when it was a café performance. I'd say that the café performance was the better one because it needed the candles on the tables and the dangerous energy.

That atmosphere was there in the concert performance at Chapter. When it transferred to The Sherman in 1982 it was clear that the work didn't suit that theatre at all.

1981, of course, when *Johnny Darkie* was first performed, was a good time for the playwright. Made in Wales was founded in that year and in those early days a group of committed writers shared ideas and hopes. There was Hugh Thomas, Gareth Armstrong, Dic Edwards and Siôn Eirian. It was a wonderful time, and Gilly Adams was there as a driving force. During the eighties Siôn Eirian and I worked on a piece called *The Rising* which dealt with the Merthyr Rising of 1831 which took place outside the house I grew up in. Geoff Moore, of Moving Being, Siôn Eirian and I wanted to think in terms of Youth Theatre because we wanted to create a young image and interest schools in theatre. But Gwyn Alf Williams, on whose research and writing the dramatic work was based, was not at all convinced that this was a good idea. He said over and over again, 'It's not possible, boys.'

HWD: *And yet in a letter to* The Western Mail *in November 1987 he praised you and Siôn Eirian, Moving Being and the South Cardiff Youth Theatre for a script and a performance that was 'relevant, pointed and challenging'. He salutes you in particular for locating the action 'in a present-day schoolroom.'*

AO: When Gwyn saw the performance he was really excited. In the letter to *The Western Mail* he said that Siôn Eirian and I worked the script from his book on the Merthyr Rising and from an essay he'd written in which he had 'tried to imagine a theatrical experience which would have past and present simultaneously on stage.' After *The Rising* had toured Wales and had had a tremendous impact, Gwyn began to think of presenting his ideas on television, because he'd seen that his work lent itself to a visual and theatrical medium. In *The Rising/Gwrthryfel*, although Siôn and I had freedom to script the play, we decided not to veer away from Gwyn's ideas and vision. Gwyn, Geoff Moore, Siôn Eirian and myself decided that the medium of theatre should be used to urge 'real change, not just some measure of reform.' Indeed Gwyn Alf himself said that the play was 'not comfortable or comforting. It is not intended to be. The people it depicts and addresses find precious little for their comfort.'

HWD: The Rising *again centred on Merthyr, and the title of the Parthian publication of three of your plays is* The Merthyr Trilogy. *Clearly this other capital of Wales has a hold on you.*

AO: Being a Merthyr Tydfil boy with a saint over his heart and a king in a castle, I can't but be fascinated with the town. When I was growing up, Merthyr was a truly international town and the school register read like a register in Lower East Side, Brooklyn. I equated myself with the poor and the struggling of the tenement flats. I'm from the Bowery. In fact Merthyr is full of different Boweries. Merthyr had a Chinatown, too. And it also had an area where people actually lived underground. I wasn't conscious of this when I was growing up in Merthyr. But I was aware that Merthyr was known as 'America before America'. When Brunel built the railway a great number of Merthyr people emigrated to Cardiff and then they went from Cardiff to America. The 'Off to Philadelphia in the Morning' movement had begun. Merthyr's influence on Cardiff was considerable. You may think that this is arrogance on my part, but it's terribly funny arrogance.

HWD: *In* Tiger! Tiger! Burning Bright *you turned your attention to the working classes of Cardiff in nineteenth-century dockland. Were you abandoning Merthyr?*

AO: Not at all. A large percentage of Merthyr people had moved to Cardiff, so I was still writing about them. In the last century Cardiff was a settlement port and exported mixed nationalities from Cardiff's Chinatown and Irishtown and so forth to America. That American emigration is part of my life. There are so many Merthyr people in America. I wonder if they're the ones who have ordered advance copies of my *Merthyr Trilogy*!

In *Tiger! Tiger! Burning Bright* I wanted to capture the plight of the working class, the misery of the coalmines, the degradation and the drudgery of the Victorian Valleys and Cardiff dockland. But while I wanted *Tiger! Tiger!* to be thought-provoking, I also wanted it to be funny, entertaining, fast-moving and energetic. I was lucky enough to be able to work closely on the piece with Moving Being and Geoff Moore at St Stephen's Theatre Space. I have always admired Geoff Moore's skills and I greatly respect his wonderful visual imagination. For *Tiger! Tiger!* he assembled a cast of over fifty professional and amateur actors, singers, dancers and musicians and he created superb tableaux and a gritty, exciting production.

HWD: *You mentioned just now that, amongst other things, you wanted* Tiger! Tiger! Burning Bright *to be 'funny' and 'entertaining'. Many of your plays have been enlivened throughout with humour and wit. Was this 'home-grown' and 'home-town' humour?*

AO: It most certainly was. The kind of humour I grew up with in Abermorlais Terrace was a lasting influence. My grandmother was constantly thinking in Welsh and speaking in English and the resultant humour fascinated me. She also had a basic common sense. I came in from school one day and asked, 'What's on the radio?' And she replied 'What's on now'. I wanted titles and credits! My Auntie Ceini and my grandmother had an innate sense of fun. Just after the war they sent off for dresses they'd seen advertised in black and white in *Exchange and Mart*. They were outsize, fifty-six inches dresses and when they arrived they fitted perfectly because they stretched endlessly and they were bright yellow and black. When they saw each other kitted out in these dresses they couldn't stop laughing and Ceini went Bz-z-z-z, and this went on for ages. My grandfather and Uncle Dai were tamping because they wanted their food, but the women were too busy laughing on the rexine sofa. My grandfather finally took control and ordered them to take off their 'bee' dresses but Auntie Ceini told him, 'No Ted, we can't just yet, there are too many flowers left to pollinate'. And the laughter started all over again. My grandfather then said to me, 'Alan, go to Griffiths the undertaker and ask him to phone the doctor'. I pretended to go there and when I returned I said loudly 'The doctor's coming and he's going to give them both an injection.' And Gladys my grandmother turned to Ceini and said 'Good, the doctor's coming. I need a syringe. I need a syringe full of honey. And I need it now.' What a performance! In the end the two of them had to go to bed. Michelangelo's figures struggling out of the rock were as nothing compared to my big-bosomed grandmother and aunt struggling out of their outsize catalogue dresses. From then on, every time we wanted a laugh, we recalled that incident. So what I saw and heard at home was very influential.

HWD: *Several of the reviewers of the 1985 production of* In Sunshine and in Shadow *which toured Wales, wrote of audiences 'laughing through their tears' during performances of the play. Was this a response you expected?*

AO: The humour in *In Sunshine and in Shadow* was the sugar-coated pill, and I designed a great deal of the humour quite deliberately. I was teaching when I wrote the play and I'd been trained to deal with the educationally deprived or challenged. I wanted to show audiences what some children had to go through. I came across one seventeen-year-old boy whose voice hadn't changed and his father couldn't stand the sight of him. He locked him in a room in the house, and if the boy wanted anything he had to communicate through an intercom. Psychologists at that time didn't realise what was happening inside the power politics of families. As a teacher, I wanted to show the inside of a house and the rawness and the suffering that existed there. It was daring, frightening and very painful because a great deal of it touched on my own life and the early death of my mother. I needed to get it over with, to exorcise it. When you write a play some people think you made it all up, but *In Sunshine and in Shadow* is based on reality. It's virtually as it existed for me, although I embellished a little for dramatic purposes.

HWD: *The play* Bull, Rock and Nut, *the first draft of which won you £500 in the 1981 Play for Wales Competition Award was also based on your Merthyr boyhood experiences. How exactly?*

AO: My mother was brought up next door to the boxer Eddie Thomas and of course the day of Johnny Owen's funeral is part of the racial memory of Merthyr. I myself did a lot of boxing, although swimming took over when I was eighteen. A great many Merthyr boys did a hell of a lot of boxing. It's part of working-class culture. It was natural for me to write a play centred around the day of Johnny Owen's funeral. For Merthyr people, it seemed as if a Greek hero was being buried that day. There was a mixture of lamentation, sadness and celebration. Johnny Owen was a real proletarian hero. He's never mentioned in the play but his spirit is there. The action takes place in the Little Roma Café, one of the typical Italian cafés you find in the Valleys and I wrote about, not the punches and the blows you get in the ring, but the punches and the blows and the injuries that are dealt by unemployment, unrealistic dreams, poverty and depression. *Bull, Rock and Nut* is a situation tragedy. I tried to create characters that we know and recognise and speech patterns that Valleys people know and recognise, and form

Alan Osborne

them into a dramatic structure that was solid and time-honoured and then throw it at the audience at a speed of a hundred miles an hour.

HWD: *In this play,* Bull, Rock and Nut, *two pro-boxers and their manager live out their lives in fantasy, dreams and drugs. In this play, too, written well before Ed Thomas's* House of America *with its concerns for the need for contemporary heroes, you raise the question of this search for heroes in modern Wales.*

AO: Merthyr is full of heroes. There's Tydfil herself and there's Dic Penderyn, The town has working-class heroes. Or rather it should call them martyrs, heroes who were willing to die for a cause. It's true that in Wales we're always looking for single figures to lionise. And we're always dreaming because we have unfulfilled dreams. We know that we can never reach our full potential. As a teacher and a dramatist, my aim is to enable people to have access to that potential.

HWD: *Were you at all influenced by the plays of Gwyn Thomas?*

AO: The strange world of Meadow Prospect? Not at all. It's too covered with green for me, too Trumpton. In *The Keep*, for instance, all the characters sound the same. I preferred him when he was on the radio or on television, just talking about himself. Caradoc Evans formed more of my tradition.

HWD: *You yourself have written for radio and television. Where do you feel most at home – in these two media or in the theatre?*

AO: I like them all because, for me, each medium is just another way of writing poetry. I wrote *Mestizo (Mixed Blood)* for radio, and again it had to do with boxing. I set it in a Spanish home in Dowlais on the occasion of the World Flyweight Championship in Madison Square Gardens. Manuel Garcia, the son of a Dowlais Spanish family is out there in New York fighting for his family, but there is real action too outside the Dowlais home where the unemployed, the drunks and the deprived are looking for another kind of fight. In the radio drama I sought to catch the atmosphere of a pre-fight broadcast, but I also sought to convey the atmosphere and threat on the streets of Dowlais.

For television I invented a six-part serial *Tan Tro Nesaf*, the flagship for S4C, and I scripted *The Whistling Boy* and *The Beach Inspector*. *The Beach Inspector* was first performed at the Sherman in Cardiff, but adapting the theatre script for television meant that I was able to open it out, because on location I had the whole of Barry Beach at my disposal. *Whistling Boy* featured Rachel Thomas and it concerned the triumph of ordinary people over adversity. I enjoyed doing this piece. The clichéd image is of Clint Eastwood wielding a gun, but I had an eighty-four-year-old woman with a gun. And she triumphs, and says 'Now I've won, I can buy sixty tins of condensed milk.' That to her, is riches. The theme is that of the individual fighting against society. I'm aware that this is a well-tried theme, but I love the way individuals can change society and triumph over the land-grabbing machinery of local councils. Theatre in all its manifestations is an opportunity for people to enrich and empower themselves. People are rich inside and theatre allows that richness to reveal itself. The painter I admire most is Gustave Corbet. He created the alternative salon and fought against the Establishment. His remarkable phrase is 'The Monumentality of the Ordinary', and I love the power, the vigour that that represents. I love the richness, the courage of it.

HWD: *Dorien Thomas has said that you yourself have written poetry in your plays of 'the post-industrial south-east Wales valleys'. He says that you've created 'a dramatic poetry out of our use of language.' Were you consciously attempting to write dramatic poetry?*

AO: Yes, I suppose I was. In the original version of *Bull, Rock and Nut* every line started with a capital letter and it was all written in blank verse. Dorien Thomas edited the script. My original play was a design structure for the voice. It looked like poetry on the page. I'm basically a design technologist. All my works are design pieces. Edward de Bono makes the point that sometimes with inventions you learn to read backwards. If you try to create on a sequential level and try to think of the next step, you're easily stumped. When ideas flow and you slap them into your writing and you read it all backwards, it makes good sense.

I'm not a conventional dramatist. I've learnt at the pick and shovel level in a rough, tough way. There's no sophistication about me whatsoever! What I do is come up with ideas. I'm an Ideas Bank. As long as what I do influences society, and people learn from my work then I've opened the sluice gates and I'm happy because I'm doing what I enjoy most, namely teaching.

HWD: *What has the 'Ideas Bank' come up with lately?*

AO: I'm working on a piece called *The Best Defensive Boxer in the World*. It's about a man who wants to win the World Record for losing. It's a monologue that will be done at Dempseys in Cardiff at the 'Theatre Upstairs' which was started by Clare Isaac. People thought I'd made it up until they saw the newspaper cuttings reporting how the British Boxing Board of Control stopped this boxer from fighting on his one hundredth fight because he'd had a record of about eighty-nine knock outs against him. It's a comic story with serious connotations. As one sports commentator I've invented says 'Attlee [the boxer] has in fisticuffs got Gandhi's philosophy of pacifism dead right.'

I'm also working on an illustrated novel about the painter in society. It's title is *God Forgive Me Little Chicago*. The words 'God forgive Me' are written across the grave of

Robert Crawshay in Merthyr, a grave that has an enormous slab of stone over it so that his workers couldn't get at the body. 'Little Chicago' was the name given to the Docks in Cardiff and to Merthyr too. Not so long ago a group of young people were discussing the idea of taking a JCB up to Robert Crawshay's grave and demolishing the stone in an attempt to rid Merthyr of the Egyptian curse Crawshay had placed upon it. They wanted to eradicate the words 'God Forgive Me'. If that grave with its huge stone was somewhere in America, Stephen King would have written about it or it would have featured in a Sam Shepard play. They would have seen its possibilities.

HWD: *It's interesting that you, a dramatist, see the possibilities for yourself in terms of the novel, not the stage. Is that because Theatre in Wales offers very few possibilities in the 1990s? Where is Theatre in Wales at the turn of the century?*

AO: In the hands of the administrators, gatekeepers, Welsh-concept window designers (the hidden *gorsedd*). These are always in the forefront, it seems, while the 'real artists' – to quote the late Bryan Jones, founder of Chapter – 'are left down in the boiler-room'. A new publishing house for fiction is greatly needed – I endorse the outcry made by Tom Davies, the writer and journalist. The world will know us more by our books.

Alan Osborne

Interview Two
September 2004

HWD: *In 1999, a year after I interviewed you for* New Welsh Review *I brought a coachload of students from Aberystwyth to the Queen's Hall in Narberth to see a performance of* The Redemption Song. *In a post-performance discussion you told the audience that you'd never imagined that it would be 'resurrected' so quickly. Who initiated the production?*

AO: Towards the end of 1998 I'd thought I'd seen the last of the *Merthyr Trilogy*. But no, along came the mature students of 'Come Support' the Bridgend College company. They were enthusiastic about *Redemption Song* and they set up a tour. I added a second act to the play. Being strapped for cash wasn't a problem. It was great fun and it had excellent reviews for such a brash, wild performance. I think the publication of the Trilogy by Parthian made a difference. A published book puts the dramatists back in the swing of things. In 1999 the Trilogy was activated again by Russell Gomer and Jeremi Cockram, and we worked ceaselessly, and with new direction on *Bull, Rock and Nut*. Unfortunately for me, both these gifted performers were called away on major projects, but they still had enough energy left to showcase a well-rehearsed reading at a 'RAW NIGHT' in Dempseys, Cardiff.

At about the same time Gillian Elisa asked me if it was possible to put on a production of my musical comic horror, *Precious*. It was made possible on a pittance (two planks and a passion). It was a very successful event because Gillian Elisa is such an amazing motivator.

HWD: *In 2001 you were commissioned by the WNO to work on their educational and outreach project in the Merthyr Valley. What exactly was that project?*

AO: Before I received the commission from the WNO I had been concentrating on my painting. Painting is a good exercise in keeping the mind focused on arrangement and composition. The new Millennium gave me time to work on large-scale canvases at our allotment. Val, my partner, did the organic work on the garden while I was practising 'the force that through the green fuse drives the flower'! My painting flow was interrupted by a call from the WNO. A large-scale opera plan for Bristol had collapsed and the WNO asked me if it could be done in Wales – immediately. The composition became *Katerina*.

HWD: *And so* Katerina *wasn't planned for Wales in the first instance?*

AO: No it wasn't. Wales was the second choice. It turned out to be a wonderful, life-enhancing event. I remember you with tears in your eyes when you watched the kids rehearsing. There were two hundred and twenty kids from the Merthyr Valley and seven singers from the WNO. Janáček provided the characters and story which were based on a Russian play. In our version we moved with the spirit of rivers and hills. Some time later kids from Gwynedd and Denbighshire repeated *Katerina* with flare. In 2004 the WNO won a prestigious award for *Katerina*, but I was never broadcast as having anything whatsoever to do with it – perhaps it was only an accident from the beginning?

HWD: *You also made an important contribution to the International Celtic Festival in Brittany in 2002. What exactly was your brief?*

AO: It was 'The Year of Wales' at the International Celtic Festival and Dave Peterson, the Head of the Welsh delegation to the Festival asked the question, 'Has Wales an exciting dance and folk history?' The answer was 'Yes', and a design was proposed and funding came from the Welsh Assembly Government for a 'Wales' presentation at the Festival. A team was selected under the direction of Geoff Moore and I contributed to 'The Year of Wales' at that international event. You could hear the applause from Brittany to Holyhead, but we'll never see the Welsh production of *Fire Tree/Coeden Dân* in Wales. That's a great pity.

It doesn't seem to me that Wales appreciates its indigenous talent. Janácěk deeply believed in his own country's traditions, in its folksong and language. We have more than enough talent and history here in Wales; we don't have to cash in the Czech to pay the Welsh! I continue to believe in the cultural potential of Wales. Big time – big scale.

Gareth Potter in *Marriage of Convenience* by Ian Rowlands

Ian Rowlands

Interview One
March 1999

HWD: *I'd like to ask you first of all, before focusing on particular questions, to give your general impression of your own work. Perhaps we can take some of our bearings from there.*

IR: My first plays were crazy, surreal adventures. They were the kind of first works any young playwright would use and they were irreverent snipes at one's own country. They had little depth. I was just exorcising a great many ghosts. *The Sin Eaters* was nominated 'Best Regional Play' for 1992 by the Writers' Guild of Great Britain. But really it was no more than the ravings of an angry young man.

My first true play was *Solomon's Glory* which opened in Dublin in 1993. It deals with a man who attempts to build a cathedral to worship God, and ultimately realises that there is no God. I myself am not religious, but I am a seeker. Most of us are seekers. The play was an attempt to present that fact theatrically. People complained that there were no characters in the play, only facets of an argument. They were looking for something very different from what I had presented on stage. As an actor, I had been greatly influenced by the Commedia Dell' Arte tradition. It was a theatre of ideas and almost, as it were, the newspaper of the people. I consequently wrote plays that were concerned with discussing issues rather than with presenting characters.

In my plays, therefore, I dealt with debate rather than with emotions and characters. In *The Great Adventures of Rhys and Hywel*, *The Sin Eaters*, *Glissando on an Empty Harp* and *Solomon's Glory* there's an archetypal man and woman and, through archetypes, I dealt with the questions of identity and of being. I presented, as I say, facets of a debate and allowed the audience to contrast and compare. I had, have, no answers. My work is a series of questions.

In *Glissando*, *Blue Heron* and *Love in Plastic* what I have tried to do is illustrate the fact that anything I write or portray on stage is merely second-best. I've been greatly influenced by the work of Umberto Eco, and his explication of the complicated process of communication. In view of the complexity of the system of communication, how can we make ourselves richly understood? *Love in Plastic*, *Blue Heron* and *Glissando* deal with our futile attempts as human beings to communicate and to be understood. People use language in order to appropriate and so, in my plays, I say that language is a lie when it is used as a means to control.

HWD: *You began your career in the theatre as an actor. What prompted you to become a writer yourself?*

IR: Writing for the theatre is, for me, a means of exorcism. I trained as an actor but I reached a point where I became tired of speaking other people's words. I found that I myself had something to say. It wasn't that I had anything more or better to say than anyone else. It was just that I felt I had an equal right to say it. I had always written poetry, as many people have, and thankfully my poetry is lost. There's a tribe in India who, every year, throw their art work into the Ganges. They believe that only by sacrificing their art can they guarantee that the gods will continue to replenish them with creativity. Most youthful poems and plays should also be thrown into the Ganges. Certainly the first plays I ever wrote, *The Great Adventure of Rhys and Hywel Part I-V*, no longer exist. I don't want to see them ever again. But those plays were an expression of my need to express myself in dramatic forms. I didn't write the plays with backing from Made in Wales, Dalier Sylw or any other company. Only by doing something on my own did I feel absolutely free to say exactly what I wanted to say, to make mistakes and grow, without being guided down avenues that would lead to the realisation of other people's aims and ambitions.

I have, of course, been immensely lucky inasmuch as I am one of only two English-medium dramatists in Wales who have consistently been given money to write and direct their own work. Some people within Wales are of the opinion that a dramatist should never direct his own play. Try saying that about Brecht! In France they approach their theatre in a very different way. The writers themselves are given the freedom to choose the team that will best realise their work. French dramatists can opt for, not a *directeur* who interprets the work but a *réalisateur* who can realise the playwright's vision. In Wales we have too many directors who insist on making their own statement. I want to hold on to the right to be the first to direct any new play I've written.

HWD: *Is that why you have your own company, Theatr y Byd?*

IR: Yes, entirely. We have too many theatre people in Wales who are not creative but who firmly believe that they're more talented than the people who create. As Artistic Director of Theatr y Byd I can create my own visual metaphors on stage, bring 'layers' to my work, and relish 'using language', rather than 'being used by language'.

HWD: *One critic in particular has underlined what he sees as your tendency to revel overmuch in the language of your plays, and has drawn attention to, as he sees it, your inclination to 'overwrite', to luxuriate in words. How do you react to that criticism?*

IR: I could reply to that by drawing attention to the fact that the Austrian Emperor Joseph II criticised Mozart's work for having too many notes. I write the words that are necessary to what I have to say. I create texts that are scores from which I suspend those visual images I create for the stage. Yes, some people have had problems with my work inasmuch as they have found it difficult and alienating. Some have been annoyed by it. They can't fully grasp the meaning of my images before they flash by and are replaced by yet more images. The audience are bombarded by these images and they can't make head or tail of what they've seen or what they've heard. What I say to people who've been alienated by the product is 'forget the words, in themselves the words are unimportant. All my words is is music. Sit back and let the atmosphere of my theatre wash over you. Don't seek to concentrate only on the words'. Sometimes, of course, a particular word will pierce through and make the impact of a particular note in a symphony, and an image here and there will illuminate the entire text. I'd like to tell an audience to go away from a performance of one of my plays with a set of impressions, not literalism.

HWD: *Your references to music and images are interesting because, under your artistic directorship, Theatr y Byd has had a definite multi-media policy. You've commissioned artists to create installations for your work, and your play* Love in Plastic *was actually performed* *within an installation at the Glynn Vivian Gallery in Swansea. Why did you embrace the tradition of involving artists in performances?*

IR: Because the artist's vision offers the audience, and those involved with a performance, different access points. It all began with my play *The Sin Eaters* in 1992. I've always had an immense interest in art and I commissioned Stephen Young, who was a lecturer at the College of Art in Cardiff, to produce a suite of drawings during the rehearsal process, visualising the actors and placing them in the imaginary landscape created by his idea of the dynamic of the play. The exhibition of the suite of drawings toured with the production. For my next play, *Solomon's Glory*, I commissioned five artists to create works inspired by the text. Linda Black (Fine Art Abstract), Stephen Young (Fine Art Figurative), Emma Lawton (3D), Andy Dark (Graphic) and Dave Heke (Art Photography), produced two or three works each and exhibitions were held at St David's Hall, Cardiff and The City Arts Centre, Dublin. In Dublin there was successful integration between the exhibition and the performance and the audience walked through a totally white exhibition environment into a totally black performance environment. Three days before the play opened in Dublin we gave a performance just to the five artists, and that night we saw what an amazing process of giving and collaboration it had been between us. It was a mutual enrichment.

In *Glissando on an Empty Harp* I took the process a step further. I commissioned Martina Galvin, the Dublin-based artist, to create an installation within which we filmed 'Head', a character in the play. This character was video-projected during the performance. I, as dramatist, didn't dictate the installation inspired by the text, but I worked within the parameters created by Martina Galvin. *Glissando* became a multi-layered interpretation. There was a further leap forward with *Love in Plastic*. With the aid of the Arts Council of Wales, Tim Davies was employed as artist in residence within the company and his installation *Caress* became the environment within which *Love in Plastic* was staged. This was an organic collaboration since the text was the base for the artist's work, and the artist's installation dictated how the play could be directed and the movements of the actor within the piece. Also, as I usually do, I commissioned new music for the play. Since then, unfortunately, budget restrictions have not allowed me to pursue further this creative structure of multi-media collaboration. Artists tend to be fairly isolated people, but working within a theatrical context (and in my case the artist's work is always inspired by the text) allows that artist to work organically with actors, and musicians. The text therefore feeds and unites the actors, the visual artists, the musicians and the audience.

HWD: *That uniting of different art forms obviously raises the question of what takes place at the original moment when you come to write a play. Do you think predominantly in terms of ideas or themes, or in terms of movement, sound and images?*

IR: First, always in terms of pictures. I have images in my mind. Some dramatists write without having any idea of what their play will look like on the stage. I see my work clearly as I write it. I visualise it all. But I also see my text more as a piece of music or theatrical poem. I tend to write seventy-five-minute-long plays. Indeed it's almost obsessional on my part to write for that specific length of time. I don't write for characters but for ideas where each word is chosen after great deliberation. I may go over a paragraph two or three hundred times before I reach the final version. Sometimes, although I work continuously, I only produce thirty seconds of texts a day. That is how slowly and how specifically I work. It would take me about a hundred days to write a full text. As my plays are, in a sense, poems, the choice of words has to be exact. I don't leave an attitude there for the actor to interpret. Some writers script for characters and they let their actors grow into that character and influence the text. For me, as a writer of ideas, that is not an option. I think that sometimes actors want to find out what is easiest for themselves rather than what is in keeping with the idea of the play. I am interested in ideas. I'm certainly far more interested in aspects of a debate than in naturalistic characters.

HWD: *Is it therefore an irony to you that you are currently Artistic Co-ordinator for Bara Caws, a revenue-funded, Welsh-medium theatre company that has traditionally been associated with plays and productions that are a world apart from yours?*

IR: I probably will not write plays for Bara Caws, and I will not direct everything, either. I see my role as very much a development one. I'll seek to expand the company, bring in new writers and directors and strengthen the structure in this most important period in our theatrical history. Working with the company gives me the chance to redefine its audience and its theatrical response to a growing nation. It's very interesting being with Bara Caws at the moment because it's also given me the opportunity to read a great many plays by youngish writers and I've discussed them with other directors. The sad fact is that not many of these scripts are theatrical. It's a disease that has come about because of S4C. The channel has stopped us from becoming a theatrical nation. It is important therefore that we bring into Wales good translations and adaptations, not to enrich our culture, but to enlarge our library and to demonstrate to Welsh audiences what a good play is all about.

There has been too much of the mundane in Welsh-medium theatre over the last decade or so. Theatre has tried to ape television. Audiences have declined because what is the point of going to the kind of theatre that bores you? Theatre should be an event, a *son et lumière*, a happening, an exciting moment and an experience that you can never get through any other medium. Welsh theatre has not offered that experience for a long time. That is sad. When was the last time you or I went to a piece of Welsh-medium theatre, not out of duty, but out of the knowledge that what was awaiting us was a powerful theatrical event? The last time I saw that kind of Welsh-medium theatre was back in the 1980s with *Cofiant y Cymro Olaf*. The Brith Gof performances were interesting, but I am now talking about the dearth of powerful text-based theatre. There are limits to what physical theatre can do. A nation can only truly express itself through language and through the conjoining of language and physicality.

It's a great pity that we have not matured as a theatrical nation. The old Cwmni Theatr Cymru was there with a dual purpose. It was to give Welsh audiences Welsh-medium theatre. Secondly, it was there as a political statement. Audiences were making a political statement by attending performances and the actors were also doing the same by being part of the company. With the advent of S4C things changed because television took on the evangelising role of the theatre. Now this was a great moment of release for Welsh-medium theatre. It was a freedom granted to become truly theatrical. It failed to take advantage of the moment. Actors and writers and audiences have turned towards S4C. I myself have been committed to theatre. This year I have refused a great deal of television and radio work in order to remain in the theatre. I have never found money that important. I'd rather be poor in the theatre and rich in its experience than rich in television while existing on a vacuous plane. That does not mean that I ignore the media within my productions. *Love in Plastic* could not work without radio microphones because one character lives totally within a bubble and the audience hears his voice through loudspeakers. And in *Glissando*, as I've explained, one character is entirely video-projected. Through using other media I explore the medium of theatre itself.

Ian Rowlands

HWD: *You are Welsh-speaking. Is your bilingualism important in terms of your writing?*

IR: Definitely. Brian Friel has said that Synge was the only true Irish writer of the twentieth century. What he meant was that Synge took the Irish language and imposed it upon an English syntax to create an epic Irish voice. Writers such as John Macardel dispute this, but I go along with Friel who has described Synge's process as 'a process of syntactical shock'. I come from the Rhondda Valley where it is said that Welsh is still spoken, but through the medium of English. It's interesting that nearly all the male writers who have risen out of South Wales recently – and it's the nearest thing we have to 'a school of writers' – were either bilingual or had been brought up with having Welsh-language influences. That has coloured our use of language, our appreciation of language and our perception of the world. Monoglot people see the world in one way only, but bilingual people see that there's more than one way to put the world to bed. In my work, I put the English language through a process of syntactic shock. That is a legacy of my upbringing. And in this I'm just a small part of a continuous line stretching from Caradoc Evans and Dylan Thomas. There is an odd tendency for many people in Wales to dismiss and condemn Dylan Thomas, but linguistically there is no doubt that he is the most powerful voice that Wales has produced this century, and I'm certain that part of this power comes from the fact that he grew up alongside a Welsh-language culture. That fact dictated the way he used the English language. Through my use of language I try to create an 'epic' Welsh voice with which I can discuss the common experience.

HWD: *But though you're bilingual you haven't written a play, from scratch as it were, in Welsh?*

IR: No I haven't. But in *Marriage of Convenience* I talk about the nature of growing up as a bilingual person in a monoglot area, namely the south-east Wales valleys. In that play I also talk about the reactionary forces in Welsh society, and the prejudice demonstrated by first-language Welsh-speakers towards those who have gone through the bilingual education process. Thankfully that is now diminishing. We have a great many things for which to blame S4C, but one of the good things it has done is to legitimise the south-east Wales Welsh accent. It has made people realise that it is not simply *l'argot* but a *bona fide* accent. If the Welsh language itself is to survive it has got to embrace an 'urban' deployment of language. The south-east Wales urban language mirrors the exciting development in some of the post-industrial regions of South Wales.

As a child of the Valleys my Welsh is thin inasmuch as it's not idiomatic, not my *mamiaith*, my mother-tongue. But it's not a second language, either. It's a kind of half-way house. This has affected my attitude towards writing in Welsh. I use the English language like plasticine. I'm scared to do that in the Welsh language. When I translated *Solomon's Glory* into Welsh I got flak because of the standard of the Welsh language within it. Critics didn't discuss the nature of the play or its themes. This inhibits me, and I know of another playwright who suffered flak because of the nature of a Welsh-language play he wrote. That playwright is a huge loss to the Welsh-language theatre scene. The Welsh language has been so exclusive in the past. I feel that it has excluded me. It's therefore a major step for me to write my first full-scale Welsh language play for the millennium Eisteddfod in Llanelli. I'm very pleased with that commission.

HWD: *Talk of language, or languages, within Wales reminds me that you've been described not only as 'a dramatist who forms a bridge between the two languages in Wales' but also as 'one who forms a bridge between Wales and other countries'. What are your thoughts on that?*

IR: Take Quebec. There they spend a billion dollars a year to promote Quebecois culture. They realise that by promoting their culture on an international stage they are legitimising their country and creating a nation out of a cultural movement. I think artists in Wales can play a vital role in the perception other countries have of us as a nation. If money was pumped into the Arts and the Arts were allowed to become a bridge between Wales and the rest of the world then as a nation we could play our part on the international stage. As a nationalist, in the Orwellian sense, I want Wales to stand shoulder to shoulder with other nations in an atmosphere of mutual respect as opposed to an atmosphere of mutual antagonism. I think that through the Arts a group of disparate people can become a nation and a new vision of Wales could be created.

HWD: *Is there therefore a 'new vision of Wales' within your work?*

IR: I hope that my plays can contribute in some small way to the consciousness of a developing nation. Parnell said that no one should say to a nation 'Thus far shall you go and no further'. I'm very excited by the new political landscape in Wales and by the image of a forward-looking nation prepared to cast off the reactionary elements within it. When I was preparing a paper for the BBC on Welsh novelists, I read a great deal of Mihangel Morgan's work. What was attractive about it was the fact that here was a gay writer writing about Welsh issues without ever drawing heavy attention to the fact that his characters were gay. It's that legitimisation of something by the fact that it's not considered an issue that is refreshing. If Welshness on the international stage is not a problem then we don't need to make an issue of it. In my work I don't deal with Welshness in crude terms. I don't deal with 'Welsh identity' and I don't use the jargonistic terms that some people use. My work is inherently Welsh. I come to my work from a Welsh perspective, but I don't make Welshness an issue. As a nation we should stop bemoaning the fact that Welshness is our greatest problem and concentrate, as Welsh people, on becoming citizens of the world. I am looking forward to an unselfconscious cultural future.

Nor should we talk in terms of 'reinvention' because the very term pre-supposes that we've been allowed to invent ourselves in the first place. We've been able to change only in the ways that a London-based government has *allowed* us to change. The contempt a London-based government feels for Wales is reflected in the way Alun Michael has been parachuted into Wales by Tony Blair. You might as well give him the title 'Governor General' and make him wear a cockatoo hat. Nevertheless, devolution has granted us the opportunity to create afresh. It's not a 'Renaissance' but a 'Naissance', a birth. There you have it. I'm a 'Naissance' Man!

HWD: *Everyone seems to be heralding the dawn. But will the new political scene change attitudes? Our attitude towards theatre within Wales, for example?*

IR: I certainly hope so. The attitude towards theatre in Wales is so very different to what you find in cities like Glasgow and Dublin. Glasgow is an incredibly theatre-conscious city and Dublin too is theatre-orientated and shows its appreciation of the written word and of the artist in general. In Ireland they see their artists as national treasures, and regard the words of writers as things to be shared. They realise the importance of the artist within a culture. We in Wales haven't quite realised that yet. We are still, in several ways, a nation of amateurs. Here so many people think they are talented writers. S4C has of course encouraged them in this. It seems that just about anybody can script for some of the soaps, given a word-processor and a plot. But with the confidence that's growing in our capital city I hope the appetite for good writing and professional theatre will grow.

Ian Rowlands

HWD: *A 'nation of amateurs'. One aspect of the reverse, of course, would be the establishment of a national 'professional' theatre. What is your opinion of the Arts Council of Wales's consultation document relating to future policy for theatre in Wales?*

IR: Yes, it seems from the Draft Drama Strategy that there is a definite move towards a National Theatre and towards a definite structure for the profession in Wales. I think it's a very brave document. Many people have been calling for a change for years and now the Arts Council has become pro-active and is seeking to provide ladders of opportunity within the profession. I see the new plan in terms of a pyramid. At the base there would be a project sector, reacting far more quickly than it has done in the past to new work. The exciting developments within the project sector could feed into a new, bilingual Welsh Writing Company based in Cardiff. That company would have a studio and a main stage and would be feeding in talent to the two main stages in Gwynedd and Clwyd. That would be its domestic role. Its international role would be to represent Welsh dramatists as the Centre des Auteurs Dramatique does in Quebec. I value greatly Yvette Vaughan Jones's effort to export Welsh culture globally but her efforts are mainly on behalf of all art forms. We need a specific bureau to promote Welsh *theatre* on the international stage.

We also need a clear dramaturgical policy in Wales which will allow dramatists to work with the two main stages and with the Cardiff-based Welsh Writing Company. At the moment we have so many courses for writers in Wales, so many 'creative writing' programmes, that we are in danger of thinking, especially in Welsh-medium theatre, that we can produce a crowd of young Welsh dramatists. In Welsh-speaking Wales we have a population of six hundred thousand and, realistically, from that figure, we could expect to produce one or two dramatists of value. Dramatists of note are another thing, and are going to emerge regardless of the system, or despite the system. You can hold your creative writing courses until kingdom come. Writers will only come through when they themselves develop their own talents.

HWD: *So Tŷ Newydd and Made in Wales can just lie down and die?*

IR: What I would ask Made in Wales is 'What, in all honesty, do you feel you have done of real quality over the past decade?' Real quality in text-based work in Wales has come from outside the revenue sector. Surely, that's a damning indictment of the revenue sector.

I wasn't *taught* to write plays. For me, as I've said before, writing is a means of exorcism. If you knew me well enough you could trace my history through my plays. In just one paragraph I could take maybe fifteen or twenty incidents from my life and place them side by side to create something entirely different, but still part of an unified whole. And so I create hybrid histories, fractured moments from my past. I put them all together to create an epic history of myself. As I continue to grow I see things from different perspectives, and I hope that my plays will reflect my development. Our personalities are collections of our fears, and in my plays I seek to exorcise those fears.

HWD: *But you have written that your plays contain not only your fears, but also your* 'dicter a chwerwder' – *your 'anger and bitterness'. Anger and bitterness at what, exactly?*

IR: I'm referring there to the canker within any Welsh person's soul – the canker of inculcated inferiority. I've also felt a great deal of anger and bitterness because, for ten years I've been working in an extremely stagnant environment. There has never been a firm ladder for me, a clear pathway as a dramatist, towards proficiency and improvement. Welsh theatre for the past ten years has been stagnant and I've felt very angry about that. But now I can use that anger and bitterness in a positive way. I now see myself as a citizen in the birth of a nation.

HWD: *On that optimistic note, how do you now view, on the British and international stage, the 'Welsh' theatrical voice?*

IR: Strangulated.

Interview Two
October 2004

HWD: *In your 1999 interview you mentioned that there had never been for you 'a clear pathway as a dramatist, towards proficiency and improvement'. Has that situation changed during the past five years?*

IR: I feel like an interloper in this volume for I have written only one play since being interviewed in 1999 and that has yet to be produced. The past five years have seen me drift around Artistic Directorships. As a consequence I have spent more time on rehearsal floors realising other dramatists' visions than I have in front of the computer screens realising my own.

When I was initially interviewed, I was the Artistic Director of both Theatr y Byd, a project company, and Bara Caws, a revenue-funded community theatre company based in Gwynedd. Within the year, I had resigned from Theatr y Byd in order to concentrate on my work up north. Ed Thomas asked me 'What the hell are you doing working in Caernarfon?' The answer, Ed, is that, at the time, Bara Caws was meant to merge with Cwmni Theatr Gwynedd to form the National Theatre in the Welsh language. I was simply keeping my eye to the main chance! In 2002, I also took up the Artistic Directorship of Cwmni Theatr Gwynedd. I was therefore the Artistic Director of both companies for a period and ideally placed. That was until a new Arts Council of Wales decided to be a new broom! Realising that the initial vision was to be swept under the theatrical carpet, I resigned from Bara Caws preferring to concentrate upon mid-scale work.

HWD: *You are now Artistic Director of a new company, Llwyfan Gogledd Cymru. What led to the formation of this company?*

IR: In 2003 I was charged by the Arts Council of Wales to separate Cwmni Theatr Gwynedd, the production company, from its host venue, Theatr Gwynedd. This was achieved in 2003 and a new company, Llwyfan Gogledd Cymru, was constituted. With a new name came a new ethos. Llwyfan Gogledd Cymru's brief is to produce theatre in the north, of the north, for the north and the whole of Wales. As I was embroiled within the creation of this vision, I did not choose to try for the Artistic Directorship of the Welsh-language National Theatre Company when it was eventually advertised.

HWD: *Tell me about your own company's work to date.*

IR: 2004-05 is Llwyfan Gogledd Cymru's first full year of production. To date, it has collaborated with the Sherman Theatre Company on a Welsh language production of *Pinocio*, staged *Deinameit!* – a ground-breaking production based upon the Friction Dynamics strike in Caernarfon, and has collaborated with The Stiwt, Rhosllannerchrugog, on *Faultline* – a show based on the Gresford pit disaster of 1934. In the new year it will tour a tri-lingual production based upon events at the Frongoch Prisoner of War camp. It was in Frongoch that over 1,800 Irish volunteers were imprisoned after the Easter Rising 1916, and it was there that Michael Collins rose to prominence. *Frongoch* is to be a collaboration between Llwyfan Gogledd Cymru and Project, Dublin.

Work next year includes the creation of a Labyrinth in Llanrwst. This bi-lingual site-specific project will trace the linguistic and social shift within the town over the past century. It will also stage a Welsh adaptation of *Blink*, a show inspired by elements of the Clywch enquiry and a Punjabi/Welsh/Hindi/English production juxtaposing the Sgubor Goch council estate in Caernarfon with the Manningham district of Bradford. Llwyfan Gogledd Cymru believes that Welsh language culture has, for too long, been an invisible one. It needs to reach out, to become inclusive without compromising its own future. The company has taken up the challenge to offer access points for non Welsh speakers, through its work, into Welsh language theatre/ culture. Our intention is not to compromise the language, rather it is to consolidate and strengthen it through juxtaposing it with other languages/cultures and, in so doing, legitimize it on an international stage.

Llwyfan Gogledd Cymru is rapidly laying its foundation on the shifting sands of the Welsh theatrical landscape. Recent developments within that landscape include the consolidation of the Theatre in Education Young People's Theatre, the Boyden Report on English-language Theatre, which did not back the development of an English-language National Theatre, and the creation of that which the non Welsh speaker will be denied, a National Theatre Company in the Welsh language.

HWD: *You recently took part in a round-table radio debate which discussed the development of the Welsh-language National Theatre Company a year after its creation. The interviewer introduced you as one who was opposed to the concept of a National Theatre provision. This was a very odd introduction, especially to those of us who have read your articles and listened to your lectures on the desirability of that provision. Any comment?*

IR: The interviewer's researcher should be shot, for I have consistently called for a national provision. He or she need only have read my original *New Welsh Review* interview, transcripts of my keynote speech in the Llanberis conference 'Towards a National Theatre' or my papers at the Dramatists' Conference at The Royal Welsh College of Music and Drama and at the Academi Theatre Conference (November 2003) – published in *Taliesin* (Summer 2004). I have backed a national Welsh-language provision time and time again. My concerns regarding the current national provision are based on the foundation upon which the company was built and its lack of integration into the bi-lingual Welsh theatrical landscape.

After the débâcle of the last Arts Council of Wales theatre strategy which, though it had its strong points, floundered on its inability to implement a quality control process (an inability which one could argue still hampers sector development), the Arts Council has attempted to reform the sector by taking separate elements and band-aiding them in isolation! An ad hoc, piecemeal approach. There are no paths of integration enshrined within an overarching drama strategy. Indeed, there is no umbrella drama strategy and no clear vision.

I therefore stand by my original interview and call once again for the integration of the Welsh theatre landscape. We need to unify the theatre cultures of our nation and bridge the linguistic and social divides that exist within our communities. For I still believe that theatre has the potential to influence the course of a nation and has a contribution to make to the course of this fledgling bilingual/multilingual one. Wales needs an integrated theatrical vision, one based upon a pyramid model of development which offers viable career paths for practitioners both young and old. Wales needs a vision, full stop! Witness the calls of current Theatre for Young People directors for the right to tour community and main-stage productions. One could interpret this as a manifestation of artistic frustration. Having been with their companies for a decade or more, they have nowhere to go, no development paths to tread. We live in a dead-man's-shoes culture where dead men do not relinquish their footwear, and who can blame them! They have artistic ambitions and no way of realising them; hence stagnation. One could not expect them to give up their security for the sake of youth when they have youths of their own to feed!

It was therefore heartening to read in the recent Boyden Report on English Language Theatre the recommendation that integration and career development should be a factor in the creation of a long term strategy. I hope that the consideration is not a two-dimensional one and that strategies are made 3D and implemented. Joined-up thinking is needed. The trouble is, few have mastered joined-up thinking this side of Offa's Dyke. It is a sad fact that there is little communication between the theatres of both languages. Few, if any Welsh language plays are translated into English and vice versa. We will only move forward as one. If partitioned, we will flounder; integration and cross pollination are essential. Less speculation, more action is needed.

I am bored and worn down by the debates and the constant consultation processes which are the product of a culture of fear incubating within the corridors of the Arts Council of Wales. Accounabtility has gone crazy; the need to wring the very last drop of life out of every pound of arts funding sacrifices both administrative and, more importantly, artistic integrity. Whatever happened to the hands-off culture that believed in the right of an artist to dream? Artists have fitful sleeps in Wales these days, and the prospect of deep dreamy slumber seems even more distant. This is especially true if the Arts Council of Wales is swallowed up by the Assembly and we live in a culture of ballot box funding. For the nightmare has already begun. Consider the controversy surrounding the funding of a certain chamber orchestra! I am led to believe that when the Assembly Culture Committee recently visited the Aberystwyth Arts Centre, their first question was 'Where's the shop?' A culture based upon such touristic priorities and political cronyism will only lead to the obliteration of any further dreamtime. In the meantime 'we dream on. For in our moments of light lie our reasons for living' (the closing lines of *Marriage of Convenience* – 1996).

HWD: *You've mentioned your new play which has yet to be produced. Can you say a little about it?*

IR: My latest play, *Blink* deals with the institutional abuse of power and trust. I was a pupil at Ysgol Gyfun Rhydfelen and suffered under the influence of a certain late abuser. The narrative within *Blink* turns upon an incident of abuse which was, sadly, far from being an isolated incident. I am a writer who writes from the heart; I could not envisage any other way of writing. *Blink* will, I hope, shed light into dark places. It is a painful play, one written for the 'friends' who suffered in silence and continue to suffer.

Blink has already been filmed for BBC2 Wales and Gareth Miles' Welsh adaptation of my text will be produced next Autumn. There are, as yet, no plans to stage it in its original English form. Regarding the next five years, I have other dreams which will, I hope, take form if I can peel myself off the rehearsal floor and away from the growing pile of administration.

In the 1999 interview you asked me for a word which summed up the Welsh theatrical landscape. Five years on and 'strangulated' still comes to mind. The only consolation is that at least it's not dead! Whilst there's life there are dreams, there is hope, the hope that in five years' time my prognosis will be a more positive one and that I will be less of an interloper amongst my peers.

Lucy Gough

Interview One
October 1999

HWD: *You spent your childhood in Beddgelert. Immediately, folk myth and a particularly characterful Snowdonian landscape come to mind. But did those early years in Wales really have any influence on your writing?*

LG: Although it's not apparent specifically in my theatre writing, the ruggedness, the richness of the Beddgelert landscape and the romanticism of wild weather entered early into my imagination as did the sea and the coast near Criccieth, where my family lived for a while. But the thing I notice most in my work that I can attribute to my living in Wales, is the rhythm of my writing. When I was studying for an MA in Playwriting at Birmingham University I and my tutors noticed that my work was very different from that of the other students precisely because of where I was writing from. My work incorporates elements derived from the rugged landscape and contains a particular rhythm and a strong emotive force.

But I'm very nervous about claiming that I'm Welsh because I don't want to appropriate anything without feeling that I have a right to it, although my father's family lived in Beddgelert all their lives. It's this hesitancy about a sense of belonging that accounts, I think, for the fact that I write out of a slight sense of dislocation. I have spent most of my life in Wales and I feel at home here but I cannot lay claim to the deep and secure rootedness of a dramatist like Sera Moore-Williams. Her writing is really concerned with where she comes from and with a clear understanding of place and tradition. My writing comes from a wanting, a *need* for rootedness. *That* is the sense in which the seeds of my future career were sown in Beddgelert.

HWD: *So a sense of place nurtured a sense of possible rootedness. But what about writing itself? How did that start?*

LG: It started not with writing but with imagining. I made up stories and told them to my sisters every night, and I'm ashamed to say, it proved to be fairly profitable because, now and then, I used to charge my sisters a fee before I would consent to tell them the ending. I could never understand why it didn't occur to them to make up their own ending – or expect to pay. I told these stories to my own children when they were little and they now tell them to their step-brothers and sisters. So the stories have been efficiently handed down. It helped, of course, that my mother, Christine Harrison was interested in literature and in writing. Her creative talents began to flourish when we moved to Fishguard. She's a winner of the *Cosmopolitan* short story competition and she has published a novel, *Airy Cages*. Her writing is unusual and strong and some of her stories have appeared in a recent Honno Press volume, entitled *Power*. Some of my favourite ones are in there.

HWD: *'Airy cages'- a phrase, of course, from a wonderful Hopkins poem of place – shows that your mother, too, has this sense of the language of place, a lyrical motivation. But what about the urge towards drama as such? Unlike some of the dramatists I've interviewed in this series, you seem to have known from an unusually early age that you wanted to write for the theatre.*

LG: I left school at fifteen with no qualifications but with a passion for the theatre. My first son was born at Fishguard when I was eighteen and I imagined then that my life was going to turn exclusively around the home and children. But it wasn't long before I began to feel trapped. Since I'd always been fascinated by the theatre, I enrolled in an Open University drama course. It wasn't easy. My daughter was born a week after the final exam and I remember once frantically writing an essay which my small son, in play, proceeded to tear to shreds. That Open University course was my first introduction to real education. But I knew instinctively that I wanted to write and I knew that I needed to study further if I was to write well dramatically. And so I moved with the children to Aberystwyth where I graduated at the Department of Theatre, Film and Television.

HWD: *You referred earlier to the Birmingham University Playwriting MA course. I don't want necessarily to raise the old question as to whether creative writing can actually be taught, but it would be interesting to know what impact the course had on your own theatre writing.*

LG: It was a turning point. The course was set up by David Edgar who has continued to be very kind and supportive over the years. I took that course in the late 1980s, in the very first year it was set up. It was a special year. My tutors,

Ann Devlin and Olwen Wymark, were both well-established writers and I was taught by John Arden, Alan Bennett, John McGrath, Howard Brenton and many other influential playwrights. They all said something different. I remember in particular Anthony Mingella commenting that whenever he's writing he creates for himself a series of obstacles that he has to surmount. During that year I felt that I'd been given enough guidance to be able to write and – just as important – I'd learnt to believe in myself. I was also given the confidence to convince people that I could write plays. Getting a novel published is hard enough, but with a play you've got to convince funding bodies, companies, directors and actors that your play is good enough to be performed! As a playwright, you have to be, not only pro-active, but pro-active through so many stages.

HWD: *When did you have your first break-through after graduating from Birmingham?*

LG: Almost immediately. *Joanna*, the play I'd written as part of my course had gone down well when it was performed at the Allardyce Nicoll Studios in Birmingham. Soon afterwards it was short-listed for an RSC New Writing festival. It ultimately wasn't done because I'd made the classic mistake of having too many characters in it. You soon learn not to do that. But the fact that it was short-listed gave me confidence and in Joanna Southcott, an eighteenth-century prophetess and my grandfather's great aunt, I'd found a congenial subject. She came from a totally uneducated background but since she had prophesied the Napoleonic War she had an enormous influence. She preached for twenty years, holding people in the palm of her hand. Even Blake wrote a poem to her. At the age of sixty-four she announced that she was pregnant with the New Messiah and the 'pregnancy' lasted eighteen months. She eventually died of dropsy, but before her death crowds gathered in the streets to await the birth of the New Messiah. All things in the play are relevant now at the turn of the Millennium. At the end of the eighteenth-century people were panicking and craving for some sort of spiritual feeling. Although *Joanna* wasn't produced by the RSC it was broadcast as *The Prophetess of Exeter* by the BBC World Service under the direction of the excellent producer Gordon House.

HWD: *Your mention of Blake's epigram, 'On the virginity of the Virgin and Joanna Southcott' reminds us of course of the young Dylan Thomas's poem on Southcott where he asks 'May a humble village labour,/And a continent deny?' I'm interested that you emphasise that Joanna Southcott was totally uneducated. Most of your plays show a concern for the deprived and the uneducated. Could you comment on that?*

LG: A great deal of my writing is about lack of education. I want to write for people who haven't got the confidence that education brings with it and about people who are trapped socially because of their lack of education. I enjoy plays that struggle with intellectual issues but I'm more interested in writing plays for a whole generation of lost young men and women who have been grossly neglected by society. They live in an imprisoned world and I feel driven to write for them. I've recently completed a play called *Wolfskin*. It's about a young man who wants to pack with the other boys and become a wolf. Unfortunately, his girl-friend has put his wolf skin in the washing machine and shrunk it. Without his wolf skin he's trapped indoors in an imprisoned world.

HWD: *Do you think these 'lost young men and women' would actually have the opportunity to go to see a performance of* Wolfskin *or of* Crossing the Bar, *another play that deals with an imprisoned boy? If not, what is the audience the plays are addressing or getting through to?*

LG: I wrote *Crossing the Bar* to be performed in prisons and I'm hoping that that will happen one day. I wrote it because no-one was addressing the problem of the number of young men who commit suicide in prison. Stick a young, uneducated man in a tiny cell and he has no hope whatsoever. Suicide seems to be the obvious way out. The play was written to draw attention to this problem. *Crossing the Bar* is about a young boy who hangs himself in a prison cell. In that split second in the noose, he meets a medieval nun who starved herself to death to see God. The cell turns into a sailing ship and the boy discovers the power of the imagination and opts for life, not death. I hope to re-write it for radio, because through that medium, it's more likely to reach prisoners. It's a very physical play, so at the moment it won't work for radio, but the subject matter is translatable.

When I began my Playwriting course at Birmingham Ann Devlin told me that all writers had their own territory. As a writer you don't choose your territory but you discover it, on the road as it were. The landscape changes sometimes, but the territory remains constant. My territory is that of marginalised and dispossessed young people and the way to expose them to plays is to stop performing them in theatre buildings. Performances should be taken to the places they frequent. And plays should be written in a language to which the dispossessed can relate. They can't be expected to grapple with words and constructions with which they are unfamiliar. If you yourself have been deprived of education, people with education can be very frightening. When I was fifteen I imagined that University was somewhere you went to if you were extraordinarily special. If I, someone who was brought up in an artistic family, thought that, what hope is there for the unprivileged? None whatsoever. It's this concern that made working with young people's theatre in Wales so important to me.

Lucy Gough

HWD: *Which companies have you worked for, and what kind of plays did you write for them?*

LG: I wrote *Catherine Wheel* for Scallywag Theatre Company, Machynlleth, and two plays for Theatr Iolo, a company based in Cardiff. *By a Thread* was a love story set on a mountain where the young characters saw the rest of the world disintegrating below them. The play was about guilt, the search for identity, war, and the need to face up to responsibilities. Before I started writing, I toured the schools and deliberately incorporated some of the things the kids had said so that the material would come back forcefully at them. I also wrote *Stars* for Theatr Iolo. The brief, namely 'The Cosmos', was frightening since I have very little scientific knowledge. But what I quickly worked out was that nobody knows anything for certain because it all changes so rapidly anyway. I would read one authority only to find out in the next that the first theory was outdated. So I decided to write a play about an old woman, knitting a pair of socks, who is driven around the universe by a man who has a little machine to trace radio waves. Some of the schools were unhappy because the play had God in it and God was a manic depressive, because the 'Big Bang' theory had stolen his thunder, as it were. The play contained all the information about the Big Bang, but since there was so much shifting sands in the Cosmos theories I felt I couldn't give the children any absolutes.

The play I did for Arad Goch, *Rushes*, originated from an idea I had when my children brought home material from a school history project on the Holocaust. I was taken aback by the material they were given. It all seemed to be a series of harrowing and unpleasant photographs. No guidance was given as to how to digest it all. I felt it needed a context. It would have been very easy to write a play that contained a series of upsetting images that would make an immediate impact. I didn't want to do that. I decided to allow the children to use their own imagination. That's less dangerous because their imagination can take them only so far. I'd also heard Stephen Spielberg on the radio discussing his decision to base *Schindler's List* on the original death camps. I was interested in this interweaving of reality and fiction and so I located my play on a film set, where a film was being made on the Holocaust. The characters were a young boy from Wales, a young Jewish girl and the ghost of a German SS soldier. All three were trapped in a truck. I explored several things but I also analysed how it was that we could record such events as the Holocaust, asking whether we could or should make Art out of such events. In fact, I challenged myself as a writer about whether I should be writing the play at all. I used my problem as a writer in order to initiate discussion after the performance. In a review, it was described as interesting but too complicated. But I wanted it to be complicated because there are no easy answers to all the issues raised. In *Rushes* I used contemporary language and images from the films *Pulp Fiction* and *Reservoir Dogs* as a way into the play. That made the children lock into the action immediately.

HWD: *You mentioned that you were thinking of adapting the stage play* Crossing the Bar *for radio. Are you equally at home in both mediums?*

LG: Very much so. I like radio as a medium because it forces the imagination and it's very much about the writer's relationship with the listener. You can't afford to forget the listeners for a minute, because, if you do, they switch off. What I try to do is release their own imagination and take them to places they wouldn't be impelled to go to otherwise. I'm also, of course, saying something. I like certain things on television but, as a medium, it doesn't fire the imagination as often as radio does. The sad thing about plays on radio is that they don't get reviewed well or often enough; the medium is treated as a poor relation. This is a pity, since most good playwrights started by writing for radio – Pinter and Beckett for example. I've been lucky with my radio plays because I've worked with some interesting directors who have been in radio for a long time. For example my play *Our Lady of Shadows*, broadcast by BBC Radio 3, was done by Richard Wortley who does Howard Barker's work.

HWD: *With* Our Lady of Shadows *you take as your starting point Tennyson's 'The Lady of Shalott', and for the Radio 4 play* Head *you took Keats's 'Isabella: or the Pot of Basil'. What was the attraction of taking a famous poem as your base?*

LG: I wrote *Our Lady of Shadows* because, although like many teenage girls I had enjoyed 'The Lady of Shalott', I was very annoyed that she had died, that she had given in as it were. I felt that she had to escape, to survive, as the girl does in my play. It made sense to use sections of the poem as part of the beat, the rhythm of the play. Having done that, and enjoyed it, I tried the formula again with *Head*. One of the images I use a great deal in my work is the image of the head. I'm fascinated with heads! I have a skull in my study. My husband's aunt drew my attention to Keats's 'Isabella' and said 'I think you'll like this poem. It's got a head in it.' And so I rang the BBC and told them that I'd like to write a play about a head in a pot. It must have sounded different because I was commissioned to write *Head* which was broadcast in 1996 by BBC Radio 4. It was a real challenge to me as a writer because I had to give an early nineteenth-century Romantic poem a modern relevance and interpretation. The play has an urban landscape, high-rise flats and a smelly lift. This urban landscape is there also in *Wolfskin*. The landscape is a metaphor for the territory which deprived young people inhabit. It's bleak, lifeless and hopeless. Often this is the landscape I go in for in my writing.

HWD: *And yet, in* The Red Room, *the play you've written for BBC Radio 4, you've gone for a totally different landscape. How did you come to choose a land of ice and snow?*

LG: When I was invited to do *The Red Room* by the BBC, I was given some information contained in a biography of Charlotte Brontë by Glyn Hughes. He notes that during the mid-August when she was writing *Jane Eyre* Charlotte was living in a stiflingly hot room in Manchester. Her father was undergoing a cataract operation and she herself had excruciating toothache. That's all I was given. I didn't want to write a drama documentary and so I read *Jane Eyre* again and tried to imagine what Charlotte as a woman would be feeling during that hot August. She'd just had one of her novels rejected, and as a writer I know what those rejections mean. I imagined her disappointment, the heat, the intensity of the room. The claustrophobia of it all would lead her to look in her imagination for an escape. This is what writers do. The escape for her, since it was so hot, would be the world of the clean, cold ice of the Antarctic.

This world of ice runs through *Jane Eyre* anyway, so I felt that this was a fair assessment of where Charlotte would have escaped to. I saw her tramping the frozen wastes and discovering under the ice the image of her dead sister. It was a metaphor, too, for the frozen state of her mind following the death of her sister and her father's operation. I saw her also shattering the ice and recovering her sister's body. Once she had broken the ice she was free to create. And we know that she completed *Jane Eyre* in six weeks of intense creativity. What I was saying was that Charlotte as a writer had used her imagination to escape the confines and pressures of her day-to-day existence and on succeeding to escape somewhere else she found the means to create *Jane Eyre*.

HWD: *Many of your plays are set in small, confined spaces suggesting imprisonment and enclosure. Why is this?*

LG: The practical reason is that I like the challenge of being confined and then breaking out. I enjoy taking the audience to a small, bare set and allowing them, through the images, to build a landscape that opens out the claustrophobic. I don't wish to get too personal here, but I myself for a long time felt trapped, and understood how the imagination could release me from that entrapment. When I was at school my reports invariably stated 'Has a vivid imagination', as if that were a disease! I really thought there was something wrong with me, and that I had to find a cure for this illness. But I discovered that the imagination can change your life, if used positively. Not so long ago I also discovered that I was dyslexic. I've always had problems with writing – which is why, I think, I am a writer. When I was at school I was trapped by the fact that the dyslexia meant that there was a gap between what my mind thought and what appeared in my school written work. I therefore understand the frustration of entrapment. That's why I think my work has enclosed spaces and that's why, too, they show how the power of the imagination can open up those spaces. It's also why, now and then, I invent a particular kind of language, as I do with the 'medieval' language of the nun in *Crossing the Bar*. I like language that is sparse and powerful. I hear the rhythm before I hear the words. My dialogue isn't right until the words work in harmony with the rhythm.

HWD: *The playwright Meic Povey, as one of the judges in the BBC Wales 'Writer of the Year' award in 1994, praised your 'innovative use of language' in* Crossing the Bar. *What exactly is the nature of that 'innovation'?*

LG: I think he also said that the language embraced the sacred and profane. In that play I mix the rich spiritual material with the earthy stuff. The medieval language of the nun contrasts with the gritty language of the boy. The young man's swearing in *Crossing the Bar* had nothing to do with trying to shock people. He uses the swearing in a way that suggests his impotence. It's not aggressive. It's the juxtaposition of the spare language of the boy and the visual language of the nun and the way they slowly begin to work together that interests me.

HWD: *I remember that as part of your degree course at Aberystwyth you wrote a play about a naughty nun, and nuns have consistently featured in several plays. Why?*

LG: Nuns made quite an impact on my life. When we lived in Box, outside Bath I attended a convent school but I wasn't a well-behaved convent girl. I was terrified that if I behaved in an exemplary fashion I too would become a nun. So I did my best to prove that I wouldn't qualify. And for somebody with a vivid imagination, a convent school which had images of the Virgin Mary staring at you all day was an awesome place. Some of the nuns, however, were intriguing; but on the whole the school was positively Dickensian. It was like *Frost in May*. The nun who tried to teach me History at the Bath convent school is responsible for the difficulties I have with writing a linear narrative. This very angry and very old nun didn't think in linear time so I had no sense of the development of historical events.

HWD: *I would imagine, though, that being freed from the tyranny of a merely linear narrative would be an advantage with your actual plays. But I suppose your difficulty with the linear could be problematic when fashioning an ongoing narrative such as the one you have to write for the highly popular Channel 4 Teen soap* Hollyoaks, *which was nominated for a 1999 BAFTA award.*

LG: I enjoy the work I do for *Hollyoaks*, and writing for a soap of that quality requires a great deal of time, skill and commitment. And television does recognize the enormous amount of work a writer has to do, and the expertise involved. You couldn't feed a goldfish on what you earn from theatre and radio. When I read an article about Phil Redmond's *Hollyoaks* I knew immediately I wanted to write for it. I've always admired his work: *Grange Hill* and *Brookside*, for example. The fact that *Hollyoaks* was about young people was also perfect for me. I sent in some scripts, had an interview with Phil Redmond and was then asked to do half a transcript. Within a few days I was offered the job. I was fortunate because when I arrived *Hollyoaks* was fresh and new, and it has continued to be an exciting venture. We're quite a small group of writers and it's very much team work. We're all involved in the story-line and in the entire process. It's not as if the writer was given a plot synopsis or a pre-packed story-line. I wouldn't want to tackle a soap where a synopsis was sent through the post. With *Hollyoaks*, writers, producers and script-editors work together for two days each month. The company is writer-led and we all have an investment in the programme and care about it. It's pretty full-time and means that I probably do less than I would do otherwise for radio and theatre. But I find it works very well to be writing for different media. Theatre and radio keep my *Hollyoaks* scripts fresh, and it also works the other way.

HWD: *This two-way current is interesting. Several critics in reviewing your theatre plays have highlighted the visual nature of your work. Is that aspect due to the influence of television, or (paradoxically) radio – where things happen, not before your eyes, but, in Shakespeare's and now everybody's phrase, 'in the mind's eye'?*

LG: It comes partly from the fact that I've had to think visually for my radio plays. For radio you *have* to think visually. And when it came to writing for the stage in *Crossing the Bar* one of the challenges I gave myself was to make the action, which takes place in a prison cell, visually exciting. The stage itself is bare and plain but the audience is asked to imagine the bed becoming a sailing-ship. It doesn't happen before their eyes. It presents the audience with a challenge and their visual imagination is exercised. What fascinated me in the theatre I saw as a child was the magic, the transformation, the idea of the casting of spells, and of changing forms. I also liked its boldness and its flamboyant courage. I think theatre is at its best when it is bold.

HWD: *'Bold' is certainly a word that could be applied to your stage play* As To Be Naked, *based on the life of the Ladies of Llangollen.*

LG: Most people enjoyed the play but, yes, there were a few letters from the 'shocked' of this place and the 'shocked' of the other. Nobody in the play stripped, but there was a phallus in it, worn by the actor who pretended to be the Duke of Wellington. I didn't choose the subject. I was offered it by the curator of Llangollen museum. When I first looked at the material I wondered what on earth I was going to do with the two ladies. They didn't achieve anything that could be called extraordinary. They were in love with each other and were perfectly happy. Their elopement was dramatic but I felt that people could more easily read a book to know about that. Why write a play about it? I felt it needed a modern, contemporary angle. What was interesting, of course, was that nobody knew for certain whether or not they were indeed lovers. That uncertainty was far more interesting than if they had declared that they were, had 'come out'.

What I did was to write an eighteenth-century Sheridan-style play and I placed that once again in a contemporary setting, where a director, doing a play on the Ladies of Llangollen wants to set up a sex scene to spice things up. My play asked questions about the rightness of that. The two actresses in the film were entirely opposed to the scene. I was in a way playing with the audience. There are in the play arguments about cross-dressing, about love, friendship and male and female roles. The very last scene is concerned with the presentation of the sex scene which is scuppered when the two actresses draw the curtains around this eighteenth-century bed. So the director and the audience have no means of knowing whether the ladies 'do it or don't do it'. Theatre allows you that kind of ambiguity and it makes the audience work hard within a performance. Television doesn't often allow for that. It's more naturalistic.

HWD: *Your theatre work is more experimental?*

LG: Well it's certainly not naturalistic. When I write for the theatre I just don't think naturalistically, and, yes, I see myself on the experimental fringe of theatre. When I'm writing a stage play I feel as if I'm hacking away at a piece of stone. I don't think of it as writing words on a page. It's a very physical activity.

HWD: *'Shocked' or 'Disgusted' of Tunbridge Wells or wherever is an occupational hazard for anyone publishing anything at all. There will always be somebody wanting to change something. Directors and actors for example – do they meddle with your scripts?*

LG: They're not allowed to. There must be respect for the writer. If, when I'm in rehearsal I see something that doesn't work then I'll go along with a change. But there was one director I worked with who thought that the script was something he could shift around, willy-nilly. I was close to murder then. Most of the time I've enjoyed working with directors, such as Ashley Wallington, for example. I did *Crossing the Bar* with him. With my radio plays there is total trust. Richard Wortley of Radio 3 once asked me to delete a swear word from *Our Lady of Shadows*. But that was only because there was a limit to the number of swear words you can use on radio. And since his next production was a Howard Barker play it was essential that he reserved his quota of swear words for that one.

HWD: *You attended an Arts Council of Wales meeting recently, on New Writing. What do you think is the best way forward, of nurturing new writers and new writing?*

LG: I hope that new writing will be nurtured in other places besides Theatr Clwyd and the Sherman. There isn't a great deal of experimental work being done at the moment in the main theatres. There should be room within a theatre budget to allow for the more challenging, and maybe scary, stuff. That's where the future lies. I think for example that Dic Edwards's work should be produced at Theatr Clwyd and the Sherman. So should mine, for that matter, but I'm far more cross about the absence of Dic's work from these stages. And we've had far too many adaptations in our theatres. The audience know in advance exactly what they're going to get, because to a large extent, the dramatist has to stick to the text of the original.

In Wales a new and challenging play is not allowed a long enough run. A play's reputation takes time to build up. In Wales, a play has one run and that's it. It's encouraging that Seren and Parthian are now publishing plays, because it gives the work an extended life. Perhaps, too, The Welsh Playwrights Company should be revived because it's important for a dramatist to share experiences with writers in the same field. And it's of crucial importance that young, inexperienced writers have contact with professional dramatists. I myself came back from the Birmingham University course with a bag of tricks. There, too, I learnt that as a writer you have to make a great deal of noise. It's like being a warrior, daubing on the war paint and going out there to shout. When I'm fighting for work I can get quite fierce. I always worry that it comes over as arrogance, but it's not meant to be that. It's commitment to the work. And of course it's much harder for a woman. There are very few women playwrights, and when I started working there was a tendency to offer women workshops instead of commissions.

On the positive side, I'm very glad that I grew up with the Welsh theatre tradition because there's an element to it that is very physical and very energetic. When I go to theatre conferences in England I realise that they are addressing different problems from the ones we have in Wales. We have a better grasp of the physical nature of theatre as exemplified by the work of Volcano and the early work of Brith Gof. There's a lot of courage in Wales and I wish the funding was there to encourage young people to write for the theatre.

HWD: *'Bold', 'physical', 'going out there to shout': these are wonderful clarion calls for the world of theatre. Given your own commitment, what can you tell us of your writing in the immediate future?*

LG: At the moment I'm working with documentary material by Marina Warner on a radio play about mermaids and with material by Germaine Greer on a play about a painting in the Uffizi, Florence, entitled 'Judith and Holofernes' by the sixteenth-century artist Artemisia Gentileschi. I'd also like to write for the hour-long radio slot on Friday nights. (The only one-hour radio play I've had is *The Prophetess of Exeter* in the 'Play of the Week' World Service slot.) I've started writing a play seeded by Made in Wales called *Sheol* which I've workshopped with Red Shift in London. *Sheol*, too, draws for its texture on the landscape and influences that have been opened to me by living in Wales. It's about Lady Macbeth after death, carrying Macbeth's head around in a suitcase. That's yet another head!

**Interview Two
October 2004**

HWD: *In the final answer in your 1999* New Welsh Review *interview you mentioned that you were working 'with documentary material by Marina Warner on a radio play about mermaids'. You hadn't at the time decided what to do with the material. What finally evolved?*

LG: That was a wonderful experience. Having read Marina Warner's transcript on the mythology of mermaids I decided to find contemporary touchstones to give the material a modern relevance. I came up with the idea of centering the play on an anorexic girl, living in a tenement flat. At the opening of the play the young girl is having a bath and listening to Marina Warner on the radio talking about the mythology of mermaids. As she listens, the girl finds herself swimming under the sea.

I remember as a kid listening enthralled to the shipping forecast and to all those wonderfully evocative names. In *The Mermaid's Tail* I used the images that came to my mind from all those seas conjured up by the shipping forecast. In those seas were children bound in gossamer, souls did sequence-swimming and the young anorexic girl swam re-inventing herself. When she finally reaches the bottom of the sea she re-discovers herself through the power of the imagination.

HWD: *I have the same early and lasting memories of the names of the sea areas as they tolled on the shipping forecast: 'Rockall. Malin. Dogger. Finisterre....' In fact those four names comprise a whole line in a poem by Carol Ann Duffy, and of course Seamus Heaney too has written a fine poem about the names.*

LG: I'm not at all surprised. The shipping forecast is magical and contains the rhythm and the images of poetry.

Lucy Gough

HWD: *In 1999 you were also working on another radio drama for BBC Radio 4 based on documentary material, prepared by Germaine Greer on Artemisia Gentileschi's painting 'Judith and Holofernes'. With your self-confessed fascination with heads that commission must have appealed to you.*

LG: It did and the commissioning editor must have known I'd be interested because I was told that the BBC had 'the perfect play' for me because it had to do with a woman sawing off a man's head! The idea was that Germaine Greer would do a commentary and then I would find a way into the painting. My problem with this one was that Germaine Greer was a cracking performer in her own right and I felt that she didn't need the additional element of drama.

I decided therefore that my play would need to have a new element and a new angle. I took as my starting point the moment when Artemisia was setting up her studio in order to begin work on 'Judith and Holofernes'. I involved the audience in what happens and what goes through the mind of an artist confronting a blank canvas. I also decided to introduce an element of comedy. Artemisia Gentileschi employs a male model for her study of Holofernes and since what she has to represent is the chopping off of the head she has various 'try-outs' and frightens the living daylight out of this model. Comedy therefore counterbalances the passion. Artemisia Gentileschi is such a passionate painter and Germaine Greer is such a passionate critic that I needed to strike a balance. But I also provided serious, quiet moments when the listener shared the artist's thoughts about the process involved in creating a painting and what it means to be an artist. A great deal of the painter's personal history is woven into it.

HWD: *It seems to me that you're at ease with all three media, television, radio and theatre, and almost every year you are commissioned to write scripts and plays that give you the opportunity to experiment with the different requirements of these media. In the year that* Judith

Beheading Holofernes *was broadcast your stage play* Wolfskin *was performed and you were also working on yet another stage play* Mapping the Soul. *Were these commissioned pieces?*

LG: The short *Wolfskin* play was commissioned by The Machine Room Company in London for a festival of short plays. It was performed at the 'Lion and the Unicorn' in London and subsequently I decided to produce it for the inaugural production of my newly-established theatre company, Lupa Theatre. I chose the name Lupa because it means 'she-wolf', but lately I've discovered that it can also mean a 'whore', and a 'looking-glass' or 'magnifying glass'. All those images work for me! Lupa Theatre performed *Wolfskin* in the Aberystwyth Arts Centre Studio as part of the 'Theatre Wales' weekend at Aberystwyth.

Mapping the Soul was a commission from Castaway Aberystwyth Arts Centre Community Theatre Company. The play concerns Adam (trailed by Eve), who having written the Genome book, has discovered there is no DNA for the soul. He is cast out into the wilderness and he and Eve go on a journey through a bizarre landscape in search of the soul. During this journey they come across an anatomist sawing through the head of a dead poet in a vain attempt to find the soul in the brain. Finally Adam and Eve find the soul hidden under the earth at the Feast of the Dead. What in fact I'm trying to say is that you can't map the soul. It's our imagination, our human creativity that reveals the soul to us.

I had over twenty characters in that play and it was so liberating to be able to think in terms of a large canvas and a large cast.

HWD: *In* Mapping the Soul *you've once again introduced another 'head'!*

LG: That was no accident. As the title indicates, *Gryfhead*, a play I took with Lupa Theatre to the Dublin ESB Fringe

festival recently, is also about a head. It's based on my radio
play *Head* and it's a play where, in an urban landscape of run-
down housing, a woman comes to terms with a life defined
by the loss of love. But in Dublin, in the autumn of 2004, the
play had a whole new relevance. It was performed at the
time when the beheading of Kenneth Bigley in Iraq was
fresh in the mind. I'd actually written the play some years
ago, but I still felt very uncomfortable with a play that
showed the power of the head, because images of people
holding up a severed head were becoming an unpleasant and
horrific part of life.

HWD: *What kind of audience and critical response did* Gryfhead *get
in Dublin?*

LG: It got four stars in the *Irish Times* and the *Big Events Guide*
described it as 'a phenomenal show that you were swept
away by'. I loved it when members of the audience came out
laughing or weeping. The important thing for me was the
fact that audiences had been moved by the power of theatre.
The experience was also a huge learning curve because it
was the first big production for Lupa Theatre Company.
We'd done *Wolfskin* in 2000 but that was a two-hander.
Gryfhead was also the first production I'd directed and I
learnt a lot about working on stage with the *rhythm* of a
play.

   I love writing for the theatre and I'm pleased with a
recent commission from Sgript Cymru to write a full-length
play based on the twenty-minute long *Wolfskin*. It's proving to
be a fascinating process because the story is going somewhere
I didn't expect. It's crazy, but it's right.

HWD: *You mentioned to me before this interview, that you'd re-read
your first interview to see what your territory was at that point. Has
anything changed?*

LG: Heads are still there and the disenfranchised are still there but I'm now also fascinated by the soul and by savagery. In 2003 I was commissioned by BBC Radio 4 to write a four hour dramatization of Emily Brontë's *Wuthering Heights* for the Woman's Hour serial slot. That novel opened my eyes to the nature of cruelty. *Wuthering Heights* is certainly not a love story. It rather deals with uncompromising cruelty and savagery. I can't understand why people have great sympathy for Heathcliff. Tom Goodman Hill who played Heathcliff in the radio serialization said 'I just don't like Heathcliff.' In fact both Catherine and Heathcliff are highly egocentric, selfish people, and both are cruel in their own way. A great deal of my work is about werewolves and the animal tendency in people. It was that wild and primitive savagery I saw in *Wuthering Heights*.

HWD: *You received lively and appreciative feedback for your version of* Wuthering Heights. *What elements in particular engaged the listeners?*

LG: What they responded to mainly was the savagery. They mentioned that the film version concentrated on the love story, but that I had identified the cruelty of it. Most of the characters are vengeful, selfish and damaged and I concentrated on that aspect. The other thing listeners and critics liked was the fact that I used the house as a character throughout. In fact the first voice you hear is that of the house. The house itself was able to give listeners light touches of the psychology that underlies the action and the characters. I felt the house was central to the novel and that you had to make its presence felt. A house is at one with our psyche – it has attics, basements, corridors and windows, it harbours so many emotions and secrets. However, one woman in her feedback disliked the use I made of the house and wrote in to say that she very much hoped that Emily Brontë would haunt me. I felt like replying that I would very much appreciate being haunted by Emily Brontë. I do believe that in having the house talk I kept to the heart of the matter.

HWD: *You mentioned that you are now also fascinated by the soul. How has that fascination been exemplified in your work for radio?*

LG: I was commissioned in 2002 by BBC Radio 4 to write a play set in a women's prison. That play was *The Raft* which was nominated for the Prix Europa. I mentioned in my previous interview that I wanted to adapt my stage play *Crossing the Bar* for radio. Well I didn't, but what I did do was to take the same broad theme and construct a whole new story, based again, sadly, on truth. I heard a radio programme about a prison in Glasgow for young seventeen and eighteen year old heroin addicts. Most of them were single parents but were separated from their children once they were imprisoned. I was horrified at that and at the fact that their daily task was to sew shrouds. I don't think that happens now. I felt that there was no hope for these young girls and that we had got it so wrong.

The Raft is a crazy play about a girl who falls into the Sea of Dread and is separated from her soul. She sees her soul drift to the bottom of the sea where it gets caught in a shipwreck. The girl is picked up by a submarine which will take her to her Death, but she opts for life and makes the Ancient Sub-Mariner who controls the submarine take her back to the shore, to life and to a reunion with her soul. All this mythical material is paralleled with scenes within a prison of a young girl who has tried to take her own life and who is revived by the gaoler. The girl fights for her life and at the end of the play she vomits salt. For me salt represents courage, a taste for life.

I'll also be able to enjoy my fascination with the soul in my next BBC Radio 4 play because I've recently been commissioned to write a play specifically about the soul which will be broadcast in May 2005.

HWD: *In* The Raft, *as in all your work, it's the rhythm that propels the action, and a printed version of the play has the appearance of poetry on the page.*

LG: That's because I feel everything through the rhythm and I have to get at the rhythm before I begin to write anything. I was reading a piece by Alan Garner recently where he said that he knows the ending of a story before he even begins to write it. I never know the ending, but I know the rhythm. When I hear a recording of one of my radio plays I'm listening to every beat. In *The Raft* I used 'Halleluiah', a Jack Buckley song, because it had the right rhythm, the right touch of frailty and vulnerability and also the desire for hope. When I was writing the play I thought he'd died of a heroin overdose as his father had done. Later I learned that he had drowned. I found that fairly spooky since *The Raft* deals with the experience of a drowning girl.

HWD: *In your introduction to* Our Lady of Shadows, *published by Seren, you warn that 'This is not a naturalistic play.' How, then, would you describe your kind of theatre?*

LG: I really don't know what my style is. An actress friend of mine calls me an 'Expressionist'. It's become an in-joke between us but I suspect there's some truth in it because I understand that style of theatre. I enjoy using every technique to express the emotion and make it work. I also like the surreal. I myself couldn't write a 'straight' play although that doesn't mean I'm dismissive of that kind of play. As long as it works I'll enjoy it.

HWD: *You continue to script very successfully for* Hollyoaks *where you have, of course, to work within the confines and requirements of a television soap. Have you ever been attracted by the more creative possibilities of television?*

LG: For a long time television was a medium I didn't understand and for a while I felt a bit of an impostor as a *Hollyoaks* script-writer, although I knew I could do it. What I've discovered is that you have to learn its language and when you've understood that, the possibilities are enormously exciting. I still think that there isn't enough challenging television. There's too much cheap telly, too much reality TV. Interestingly enough, television ratings figures are dwindling while radio listeners are steadily increasing. People want to be challenged.

HWD: *You've been commissioned several times to write for BBC Radio 4. Have you, as a writer living in Wales, been commissioned by Radio Wales to write a play?*

LG: Not as yet, but I was commissioned to do an episode of *The Bench*, a BBC Wales series which I admired. Sadly, the money for *The Bench* was pulled. Two series had already been done and my episode would have been for the third series. It was a great pity because *The Bench* was a wonderful programme.

I feel, however, that although my radio and television work is based in London, Liverpool and Birmingham, Wales is where my home is, and where you live is bound to be reflected in some way in what you write. It could be also that there isn't enough work available for all the writers living in Wales.

HWD: *You contribute to Creative Writing courses at the Universities of Lampeter and Aberystwyth. In your experience do students regard such courses as vocational?*

LG: Not necessarily. Some students enrol in these courses in order to exercise part of their brains they wouldn't otherwise use. Some of them will go on to write after graduating but often the experience of following a creative process will stand students in good stead because they've been given the opportunity to explore, to use their imagination and come up with unexpected things. Creative writing doesn't have to be career-based.

In my case, however, the MA Playwriting Course I followed in Birmingham when it was first set up did lead to a career. Indeed, I haven't looked back since. Not that it makes for an easy life. Working continually to deadlines is scary and I sometimes yearn for the time when I was writing a play that nobody wanted. Then I could write it at my own pace, and that's a different process. Writing is extremely hard work. You have wonderful moments when you're flying but there are hours of sheer grind and of losing heart at what you've written. I then hate myself and everybody around me, but I have by now learnt not to give up at those low moments and to keep faith. Writing is bloody hard work, especially if you're driven. But when everything comes together, and your work touches other lives, it's electric. It's an exhilarating, powerful feeling, and at those moments I know why I'm a writer.

Mark Jenkins

Interview One
May 2002

HWD: *You have a definite Celtic lineage. What in particular is the Welsh connection? How did it relate to the rest?*

MJ: We all have four grandparents, and to some extent they determine who we are. Two of mine were Irish, one was Scottish and the other was Welsh. I'm always asked the question, 'Are you a Welsh writer?' It's a question I find difficult to answer. I spent the first forty years in London, immersed in London life. But Wales played a great part in my childhood. I was a pre-war baby, and when I and my brother were growing up we were shunted back and forth to my grandmother who lived in a small village called Caerfachell just outside St David's. When we were there we went to school with the local Welsh kids and returned to London as soon as the bombing eased off. So I never quite knew where I was. I was brought up in a house full of Irish women who were always telling stories. That story-telling background framed my childhood. We eventually moved from our one-room home to Watford to one of those new housing estates built under the Attlee government. I had to travel from Watford into London daily because I'd won a grammar school place and the nearest school that could accommodate me was several miles from my home. So, once again, I was between two worlds. I was conscious of being the trailblazer since I was the first in the family to get to grammar school and university. Because of that, quite a lot was expected of me.

HWD: *But university didn't follow hard on the heels of the grammar school.*

MJ: No, you're right, the army did. Had I gone straight to university I could, of course, have been granted deferment. What I really wanted to do was to read History at Manchester University. But in those days you had to have Latin in order to be accepted and I just didn't have 'A' Level Latin. After grammar school, I was straining at the leash to be a bit more independent, so I decided to go into the army to get it out of the way. It was a baptism of fire. I met people from all walks of life, some even poorer than I was, characters from Glasgow, Belfast and Liverpool. It was itself an education. After the army, I went to a teacher-training college, but after a year's teaching I decided again to set out for university. I chose to read Economics at what was then the Regent Street Polytechnic.

HWD: *That's interesting. What prompted the switch from History to Economics?*

MJ: Something extremely important happened in 1951. In that year my parents joined the Communist Party. Previously, I hadn't been at all interested in politics, but out of respect for my parents, because they were hard-working, upstanding and honest people, I gave an enormous amount of credence to their beliefs. I became a committed communist. I was reading Marx and Engels when I was fourteen, and I got fired up by the theories of Adam Smith and the competing views of how wealth was created. So I had really already discovered Economics in my teens. So great was my interest in the subject that I went, after graduating, to do a Master's degree at the London School of Economics. But while I was there I fell in love. I don't do anything by halves, so I abandoned my course to devote my time to the relationship. Later, of course, I completed a PhD thesis on 'The Bevanite Movement', and became a lecturer in Government and Economics in London before moving to Wales to teach at the University of Glamorgan.

HWD: *Your PhD thesis bore fruit in your highly acclaimed volume,* Bevanism, *a definitive standard work of reference. Does the subject, and that background, get reflected in the interest you show in your plays in the phenomenon of movements and political creeds?*

MJ: It does. It was suggested to me that I write a book, not about Aneurin Bevan, because Michael Foot had already written some wonderful volumes on him, but on the Bevanite movement which had caused so much strife in the 1950s. *Bevanism* isn't a biographical piece, but a solid and rather dark analysis of just how the movement was organized, how big it was, and what its programme was.

HWD: *So when did theatre become part of the scene?*

MJ: Very late, as it happens. I suppose it was when everything else was failing. Moving to Wales was crucial to my turning to the theatre. It got me out of the hothouse of London politics. I'd been very active in the Labour Party, and had had enough of political activity. I needed some way at that point of *understanding* everything I'd been involved with during the previous twenty years. That's why my early plays are all about socialists like Karl Marx and Robert Owen. A later play, *Downtown Paradise*, also deals with radicals, this time American radicals. In my early plays I wasn't wasting any experiences or material. Those first efforts were all to do with analysing the nature of political commitment, what it does to you, and how it affects everyone else around you. You pay a price for any all-consuming political passion. *Birthmarks*, *Mister Owen's Millennium* and *Downtown Paradise* could all, I suppose, come under the heading, Promised Lands, and although they do not mirror specifically Welsh themes they do address the preoccupation of an epoch, the epoch of a collectivist vision, which both engaged and dominated the twentieth century.

HWD: *In the two early plays,* Birthmarks *and* Mister Owen's Millennium, *and later in* Downtown Paradise, *the women in particular are shown as direct victims of male obsession.*

MJ: Owen's wife was reduced to poverty by his lavish schemes. Marx's wife was betrayed, and finally destroyed, by the husband she stood by. Later, although this does not feature in the play, two of Marx's daughters committed suicide for reasons that I think are related to their father's messianic commitment to a cause. And the heroine of *Downtown Paradise*, Rachel Bloom, paid a tragic price for her misplaced idealism. But in the case of *Birthmarks* and *Mister Owen's Millennium* the women were also victims of their times and social climate inasmuch as loyalty and unquestioning devotion to the husband was expected of them. But I also think that they shared the vision of the men.

HWD: *Would you say that* Birthmarks *and* Mister Owen's Millennium *are, amongst other things, studies in the psychology of obsession?*

MJ: Yes, and that's partly because I myself was trying to understand my own motivation for my twenty-four hours a day, seven days a week commitment to a cause and what it meant to me and others around me. In a sense I was probing my own psychology and the nature of my own thinking which I saw reflected in the lives of Marx and Owen. I research the material for my plays carefully, and during the process of research I became very interested in the psychological motivation of Owen and Marx. In my reading in preparation for writing *Birthmarks* I stumbled on something very profound about Marx which was that he was a self-hating Jew, and that what he thought was an objective, scientific study, was really an attempt to expurgate what he saw as his own Jewish essence. He sees Capitalism as essentially a Jewish thing, and by writing about the topic he erupts in boils and carbuncles. This was so obviously psychosomatic, but he himself was totally unaware of his neurosis. When a man has that much self-hatred in him he cannot create a secure, loving family unit. The Marx family were close but right at the heart of it was Marx's destructiveness.

HWD: *In* Birthmarks *you also take a fresh look at the curious relationship between Marx and Engels, basing your exploration on the correspondence between the two. One sentence in a Marx letter to his friend is particularly unexpected: 'We must re-fuck the Communist Manifesto'.*

MJ: It's interesting that he wrote to Engels in those terms, and in *Birthmarks* I make a number of allusions to a statement that Marx's wife makes, 'They write to each other as lovers.' I'm not at all hinting that there was any kind of homosexual relationship there. But there is undoubtedly a kind of sexuality there, and the idea that they created this child, this Communist Manifesto together. And then, of course, Marx fathered an illegitimate son by his housekeeper Lenchen, and Engels accepted paternity for the child and paid for his fostering. There are so many interesting connections between Marx and Engels that I found in the relationship rich material for a play.

HWD: Birthmarks *has a variety of characters but* Mister Owen's Millennium *has only one character, Robert Owen himself. It's a monologue, a solo performance that lasts for 90 minutes. This is a real challenge for an actor. How can an actor sustain, that long, the impetus of the 'play'?*

MJ: That's a question for the actor. But I have to say that the vehicle helps. The actor is telling a story, the voyage of a man's life. It's got all the elements of a good yarn. Robert Owen leaves Newtown, Montgomeryshire for London with a shilling in his pocket. By the age of 21, he's a successful businessman and manufacturer. He met the Tsar of Russia and the President of the United States and sought to change the world from top to bottom. The play is the Seven Ages of Man summed up in the life of this one Welshman. After his life's voyage, Owen in the play returns to Newtown and stays at the Bear Hotel, right next to the house where he was born. His life has come full circle. So it helps for an actor to be aware that he's telling a story with a beginning, an incredible middle, and an end. I'm not saying that there's no further dramatic art in the play. There is. But the story is the thing. None of my plays are polemical tracts. They do penetrate human relationships.

HWD: *You say there that 'the story is the thing'. Why therefore did you decide to make plays the vehicle rather than the novel or the short story?*

Mark Jenkins

MJ: My mother always used to say to me when I was a kid, 'You are going to be a writer. Are you going to write books or plays?' I never took her seriously. Even when I wrote the Bevan book she said to me, 'It's a wonderful achievement, but it's not what I thought you'd write.' In turning eventually to writing a play, I suppose I was searching for a language that I couldn't find in academe, a language which allowed me to look in greater depth into things I'd neglected. Only theatre allowed me to look beyond the surface of everything in which I'd been involved and explore the psychology of characters and how they react to one another. Theatre, then, allowed me to take psychology seriously as a way of penetrating reality. Theatre was a liberation. And also, of course, you've got to know your limitations. I've written a couple of novels, but I know they're not good. There's something immediate and direct about theatre. You can bring people to life or back to life. It's as if the playwright is a medium who can conjure up the dead and make them speak and move and relate to a live audience.

HWD: *You mentioned to me earlier that you felt yourself neglected in Wales, and yet your first play,* Birthmarks, *was certainly recognized. In 1987 it won first prize out of an entry of 120 in the national competition organized by the Drama Association of Wales.*

MJ: That's true. But then one has to ask, 'If it was good enough to win a prize, why didn't it get a production in Wales? It was rehearsed and read at the Sherman by Made in Wales but it wasn't considered worthy of development. It was first produced at Taurus Theatre, London, directed by Richard Leggatt. It then did have a production by Cardiff Everyman Theatre at Chapter Arts Centre, and then at Theatr Tribuhne, Stuttgart. I was delighted that London wanted the first production, but why is it left to London to take up a play written in Wales? Of course, it was partly to do with the priorities of Made in Wales at that time. They were looking for very specific 'Welsh' things. *Birthmarks* had nothing specifically to do with Wales. It's set in nineteenth century London and it's about German characters. But the main criterion by which to judge a play is its worthiness for production and its ability to gain an audience. What we need in Wales are, quite simply, good plays. An Englishman isn't prohibited from writing about Napoleonic France or ancient China. Shakespeare, the ultimate Englishman, was writing about the Romans, Celtic Britain and Italy. Nobody asked, 'Is this an English play?' Why should we need to ask nowadays, 'Is this a Welsh play?'

HWD: *I take, and totally agree with, your point that a Welsh playwright shouldn't need to write only about Welsh things as such. But, to take also your own chosen example of a playwright's freedom – that of Shakespeare's plays – didn't they remain very much 'English' plays, however much concerned with 'Romans, Celtic Britain and Italy' as you put it? Shakespeare's plays were, surely, inherently 'English'. The wood in* A Midsummer Night's Dream *may be 'outside Athens', but it is a very English wood. Olivia's household in the Illyria of* Twelfth Night *is a very English household. Benedick's description of the love-sick Claudio in* Much Ado About Nothing *– 'Poor hurt fowl! Now will he creep into sedges', - is imaginatively in Warwickshire, surely, not in the play's ostensible Italy. The only way out of this rootedness (should one* want *to escape from it) would be a transnational 'language', by which I mean, not literally the language itself, but a set of preoccupations, tendencies and attitudes. No such internationally homogeneous matrix exists.*

MJ: It remains a tough question. I don't think that Wales has a long enough or a deep enough theatrical tradition yet, for us to be able to look at a text – in English – and say, 'This is definitely Welsh. It couldn't be anything else.' I don't think that Wales has a sufficiently separate identity from England to make its theatre product distinct. I myself have always seen Welsh culture as a variant of English culture, a wide variant, but a variant nevertheless.

Mark Jenkins

HWD: *On the question of a Welsh theatrical tradition, I take it that you mean basically a modern English-language one. Welsh-language drama of course, has, historically and sociologically, both a 'longer' and a 'deeper' tradition than we tend to realise. But of course television and Welsh-language demography have usurped, more than would be the case in English anywhere, the role of actual physical theatres. Even so, the presence in the background of an alternative national language at a level not approached anywhere else in Britain, surely can't result in Welsh culture being a 'variant' of anything else.*

MJ: This appeal to traditional Welsh-language modes of writing that are distinct from the English tradition is interesting. I've read Welsh poetry in translation. One poem in particular I remember, about a man and a woman making love in the grass. The verve of that poem has got nothing to do with the puritanical Wales that emerged through the Methodist Revival. The older Catholic Wales was much more akin to France and Italy than it was to post-Cromwellian England. I think Wales was blasted by two things, by the Methodist Revival and by the Industrial Revolution. These two things blew away the older tradition and placed Wales in a straitjacket. But I don't speak as a Welsh historian so I defer to scholars with superior knowledge of the facts.

HWD: *Let's return to plays and productions. In the early 1990s you wrote two plays,* Strindberg Knew My Father *(1991) and* Playing Burton *(1992). First of all, what attracted you to write about a Strindberg play – in this instance,* Miss Julie?

MJ: The Strindberg play had some connection with the Robert Owen play. The director Wil Aaron in 1992 did a telefilm in Welsh for Ffilmiau'r Nant of a script I'd written about Robert Owen's return from his American visit to find his family destitute. We were filming in this vast house that had once belonged to a quarry owner, and there, on the floor,

283

in the middle of this huge, empty library was a copy of Strindberg's *Confessions of a Madman*. It seemed a shame to leave it abandoned there, but I'd be happy to return it if its owner wants to reclaim it! Before reading this volume, I hadn't realized what a psychological mess Strindberg was. But I soon realized that for most of his life he was struggling with his own sanity. Then I read Michael Meyer's analysis of Strindberg's *Miss Julie* and I realized that the work is totally at odds with the circumstances surrounding the writing of the play. Strindberg tells us that he based the play on his experiences and his encounters with certain characters in a castle where he happened to be staying. But those months in the castle were for Strindberg crazy ones. There was a great deal of heavy drinking, guns were being fired and marriages were breaking up. So in *Strindberg Knew My Father* I wrote what I thought was the real story behind the composition of *Miss Julie*. It went down so well that the play was published by Aurora Metro. It was first performed at The Old Red Lion in Islington, and then we took it to the Sherman Arena which we booked privately for three shows. It was on for three weeks in London and for three days in Cardiff.

HWD: *Your hugely successful* Playing Burton *also had to go to London in 1992 for its first production. When you took the play to the Etcetera Theatre in Camden you went with the 'Out of Wales Theatre Company'. Was that in any way an ironic, or at least a layered, title? Is it 'Out of Wales' in the American use of 'out of', for example?*

MJ: It was meant to indicate, 'Let's get out of here and see that the show is put on *somewhere* at least'. But it also implied, as you say, that the show had actually come from Wales. It was a dual title. The breakthrough with *Playing Burton* came at the Edinburgh Festival in 1994. I'd met Guy Masterton by then. He was Burton's great nephew and knew quite a few things about the production. He was also a good actor. We returned to the Edinburgh Festival in 1997 and the play was a sell-out for three weeks, with tickets changing hands for inflated prices. Recently the actor who played the part of Burton in New Zealand won the Best Actor of the Year Award for his performance of the role, and this has opened the doors of theatres throughout New Zealand and Australia to productions of the play. It's in Christchurch at the moment before moving to Auckland. It'll be playing in the Sydney Opera House in November. But it's never been played properly at the Sherman Theatre, Cardiff. They did two nights, at our request. In Wales it's been presented in small venues, with 30% profit for the companies and 70% for us. It's hardly worth the actor doing the performance. In the New York Actors' Studio the place was packed to the rafters. *Playing Burton* has become part of the canon of Welsh plays.

HWD: *What's the significance of the title of the play?*

MJ: The play is about role-playing, hence the title. I didn't want this monologue to be just an impersonation of Burton. I wanted it to be an exploration of the man Richard Jenkins playing the part of Richard Burton who was, in a sense, an artificial creation. Richard Jenkins also appears in the play in the form of a chair which the older person addresses as if he were talking to his childhood self. I also like having a gerund in the title because it brings the play to life, instead of being 'The this' or 'The that'.

HWD: Mister Owen's Millennium *is, as we saw, also a monologue. In what way is* Playing Burton *different from the Robert Owen play?*

MJ: I'd rather not compare it with the Owen play. The play I'd like to compare it with is one that has done extremely well, namely Bob Kingdom's *Return Journey*. That play is a wonderful evening's entertainment, but it's an impersonation of the man we think we know, Dylan Thomas, reading his work, though with other words woven into the text. But

Playing Burton isn't like that. What we see on stage is the dramatic turning points in Burton's life, and the character is *acting* those moments, not just telling us about them. In *Burton* I recommended three interwoven modes of performance: (1) Burton the raconteur, talking about his life; (2) Burton acting scenes from his life, say his meeting with Elizabeth Taylor; and (3) Burton acting cameos from his most famous parts. So you've got three entirely different modes of delivery and the actor switches seamlessly from one to the other. When you're dealing with a play of one-and-a-half hours it's this variety, together again with the strength of the story that's unfolding, that makes the play work on stage. There are also of course, the thematic 'sub-plots' that bubble up through the dialogue. There's the Dr Faustus sub-plot, with Mephistopheles waiting for the soul of Richard Jenkins. Then there's Prince Hal conquering the world, and King Lear who retains his greatness despite the terrible things that have happened to him. With *Playing Burton*, you are watching a living piece of theatre.

HWD: *You've just called up examples of the tragic –* Faustus *and* King Lear *– but there is also a great deal of wit and humour in the Burton play, as there is also in the Strindberg play.*

MJ: I suppose I get that from my mother. The Irish have a way of delivering tragic things comically and comic things tragically. My mother was a master of those skills.

HWD: *The monologue has become a very fashionable form. Do you think that the financial constraints within actual theatres has forced dramatists to think in terms of one-man/one-woman shows, and to work, as it were, within the realms of the possible?*

MJ: If so, that wasn't what I was doing. I have written plays and filmscripts that are not monologues. But it is a fact, of course, that in a period of financial constraint monologues travel well. For the Burton show we didn't need a van. We could get everything into a suitcase. The only extras we needed were a chair, a bottle of vodka and an ashtray, plus of course lighting. On the other hand, a one-man show asks an enormous amount of the actor, the audience and the script. You need, in a different sense, light and shade. What you can't have is one long, chronological social historian's dirge. Only the best actors can sustain monologues. I've been lucky enough to have excellent actors such as Josh Richards to play the part of Burton.

HWD: *Your next play,* Downtown Paradise, *which received excellent reviews, was once again first performed in London, at the Finsborough Theatre, Chelsea, before moving to Chapter in Cardiff. Here you are dealing with a radical Jewish lawyer's disastrous love affair with a Black Panther client who faces trial on a murder charge. It's a true story. What drew you to it?*

MJ: Once again the theme of the price you have to pay for unquestioning commitment to a cause was right there in this very American story. But this time the theme was writ large. The woman lawyer is an idealist who has all kinds of false illusions about the ideal America she would like to see. In her pursuit of what she imagines to be the ideal, she fails to analyse the inner motivation of the people around her. She is blind to the fact that her Black Panther lover is a deeply flawed man. As I say in the preface to the published version of the play, she is unaware of the devil's art of disguise. She doesn't realise that someone with an apparently justified cause can be a nasty bit of work. I've written a film script of the play but it would need a big budget because it's also about the FBI and the San Francisco police force. It's a huge, modern story, and it's a film I want to see made.

HWD: *Your 1998 feature film* The Scarlet Tunic *had a very modest budget of one million pounds, but it was given five-star rating* *in* Time Out, *and played in major cities throughout the UK and was shown at the Cannes Film Festival in 1997. What is the film about?*

MJ: It's an adaptation of a Thomas Hardy short story called 'The Melancholy Hussar of the German Legion'. That wasn't a snappy enough title, so it was changed to *The Scarlet Tunic*. Apparently, things with 'scarlet' in the title sell well. The Hardy short story was only ten pages and my work involved inventing characters that were only hinted at in the text. Hardy is very economical with detail, so I had to develop those things that were merely hinted at in Hardy's text. It certainly wasn't a case, as it sometimes is, of which bits to leave out and which bits to retain. It was a Scorpio-Pinewood Studios production starring Simon Callow, Jean-Marc Barr, Jack Shepard, Emma Fielding, Linda Bellingham and John Sessions. A few years ago I completed the script of another film, *Tiger Bay!* This script, which received a script development grant from the Arts Council of Wales Lottery Unit, is Cardiff-based since it is about the rise to fame of that people's hero, Jim Driscoll, the Irish-Welsh boxer who won the world featherweight title in 1909, and whose funeral was the biggest ever held in Wales. I don't know whether the film will ever be made. It's a question of funding.

HWD: *Even apart from the further reaches of widespread stage productions or of film possibilities, does inadequate funding account for the dearth of new theatre writing in Wales?*

MJ: Two years ago David Clark wrote a report for the Institute of Welsh Affairs in which he suggested that theatre in Wales was at death's door – 'if it's not dead already' I think was one of the phrases he used. I don't think theatre in Wales is dead, but despite all the money and effort that has been given to theatre over the last twelve to fifteen years, we've got very little to show for it. It's not only a case of funding. I wonder how many playwrights we have in Wales of

London standard. It's just not good enough to say when Welsh plays are staged in England and fail, 'Oh well, the English don't appreciate us.' The English know quite a bit about playwriting. They appreciate Irish plays and Scottish plays. In the main those are probably better plays. We have had some good playwrights in Wales – Alan Osborne's *Merthyr Trilogy* is a case in point – but we don't have the example of a founding school where you could say of it, 'That was the heroic age of Welsh playwriting in English.'

HWD: *Many Irish playwrights write, in one way or another, of what is happening in the Ireland of their time or times. It has recently been suggested that such plays be commissioned from Welsh playwrights. How, finally, would you respond to this suggestion?*

MJ: The best plays are probably not commissioned. They succeed *despite* public funding. I think people who want to write plays are free spirits rather than breast-fed people who are comfortably commissioned. Commissioning a Welsh voice seems like 'hunting the quark' to me. You cannot 'create' a Welsh theatre. You have to wait for it to grow and develop naturally. My objection to 'cultural nationalism' is that its proponents are laying down a prescription for what a Welsh writer should be or do. At the moment, in Wales we see artificial attempts at creating the symbols of nationhood. An example is this theatre that's due to be built in the Docklands. It's just another outward symbol. It takes more than buildings and 'national' institutions to create a nation.

And I don't think in any case that a writer should be commissioned to write about 'the state of the nation'. It is, of course, a perfectly legitimate and interesting topic, and there are plays that could be written about what is activating people in Wales at this very moment. There's the issue of the Assembly, for example. My own view is that the Assembly was not embraced enthusiastically, and as a result people don't feel all that liberated. It was a cool, reluctant, sceptical acceptance by a people who felt that an Assembly was inevitable. Then take the issue of the Welsh language. Most people in Wales speak English but the top jobs in the public sector are advertised in Welsh and English. I can well imagine that an English-speaker would say, 'Oh, I haven't got the language; there's no point in my applying for this post'. That's a democratic issue. Perhaps playwrights should look at that issue as one that is agitating Welsh people at the moment. Would such a play be considered an example of a 'Welsh voice'? Some years ago I mentioned in an article on cultural nationalism that one of the major ironies was that Ed Thomas's play *A Song From a Forgotten City* was a 'Welsh voice'. But what is the play about? It's about the loss of a Welsh voice. So, here's a Welsh voice writing about the fact that we haven't got a voice. It all seems terribly confusing.

Interview Two
August 2004

HWD: *How would you summarise developments in your writing career over the past two years?*

MJ: Quite simply – all my expectations have been exceeded to a degree I would not have imagined possible in 2002. *Playing Burton*, now in its twelfth year of annual performance runs, continues to surprise me. With Swansea-born New Zealand actor, Ray Henwood, it toured Wellington, Christchurch, Auckland and other New Zealand cities and festivals in 2002-03, winning the prestigious Chapman-Tripp award, New Zealand's highest honour. It then went on to play major Australian cities, the high point being a two-week run at the Sydney Opera House theatre. I would have been satisfied had the story ended there!

But more and better things were to follow. My daughter Emily spotted Irish-American actor Brian Mallon in a show called *Secrets of the Celtic Heart*. Brian is a dead ringer for the star from Pontrhydyfen. So much so that the locals at the Miner's Arms fell deathly silent when he walked into the bar and ordered a pint. They thought he *was* Burton, back from beyond! After playing *Burton* at the New York Actors Studio before such stars as Ellen Burstyn, Eli Wallach and Lee Grant, we took the show to Provincetown for two weeks in the summer of 2002. Paying customers included Monica Lewinsky and literary legend Norman Mailer, who invited us back for a drinks party and reception. We talked theatre and boxing with the great man, who was full of praise for Brian's performance. The following year, 2003, our off-Broadway run of six weeks at the Irish Repertory Theatre had to be extended to ten by popular demand.

In July 2004, Brian performed the show at the Conference of the North American Association for the Study of Welsh Culture and History in West Virginia. In October 2004, he is booked for sixteen performances at the Celtic Arts Centre, North Hollywood, followed by a two-week run in Dublin in November, culminating in a three-week run at the Wales Millennium Centre inaugural season in Cardiff Bay. I am truly delighted with this Cardiff season, because we have only ever been offered one-night stands in my home City – till now, that is.

HWD: *Then, of course, came* Rosebud, *your new highly-acclaimed Orson Welles monologue. How did that come about?*

MJ: After *Burton*, I had silently sworn to myself that I would never, ever, write another solo show, until one day Josh Richards was doing a charity performance of *Burton* at the RSC in Stratford-upon-Avon. After the show, we repaired to the 'Dirty Duck' pub, where Josh introduced me to a young RSC actor of truly prodigious talent – Christian McKay.

291

By the end of the evening I had agreed to write a show especially for him, and Josh, a master of the technique of staging solo shows, agreed to direct it. After a whole year of writing, rehearsals and direction, we took the show ourselves to the Edinburgh Assembly Rooms in August 2004. The response was instant and overwhelming. Two five star reviews in the first week and any number of four stars in the national dailies. Christian's penetrating portrayal of Orson Welles had him surrounded by reporters and photographers from day one. Steven Berkoff called backstage to pay his respects to this brilliant young actor. A tour to Dublin was contracted almost immediately and others were lining up. The book of the play was published to coincide with the Edinburgh launch and Christian was offered a movie part, playing Welles. The high point of the run was being awarded the 'Fringe First Award', and then to our great delight *Rosebud* won the new 'Carol Tambor Edinburgh to New York Award'.

HWD: *When I interviewed you in 1992 you were working on a new play entitled* Nora's Bloke, *an adaptation of a short-story you'd written. That play was premiered in New York two weeks ago. Did you attend the premiere?*

MJ: No, I was too busy at Edinburgh. I just didn't have the time to attend the American premiere of *Nora's Bloke*, which ran from 11 to 29 August at the Blue Heron Arts Centre in New York City. The Wales International Centre in New York publicly lent its support to this production, as part of its promotion of Welsh business and culture. *Nora's Bloke* had a week's run of near-full houses with Cardiff Everyman the previous December, but the American production, so soon after, came as something of a surprise. Both *Rosebud* and *Nora's Bloke* had, need I say, been turned down for production and very modest funding requests here in Wales. But really, these days, such a negative response hardly matters. We either raise the money ourselves or from private financiers, who now

292

seem prepared to back my work. I find that very reassuring – especially as they get their money back with interest.

HWD: *So for you August 2004 has been action-packed.*

MJ: Yes, August 2004 was quite a month, really. The *Rosebud* book was followed immediately by *More Lives Than One*, a volume of five of my plays, published by Parthian. It is my hope and firm belief that this book will lead to further productions internationally. Why do I say that? Because the first Parthian publication of *Playing Burton* led directly to it being translated into four languages and contracted for three years of performance in Scandinavia.

HWD: *And what of the future?*

MJ: I have at last managed to complete a novel, which my agent is trying to place at the moment. I'm also half-way through a childhood autobiography called *Coming to Life*, which examines the way a child grows into consciousness of the world he inherits – family, friends and neighbourhood. Lurking in the background is another play, set in fourteenth century England and based around the first protestant heretics – the Lollards. It's an ensemble piece for a large cast.

You see, I truly believe that the Protestant Reformation opened the highway to modernity by challenging the stifling power of medieval Rome. Without Protestantism, there could have been no mass literacy, no democracy, no Enlightenment and no modern science. The translation of the Bible into the vernacular, which John Wycliffe and his Lollard followers began, rescued the English language from Latin and Norman-French elite domination and propelled the language of the common people of England into a position of world prominence, from which it has never subsequently been dislodged. And all of this was happening in Britain over 150 years before Martin Luther's great Protestant revolt.

HWD: *The Lollards should keep you busy for at least another year.*

MJ: 'Busy' is the key word. You know, Hazel, I used to wonder how a writer could ever pin-point that defining moment when he finally 'breaks through' to serious recognition. I now know the answer. It's when your agent starts ringing you more often than you ring her. It's when you are so busy answering correspondence that you have to fight to find the time to write fiction! It's when you log into your e-mails (as I did after Edinburgh) to find forty enquiries about three separate plays from theatres and agents as far afield as Adelaide, Los Angeles, San Francisco and the Berlin Festival, and people from Stockholm requesting translation and performance rights in languages as unlikely as Icelandic!

In early 2003, I would never have believed I would have three separate plays performed in New York within the space of twelve months, but it happened in Autumn 2003-04. As for *Rosebud*, its success had travelled to the four corners of the earth whilst I was merely getting back to Cardiff from Scotland. It is already almost booked up for the whole of 2005 and we're having to refer people to dates in 2006. Suddenly, everything just seems to open up for you. What is it they say, 'Nothing succeeds like success'? It has to happen to you before you know the truth of it. But the most gratifying thing about all this is that it confirms what I said over two years ago about the neglect of mainstream theatre. The three plays of mine most in demand are all unashamedly mainstream. There is a hunger out there for plays that are 'theatre-for-all' – no special pleading, no 'minority causes', just challenging plays that confront what it is to be human and send audiences away with something to chew on. My advice to young Welsh writers is this. Don't chase fashion. It only lands you in the pit of populist, junk 'culture'. Believe in your own vision. As the Bard says – 'To thine own self be true!'

Gary Owen

Interview
March 2003

HWD: *Your earliest years were spent in Pembrokeshire. Though a county that, in some of its parts, separates Welsh and English, for the most part it affords acquaintanceship with both languages. Was this early intermixture of languages enabling or confusing in your case?*

GO: Both. There was so much moving around during those years. I first attended the English-language Narberth Primary School and then my family moved six miles to the north and I was sent to Brynconin Primary School, Llandysilio. That was a Welsh-language school. But within six months I was happily settled and was at ease, at least with playground Welsh. Then we moved again, this time to Bridgend where I attended the English-language primary school. When I later went to Brynteg, the Bridgend English comprehensive school, my colloquial Welsh was severely criticized and corrected in the Welsh lessons. Ten or fifteen years ago, if you lived in Bridgend, the Welsh language simply didn't exist.

HWD: *And so, at the end of your sixth year at Brynteg you opted for the deeply English environment of Cambridge University.*

GO: I did. I went to Sidney Sussex to read Philosophy. I chose philosophy because I wanted to find answers to certain questions about the world that had puzzled me for some time. For me, Cambridge meant my relationship with some excellent tutors who very wisely gave me wide-ranging reading lists and left me the freedom to explore and study a good deal on my own. Socially, on the other hand, Cambridge for me was a blank. When I first arrived, there was something about the look the porter gave my family that deeply offended me. I grew to hate the British class system.

HWD: *During your period at Cambridge, the University could boast a lively theatre scene. Did that liveliness draw you, or had your interest in theatre already developed during your English courses at Bridgend?*

GO: At Bridgend it never crossed my mind to get involved in theatre in any way. I'd probably seen performances of *Macbeth* and *Othello* and I'd read *The Merchant of Venice*. In the sixth form I wrote a poem on the occasion of the death of my great-grandmother, whom I'd been very close to, and I submitted the poem to the School Eisteddfod poetry competition. The adjudicator that year was Robert Minhinnick, and his advice and comments were encouraging. But once I left school for Cambridge I forgot about writing and concentrated on my philosophy studies.

HWD: *After graduating from Cambridge you embarked on further academic studies and undertook a Master's degree at Lampeter. After Cambridge, why Lampeter?*

GO: Because I wanted to study at a place that was as far removed from Cambridge as possible. But at Lampeter it soon became clear that for me, academic philosophy as I'd studied it at Cambridge, was a waste of time, even though it was a very useful 'work-out' for the brain. Fortunately, one unit of the degree in Lampeter was a course that explored the relationship between the word and the visual imagination, and as part of that course there was a television module, taught by Carol Byrne Jones. I thoroughly enjoyed that module because it was so radically different from the kind of study I'd been involved in at Cambridge. For one thing it was a very practical course and it was also geared towards beginners. My contribution was a dreadful film entitled 'The Prospect for Rational TV', in which I forecast our digital future.

HWD: *Clearly that Master's course in Philosophy at Lampeter didn't appeal to you, because you abandoned it and moved to Swansea, to live on the dole.*

GO: That period in Swansea eventually fed into the play *Crazy Gary's Mobile Disco*. It was also during that time in Swansea that I saw in *The Western Mail* a Wales Film Council advertisement that greatly appealed to me. It advertised a Scholarship to the European Film College in Denmark, a scholarship that would give the successful applicant 'a great deal of practical experience'. I applied, was successful, and went for eight months. When I first arrived I followed the basic courses in editing and audio post-production, but eventually I found the courage to follow a course in script-writing.

During my period on the dole in Swansea I'd written a novel, because that is what I thought people with useless degrees should do on state benefit. The one thing I'd done socially at Cambridge was attend a writers' group at my college. Sidney Sussex at that time had an American novelist as writer in residence and I used to go along to the sessions where students would read their stuff to the group. I never contributed, for the simple reason that I hadn't the nerve. But in Denmark I showed the novel I'd attempted at Swansea to two friends on the course. They were Joachim Trier and Christina Rosendahl, and it was their encouragement that after six months finally made me join the script-writing course. It was one of the best things I did because Gala Antipenko, a Russian tutor, convinced me that I had an aptitude for writing and also that I would actually *enjoy* writing.

HWD: *You went for eight months from busy Swansea city to an isolated Danish village. How difficult was it to adjust to the relative isolation of Jutland?*

GO: The film school is in a tiny village and about as far from a city as you can get. But I think the place was deliberately chosen because it was felt that students should have a concentrated, intense experience of study and training. Only fifty per cent of the students at any one time are Danish. The other half comprises people from all over the world, and the student body represents a wide spectrum and level of skills and a surprisingly wide age-range. Each student is responsible for cleaning various areas of the college and you take turns at kitchen duty. At 8.00 p.m. every Saturday there's an organized party, and by January everybody's had enough of this inevitable entertainment, and every classroom is full of students avidly watching a film in order to avoid the party.

In Denmark the emphasis is on the liberal nature of education and it is perfectly normal for a person to take a four-month leave from a career and go off to a college or to a school to follow a course in pottery or alternative therapy. Indeed, in Denmark, if you want to break up your marriage you enrol in a course in a folk high-school and your partner will take it that you're serving papers. All this was an education for me.

But my eight months in the Ebeltoft film college was an astonishing and rich experience. My closest friends now are some of the people I met there. They encouraged me to try things, to take risks.

HWD: *On your return to Wales how did you put that experience into practice? What did you try to achieve? What risks did you take?*

GO: I ended up on the dole in Aberystwyth! My brother was a student at Aberystwyth and I thought it was a nice place for a person on the dole. Niall Griffiths has captured this very well in his novels. At the time Berwyn Rowlands was organising the film festival in the town and he gave me a job for a short time. I also taught for a year as a tutor on the Media and Society course for the Department of Theatre, Film and Television Studies. When I was offered the work I asked 'Does it matter that I know nothing about Media and Society and that I've never taught before? Should I get some training before teaching undergraduates?' I was told, 'Don't worry Gary, all the students have to learn in their first year is where the various buildings are.' And so I became a university tutor.

While I was at Aberystwyth I got to know Andy Cornforth who worked at the University's Theatre Department and one day he showed me a photocopied play-text that seemed to comprise just swear words. It was *AC/DC* by Heathcote Williams. He invited me to work with him and a few actors on a performance of the play at Bethseilun Hall. Since I'd had some experience of working with videos I went around Aberystwyth filming people and scenes, and during the performance, these images were projected on screen. That experience taught me that you don't necessarily have to have access to huge funds to put on a performance and draw an audience. Some things you can do in your backyard without endlessly applying for funding.

That period at Aberystwyth was productive in many other ways. Two drama students, Rob Storr and James

Topping, and I, devised a plan to infiltrate the TV world in Cardiff. Cardiff was the place where People With Money lived and it was also the hub of the Wales TV scene. I would write the script and my two friends would be responsible for the directing and the acting. As part of that cunning plan I wrote *Crazy Gary's Mobile Disco*. Our grand scheme came to nothing. I then applied for a post as trainee script editor when Pedr Jones, the new Head of Drama at BBC Wales, took on a fresh development team. I was offered the job and accepted it, thinking that I would surely be on my way to meet a Man with Money who could further my career. I stayed in that post for about twenty months.

Script-editing for BBC Wales at that time was a very curious business because essentially there was very little of use you could do. It's certainly not like script-editing for the rest of the BBC. Luckily, during my period there Dai Smith decided to commission *Station Road*, so I got to work on that. That was much more fun.

HWD: *When did* Crazy Gary's Mobile Disco *get taken off the shelf?*

GO: The one who was ultimately instrumental in rescuing it was the playwright Winsome Pinnock who was writing for BBC Wales, and who, bizarrely, had been writer-in-residence at my old college, Sidney Sussex – a weird tie-in. I'd arranged a reading of *Crazy Gary* in Cardiff and Rob Storr and James Topping came down from London to take part. Winsome Pinnock came to the reading, liked what she heard and recommended me to her London agent. He started sending the *Crazy Gary* script out and the result was that I had fifteen meetings with different people within a couple of weeks.

HWD: *Is there a lesson here for other undiscovered aspiring young dramatists?*

GO: You've got to take the initiative. I needn't have arranged that reading, but I was very bored indeed with the BBC editing work and I had to do something to change the situation. The reading of *Crazy Gary* was a low-key, after-work event at the BBC Wales drama department meeting room, but the end result changed everything for me.

My agent sent *Crazy Gary* first to Jack Bradley, literary manager at the National. He liked it but for reasons best known to himself, sent it to John Tiffany at the Traverse. Although John Tiffany really loved it and wanted to do it, the Traverse at that time wouldn't put on a Welsh play, and so he sent it to his very good friend Vicky Featherstone at Paines Plough. She decided to produce it without even having met me and I got a phone call from my agent giving me the good news that Paines Plough were interested in doing my monologues. My knowledge of theatre companies was so limited that I had to ask my agent 'Who the hell are Paines Plough?' Had I known that Vicky had commissioned and produced Sarah Kane's *Crave* I would have been even more petrified than I was when I first attended rehearsals. But, then, maybe not. I was so ignorant at that point that I hadn't even heard of Sarah Kane.

HWD: *How did working with Vicky Featherstone enlighten your ignorance?*

GO: It was Vicky who gave me confidence and a belief in my own work. She and Paines Plough made me seriously interested in theatre and in the way it works. Vicky accepted my tongue-tied, nervous silence in the first week of developing *Crazy Gary*, and when I eventually relaxed and contributed I knew that what I said was appreciated. Her trust in me led me to believe in myself and in what I was doing.

Crazy Gary was commissioned in 2000 for showing in February 2001. I worked at it a great deal during the summer and autumn of 2000. Since *Crazy Gary*, Vicky Featherstone has commissioned me twice to write new plays without ever having seen a sentence or a synopsis. On both occasions I went to her with an idea for the plays I wanted to write and the commissions were the results of those ideas. What is energising about her is the trust she places in the writers who work with her. That trust generates creativity.

HWD: *I'd like to stay with* Crazy Gary's Mobile Disco *for a while longer and ask you about the reaction here in Wales to performances of the play, performances made possible of course through Sgript Cymru and Simon Harris's support. Was the response of Welsh audiences to the play any different from that of English audiences?*

GO: On the occasion of the press night in London one of the reactions was that the play was far too long. There was a reason for that. The actors knew what they were doing, they were very comfortable with the script and they took their time to enjoy the laughter of the audience. And so the play 'grew' by about fifteen minutes. Needless to say, it shrank again when we moved to Hemel Hempstead and played to about six people and a great deal of silence. In Scarborough, at the Stephen Joseph Theatre, forty-five people out of an audience of ninety-two walked out of the performance. When it played at the Traverse Joyce Macmillan saw it, as had Paines Plough, Simon Harris of Sgript Cymru and most audiences outside Wales, as a 'cry of rage against violence, hatred and misogyny.'

HWD: *Why, therefore, do you think, did forty-five people walk out of the performance in Scarborough and why did some Welsh audiences (and critics) accuse the play of misogyny and homophobia?*

GO: At the opening of the play when Gary appears on the stage the first thing he says is, 'I'm going to spoil this for you now.' The audience immediately react to a character who has, from the outset, declared himself against them. In rehearsal one of the exercises that Dai Talbot, the actor who played Gary, did was to look at the first few rows of the audience and think to himself that he could probably beat them in a fight. The play therefore had an aggressive opener. It presents this awful character who is extremely self-possessed, sees what he wants to see and takes what he wants to take. He's not afraid of anything. In a way, he becomes quite an attractive character and I present the dreadful things he says as if they were jokes. I dare the audience to laugh. And, terrifyingly, they often do.

When the play toured to Clwyd there was yet another 'walk-out' incident. Two women walked out in protest because it seemed as if the play presented atrociously bad behaviour, and nobody was punished for it. They wrote to the theatre to explain the reasons for their protest, and declared that if this was the best that English-medium writers in Wales could do they'd better give up immediately. Tim Baker wrote back at great length to explain that, had they stayed till the end of the play, they would have seen that matters were resolved. Even so, at the time I was trying to write my second play and the women's comments troubled me. I replied to them and returned their ticket money as a measure to get them off my conscience. One of the women returned the money to me, since Theatr Clwyd had already reimbursed them. She thanked me for taking their complaint seriously and ended by saying that I should have given some indication right at the start of where the play was going.

HWD: *But theatre just doesn't work in that way. Quite the opposite....*

GO: There was no point in extending the correspondence. Theatre is a most terrifying medium inasmuch as you are physically there with whatever is happening on the stage. If you choose to walk out, ironically you become part of the event that is happening. I would have liked to have been at the Scarborough production, first to apologise to Dai Talbot for what he must have gone through that night, and secondly to have had the opportunity of being part of the forty-five people who stayed and in effect said, 'No, we're determined to see where this play is taking us.' If I had written a version of *Crazy Gary* where a character appears as some 'prologue' and says 'You know, we're not really bad people, and, rest assured, all will be well at the end', that would be no play at all. Good theatre never holds your hand to reassure you of this, that and the other.

What *Crazy Gary* says in fact is that violence and intimidation are destructive and wholly unacceptable. People like Gary are popular in the places they come from, but in my play nobody really likes him. They're scared of him. What I do is put you in his boots and then whip you out again. What you see is this self-absorbed, weak, brutal man who blames everyone else for his problems. He is obviously damaged but good for a laugh. In fact, one of the things that the ladies who walked out of Theatr Clwyd complained about was that the audience were laughing. They didn't wait to see that Gary is killed at the end. The life of his killer, Russell, is also in ruins. Nobody laughs at the end.

HWD: *During 2000 you won a playwright attachment at the National Theatre. What did that attachment require of you?*

GO: Eight of these attachments are awarded each year. You are given an office to yourself at the National Theatre Studio and you're left there to write. You are paid a weekly wage. The extraordinary thing about these attachments is that if you don't like what you've written you don't have to let them see your play. You can bin it. I found it quite difficult to write in the little office, but during the year I went to see a great deal of theatre in London. I also spent a lot of time at the Tate Modern. I also went home for two weeks to my room in Canton where I wrote a play before returning to London.

The play I developed during my attachment year was *The Shadow of a Boy*. It was produced in a studio space in the Lyttleton as part of the National Theatre's 'Transformations' season in June 2002. During the season they transformed the Lyttleton into a more intimate space by bringing the seats closer to the stage. It was a fantastic experience to be part of it all. As an added bonus, the week before we opened I found that I was joint winner that year of the George Devine Award for Most Promising Playwright, something I'd never dreamed I'd win.

HWD: *The critical response to* The Shadow of a Boy *was very mixed. How do you account for that?*

GO: The reaction to the play was divided along generational lines. *The Shadow of a Boy* is about a young lad who is brought up by his grandmother after the death of his parents and it deals with the boy's fears and concern about the threat of nuclear war. It's set in 1982 and things that happened during that year are woven into the play. People of my age who saw the play found that it embodied and reflected their own childhood fears and concerns. As a young boy, because both my parents worked, I had been brought up by my great-grandmother. I remember the period clearly because at the time I was obsessed by the possibility of nuclear war. I used to lie awake nearly every night in fear that this might be the night of total destruction. I was terrified of sharing this fear with my great-grandmother and parents because I'd realized, from watching programmes like Panorama that they were helpless, there was nothing they could possibly do. That terrible fear only left me at the end of the 1980s.

Michael Billington in his reviews seemed to think that the play was set in the 1960s. What in fact he was asking was 'Why has Gary written this bad play about the 1960s in a season of plays meant for people in their 20s and 30s?' But what I did was very relevant to that group. We had grown up in a society preparing for destruction, and because of fear we had colluded through our silence. Like the young boy in the play we had to live with the terrifying knowledge that nuclear war was a possibility, and yet we had, somehow, to get on with our day-to-day lives although we knew that things were certainly not 'all for the best'.

In 'Brompton Cocktail' in the volume *Jafsie and John Henry*, David Mamet captures exactly how my generation too felt about the possibility of nuclear war. Mamet declares himself 'a child of the first generation of the atomic age. We were raised under – it seemed to us, at any rate – the very real possibility of nuclear war.... Wait one moment, I remember thinking, the world may be ended in the next moment – everything we know may be blown away by the push of a button – and yet you can continue one moment to the next as if that were not so? In my generation and milieu we were stunned by my parents' acceptance of the inevitability of war.'

One of my proudest moments on the evening of the production of *The Shadow of a Boy* was when a man came up to me after the performance to say he really had to see the play again. He said 'I'm a Christian, and right through I was waiting for the moment when the kind and good grandmother is declared a psychopath. That never happened as it always seems to do in contemporary plays.' I was delighted he'd commented on that because one of my aims in writing the play had been to create a good Christian character who couldn't possibly be seen as a 'psychopath'. 'Nana', the grandmother in *The Shadow of a Boy*, is based on my great-grandmother.

What I realised while writing the play was that it was the middle part of a trilogy I intend to write, investigating what has happened to people of my generation. In the trilogy I also want to explore Nana's character in more detail. My mother is interested in genealogy and has uncovered a great deal of detail about our family. I'd like to investigate that.

I've never yet really written about anything I haven't known or experienced myself. Writing about newly discovered family details would be a real challenge.

HWD: *As well as the production of* The Shadow of a Boy *at the National, 2002 also saw the broadcasting on Radio 3 of* The Island of the Blessed, *your first full-length radio play, and the performance of your third play,* The Drowned World *by Paines Plough at the Edinburgh Traverse Theatre.*

GO: *The Drowned World* was a play Vicky Featherstone commissioned and it was written when I was writer-in-residence at Paines Plough. This was a post that was supported by the Pearson Playwrights' Scheme and the Peggy Ramsay Foundation. *The Drowned World* opened in Edinburgh in August 2002 and then played at the Bush in London in January and February 2003. It then toured for a month.

HWD: The Drowned World *received highly complimentary reviews, and this time Michael Billington in* The Guardian *admits that 'Owen can certainly write.' Other critics describe the play as 'masterful' and 'one of the most powerful pieces of theatre I've seen for a long time.' Were you yourself aware, during the writing of* The Drowned World, *that you were maturing as a playwright?*

GO: When I was writing *Crazy Gary* I wasn't even thinking about how or what I was writing. But when I came to write *The Shadow of a Boy* I was aware of the fact that people were investing in me and that I had to be more conscious of what I wrote. Also, I'd seen a great deal of theatre while in London and I'd read a great many plays. Vicky Featherstone all the while encouraged me to try new things.

I wrote *The Drowned World* to explore a contemporary issue, namely the wish to be beautiful and successful, and the modern concern with surface values. The action is set in a futuristic totalitarian state where 'the beautiful people', or 'the radiant' ones are persecuted by 'the citizens' or the ugly people. *Drowned World* began as a naturalistic piece, set in a recognizable Balkan nation in which ethnic cleansing was taking place. Then I began to think about why we decide to pick on a minority. It's often because we feel threatened by them. So I pushed that thought to an extreme: what if the beautiful people were so untouchably beautiful that they made us feel ashamed of ourselves. What might happen then?

With *Crazy Gary*, I'd written monologues. With *Shadow* I'd written a 'proper play'. For *Drowned World*, I decided the form would be led by the story. So I could use monologue or dialogue, narration or dramatisation. I could flash back or forward, whatever the story needed. All the actors stay on stage throughout the play, so characters can interject even when they aren't really involved in a scene, or after they've been killed. I'm a believer in something that exists beyond the material world, and this belief influences the way I write. One of the starting images of *The Drowned World* centred on the fact that a world God had created had been completely destroyed by its inhabitants. God then decided to begin the process of Creation all over again and he built a new world on top of the wreckage of the old, drowned world. It's a play I enjoyed writing and Vicky's directing was outstanding.

HWD: The Drowned World *certainly created a stir, so much so that, when it became known that you were going to write your next play in Welsh, one English theatre critic regretted the fact that she wouldn't be able to enjoy your play because of her inability to understand 'the lingo'. What or who prompted you to write a Welsh-language play?*

GO: Bethan Jones at Sgript Cymru and the Royal Welsh College of Music and Drama. The College had commissioned Sgript Cymru to develop three plays for their graduating Welsh-language actors. Initially, when Bethan Jones asked me to write one of the plays I refused because I was terrified of writing in Welsh. She persevered and eventually persuaded me to relent, and I'm very glad she did.

HWD: *The title of your play was* Amser Canser *(Cancer Time). What does it deal with?*

GO: *Amser Canser* is a play about two young women who sit on a park bench and discuss the habits of a group of skateboarders. On one level it's a homage to Mamet's *Duck Variations* – a play in which two old men sit on a park bench and discuss the habits of a group of ducks.

On the other level, it's a play about irony and moral laziness. For example, we sit round growing ever fatter while people in the Third World die for the want of a few pennies worth of rice. And we say to ourselves, 'Well, if there is a God, then we're definitely going to hell', and we reach for the next grab-bag of Doritos. We think an endearing, self-deprecating acknowledgement of our failings excuses us from doing anything about them. When clearly it does not.

Most of the plays I write have been created by a place. *Crazy Gary* is Bridgend and Aberystwyth, and maybe a bit of Swansea; *The Shadow of a Boy* is Narberth and Clynderwen; *The Drowned World* is Cambridge and *Amser Canser* is definitely Cardiff. If you walk around the city, you'll see around every office block a group of people smoking. They're having their 'Smoking Break'. So the title 'Amser Canser' was a play on the Welsh 'Amser Coffi', 'Amser Cinio' (Coffee Break, Lunch Break).

HWD: *It's good to see that your partnership with Sgript Cymru is ongoing.*

GO: I'm writing a play for Sgript Cymru at the moment, called *Ghost City*, which is really a hymn to Cardiff. It's me trying to write about the whole city and everything in the world that's worrying me at the moment. Probably I should write twenty plays to cover all that, but I haven't got time or money.

HWD: *Performances of your plays have been widely and, more often than not, wisely reviewed in English and Scottish newspapers. How informed has the critical response been in newspapers here in Wales?*

GO: That's a difficult one. To engage in reading criticism is often to wade through an awful lot of rubbish and I have to say that people who review for newspapers in Wales are generally not very good. Billington and a few other reviewers in England really care about theatre. That isn't the case in Wales. In fact, if you're a dramatist here and have any sense you probably won't read the reviews in *The Western Mail*. You can get wound up by the stupid things that are there. It's best to make a decision to ignore reviews and put your energy into your work. Writers in Wales need to have respect for professional reviewers who can give them informed and objective feedback. But that respect needs to be earned. It's certainly not earned at the moment.

HWD: *And lastly, is there enough being done in Wales to nurture and show new writing?*

GO: Clearly not. There's nobody in Wales who can enjoy the kind of freedom Vicky Featherstone has in England to decide what's worth nurturing. Vicky's position is that of an enlightened dictator. She will say, 'Yes, we will do that play', and it's done. I don't get the impression that there's a right person in the right position in Wales, namely a director who has not only the funding, but the will to stage, and that on a regular basis, new work from Wales. Sgript Cymru have been very good to me but they are shackled by funding which restricts them to producing only one play in each language per year.

Gary Owen

In Wales we need dynamic directors, people who are sufficiently sure of themselves and who believe, not only in their own judgement, but also in the ability of the people around them. More than anything, we need the opportunity to practise our craft. I work in London and in Cardiff and, much as it pains me to say it, people are generally sharper at their jobs in London. And that's because in London they produce more plays, and see more plays. They get to practise.

Nia Gwynne in *Ghost City* by Gary Owen

Siân Evans

Interview
May 2003

HWD: *You were brought up and educated in Bridgend. At the age of eighteen you left for London and since then you have made England your home. How deep are your Welsh roots?*

SE: I attended primary and secondary schools in Bridgend and after the sixth form I went to the University of London but to a college, Royal Holloway, that was tucked away in the Surrey countryside. If I hadn't thought much about identity and geography before, I did then. Living in Surrey after South Wales was a culture shock. I'd had an excellent French teacher at school, Janine James, who was actually French and had lived a long time in Senegal; somehow she made studying a foreign language seem mysterious and exotic. So I did my degree in French and spent a year in the south-west of France. I felt more comfortable there than I did in Surrey! But I think I always resented having any kind of identity imposed on me. I didn't want to feel bound by anything. I wanted to travel, to cross boundaries.

HWD: *Were you encouraged in Bridgend to take an interest in theatre as a means of crossing boundaries, and do you remember being interested in any form of creative writing during your secondary years?*

SE: I had a wonderful teacher, Ray Hollow, at Primary School who took a particular interest in me. He used to bring books from his home for me to read and encouraged me to write. But even then when I said I wanted to be a writer he told me I'd have to have 'another string to my bow.' I remember getting a lot of praise for essay work until I got to about fourteen and then I was pulled up because my spelling and grammar were so bad. Also, the English curriculum doesn't really include creative writing after the age of sixteen. I think I wrote pretentious poetry, like a lot of teenagers, but theatre was largely alien. I went to the theatre with the school a couple of times, trips that tied in to the set texts, usually Shakespeare. But before that I'd only ever seen 'Panto'. It wasn't until I graduated and moved into London proper that I started going to the theatre seriously.

HWD: *Did any of those performances fire your imagination?*

SE: All of them. One of the very first plays I saw was an adaptation of Hunter S Thompson's *Fear and Loathing in Las Vegas*. A friend had lent me the book and I was fascinated to find out how they were going to translate such an internal and surreal piece of writing into theatre. I remember they used lighting to suggest the characters' 'altered states' and that I laughed a lot. I was impressed by the acting, by the energy of it. Then soon after I went to see a piece by The Women's Theatre Group. Again this was not a typical 'play' but something devised from the letters and writings of the suffragettes; it could have been dull and worthy but instead was moving and engaging. It made me think about theatre as a political tool, a way of influencing hearts and minds, converting them to your point of view. It was also around this time that I saw Stephen Berkoff's *East* and that started me thinking about theatrical dialogue. The more plays I watched the more I understood theatre's potential. But I do think there was something inside me which was drawn specifically to drama. When someone eventually asked me why I wrote plays and not novels, I realised that I always seemed to be having an argument in my head and that putting these arguments down on paper was a terrific release. Then, life seemed to be about conflict, about defending your corner or someone else's corner. I think I've calmed down a bit since then!

HWD: *The first play you wrote was a play for radio. You've described it as 'a family story'. What exactly was that story?*

SE: I think I wrote two short pieces which went straight into a cupboard and never emerged. Then I joined a writers' group and wrote my first 'proper' play based not on my own experience but my mother's. It was about growing up as part of an Irish immigrant community in South Wales and it focused on the relationship between her and her sister. The sister emigrates to Australia and then disappears. The story was based on real events my mother had recounted to me; in fact we had only recently found out what had happened to my aunt and the profound sadness of it affected everyone in the family. Cultural identity was definitely an issue in the play. Although my mother was born in Wales other children would regularly taunt her with the curious question 'Are you Welsh or are you Catholic?' It seemed you couldn't be both. This set up a sense of dislocation within her (something I inherited), but I also think a part of this dislocation was

315

deliberate and peculiar to her. She enjoyed being different. She also embodied a yearning for 'culture' in a broader sense, something over and above male voice choirs and the only arts programme I remember as a child, namely 'Poems and Pints'. She never expressed it in this way but there was a sense that the limited culture we had access to was oppressively male and reductive.

HWD: *That's interesting: 'Are you Welsh or are you Catholic?' when one would have expected 'Are you Nonconformist or are you Catholic?' But I see your mother's point, as I can also understand your term 'oppressively male', even though, as one brought up and educated in a mining valley, and the daughter of a miner, I felt myself that women controlled many aspects of life above ground.*

SE: But you probably lived in a close-knit community. I didn't. I was brought up on a post-war housing development, and it was an extremely isolating experience for the women who lived there. My father had his work and work mates; my mother was on her own. So whilst life was slightly easier physically for women than it had been a generation before, the camaraderie and neighbourliness of the mining communities was largely absent. Many of my relatives did live that life, particularly on my father's side and though there wasn't any interest in culture with a capital C they were interested in politics, and the women, my aunts and grandmother, were as vocal and fierce as the men. My father's mother wouldn't let a Tory into the house and even my mother's mother was apparently once arrested for singing the Red Flag. A political viewpoint seemed intrinsic to being Welsh, albeit in a simplistic 'us against them' kind of way. I found the old political social clichés infuriating then, while now I feel the lack of any kind of political engagement. The ground has shifted of course and Welshness is less about political affiliation than about language and culture. When I was growing up no-one in my family spoke Welsh, though they had a generation before. The only Welsh speakers I knew were invariably middle-class. It was taught at secondary school but you could drop it completely at thirteen which I did, opting to do French and Latin instead. I think the situation's completely different now, and I'm glad. It's one of the ironies of my life that I was born with an aptitude for learning languages and never learnt my native tongue.

HWD: *You've spoken there of your mother, grandmother and aunts. Did your mother's isolation on the one hand, and your grandmother and aunts' robust sense of belonging, have any influence on the material you chose for your plays?*

SE: There is a great deal of sexual politics in my work. My way into politics has always been through feeling, through a sense of injustice and passion and pain. I also find it hard to follow any party-line. It's just too restrictive, and my views just don't fit – life is too complex. Both my parents had to leave school at fourteen. My father was sent down a mine when he was still a child really; he spent hours on his own in the dark and had to be taken out when he started hallucinating. He never went back down and became a carpenter instead, and although life outdoors was hard he enjoyed physical work and the sense of achievement that gave him. My mother was a different case altogether; being taken out of school was a blow she's never recovered from. Her disappointment naturally affected me and, yes, it did influence what I chose to write about. I often write about frustration and being unfulfilled and being an outsider. There's still a sense that the working-class don't understand 'high culture', or worse, don't want or need it. I've written many characters who feel their world's circumscribed by class or gender and who try and break though those barriers. At one point I became fascinated by women artists, I think it was when I saw for the first time a typical 'old master' and realised it had been painted by a woman. I was amazed at my own ignorance and

317

then at the extraordinary determination that fuelled these women to live creative lives against the odds. I started by writing about the women artists who orbited around the painter Sickert, putting aside the stuff that had been written in the late 1970s about Sickert's connections with Jack The Ripper. Then years after I'd written that play I came across a book in a second-hand market called *Sickert and the Ripper Crimes* by Jean Overton Fuller. The author's source was unique – her mother had been a friend of Florence Pash, herself a close friend of Sickert. For me the most intriguing revelation was that she had met Mary Kelly, Jack The Ripper's final victim at Sickert's house a few years before she was killed and that she'd worked for him as a nanny. Like most people I'd always assumed that Mary Kelly was an Irish prostitute but here Florence Pash claimed she'd left Ireland with her family at the age of two for Wales, that she'd recently arrived in London and was a keen amateur artist. This threw up all sorts of questions, not least about her relationship with Sickert. So I wrote a play about a young woman who is dirt poor but who has a certain creative ambition. She goes to London, meets a middleclass (and married) bohemian, falls in love, gets pregnant and is then abandoned by him and most of her bohemian friends, ending up on the streets. The play is about a woman trying to live the life of an artist in a society that says she has no right to do such a thing; ironically the only thing she becomes famous for is the horrific way in which she dies.

HWD: Little Sister, *the play you wrote two years before* The Journey of Mary Kelly *and now published by Parthian, is also written from the woman's viewpoint. What were you saying in that play?*

SE: I wanted to write a play about innocence and the loss of innocence. I'd read about the murder of Susanne Kaplan, a 16 year old who was killed by her 'friends'. It happened around the same time as the murder of James Bulger but received only a fraction of the publicity. I was both fascinated and repelled and eventually rejected writing her particular story because it seemed, like many true stories, almost unbelievably horrific. Instead my play was about a naïve young woman who becomes spiritually corrupted and ends up corrupting others. When I was growing up, the good girl – bad girl dichotomy was still very powerful. Good meant innocent, naïve, ignorant even, all those qualities that made a young person easier to manipulate and control. In other words, you couldn't win. If you were streetwise you were bad but if you weren't then you were extremely vulnerable. There was a pressure on young women to maintain a state of innocence. There wasn't this same pressure on young men.

HWD: Little Sister *was the first of your plays to be staged in Wales. How did that come about?*

SE: I'd been previously commissioned by Made in Wales and had written a play called *White is Not a Colour* which was workshopped but not produced. I was told it was the first play they'd commissioned from a woman since the company was set up ten years earlier. I then wrote another play for one of the Write On! festivals, but that wasn't produced either. I was then given another commission which went on the back burner because I was rehearsing an adaptation I'd done for Second Stride and had just had my first child. I think I was also a little pessimistic about ever having a play produced in Wales. In the meantime Jeff Teare took over Made In Wales and announced that the first thing he wanted to do was produce a season of three plays by women. I then wrote the play in about four weeks.

HWD: Mary Kelly *was subsequently produced and directed by Terry Hands, soon after he was appointed to Theatr Clwyd. How closely did you work with Terry Hands on the play's development?*

SE: I'd worked on the play with Deborah Bruce and already had a first draft before Terry Hands took over Theatr Clwyd. It turned out that Terry lived in Muswell Hill which was very close to where I then lived and I went round to his home to talk about the next draft. He talked at great length about the background to the play, about plays, about dramaturgy – a crash course in theatre, really, from someone who knew it inside out. When it came to rewriting he gave some of the most succinct and precise advice I'd ever received. He said something like 'you need two more large scenes and one more character. Read these two plays to show you how it's done.' I was a touch sceptical but when I went away and read the plays (by Peter Barnes and Oscar Wilde) I knew exactly what he meant. After that he hardly changed a word. I couldn't spend more than a week in rehearsals since I'd started writing for television by then and had to write an episode of something in four weeks (and my son was only four months old). I was delighted with what he brought to the play as director. It was an incredibly satisfying experience. Since then I've written almost exclusively for television but I would love to work with Terry Hands again on a play – in some ways it's a shame that new writing and new writers are seen to be synonymous since established writers need this kind of dramaturgical expertise and mentoring, too.

HWD: *An important distinction. But on a wider front do you think there is an audience in Wales for first-time dramatists?*

SE: I don't think audiences exist in the ether, they have to be created. If new plays are never staged then there will never be an audience. Much has to do with the way things are marketed. *Mary Kelly* was put on in the studio at Theatr Clwyd and got over 65% box office for the run. Of course it had the publicity machine of Theatr Clwyd behind it and people travelled a long way to see the play. But the whole point of having a studio should be to showcase new work, subsidised by a more familiar fare in the main house. I think what Wales needs are more venues. There are hundreds of fringe/pub theatres in London. You may not make any money, you may only get half a dozen people in to see it, but theatre is a live physical art, it needs to be acted out in front of an audience and really there's no other way to learn the craft than by doing it. Also these kinds of showcase are sufficiently cheap and low-key to allow people to experiment and fail, another important stage in the process. I'm not saying there shouldn't be well funded professional companies – of course there should. You can only do so much without a budget, but it's about having a vibrant and diverse base; a network of people and venues and ideas is incredibly important.

HWD: *You haven't written for the theatre lately. What accounts for the silence?*

SE: Well, nobody's asked me for one thing. Seriously, working in the theatre is in many ways about being a part of that community. Having a young family and writing for television hasn't left much time to engage with that community. I also need a certain financial security and writing plays full time isn't going to provide that. But I still hanker after doing it, particularly as some of the work I do for television is quite prescriptive; it's only now I appreciate the freedom and control that writing for the theatre gives. Of course I'm constantly working on original projects for film and television and whilst I love developing ideas it can also be deeply frustrating when projects never get off the ground. I have several treatments which I'm now thinking of converting into novels, or maybe even plays!

HWD: *What do you think is the main difference between writing for the theatre and writing for television and film?*

SE: Initially I found writing for theatre far more intimidating than writing for television. I had little or no experience of it and it was a steep learning curve, whereas I'd been immersed in film and TV since childhood. I think in many ways theatre is more rigorous. The ideas have to hold water, and there's no shorthand visually. The theatrical metaphor has to be thought through. You can also create a much less naturalistic world, be more adventurous and take the audience with you. I saw Robert Wilson's *Black Rider* a few months ago and was really thrilled by the theatricality, the weirdness of it. There's no way you could create that sense on TV or on film where there's an assumption of physical reality and you have to create a believable, if surreal, world. But in theatre we all know it's a fiction, a conjuring trick, a metaphor, and it doesn't matter.

HWD: *Would you say that your play* Asleep Under the Dark Earth *is a good example of a theatrical metaphor?*

SE: Yes, it is. The crux of the plot means you have to believe that the two young women at the centre of the play can transform themselves into birds. If it had been a film everyone would have been obsessed with how well this could be done but as it was written for theatre it was less a problem than an opportunity for creativity. The play was part of the BT National Connections scheme which involved productions by youth groups from all over Britain. Twenty-two groups chose to produce *Asleep* and I physically went to see about six, including one in the Shetland Islands; others I saw on video. Seeing so many different versions of your play is an amazing experience for a writer. Although the play was set in Wales it translated easily to parts of Scotland and England. There's a Catholic/Protestant and a rich/poor element but it's not at all simplistic. It asks questions about why we're here and where we come from; it also deals with the rich opportunities given to some and denied others. This was the first time I'd written for young people and I approached it by trying to remember what had obsessed me as a teenager. There was a lot of stuff about desire and spirituality and I wondered how they would tackle it, but of course they did it brilliantly. I loved seeing how each company interpreted the play and also seeing what they got out of it in terms of their experience of theatre. There was also a competitive element to the scheme and only one group could go on to perform each play at The National Theatre; co-incidentally the company chosen to do *Asleep* turned out to be a Welsh company.

HWD: *In writing for the theatre have you found that funding restrictions have limited you to scripting for a maximum of, say, four characters?*

SE: Not really. *Asleep* had a core cast of about six or seven characters but it had a great many group scenes, feasts and weddings, crowd scenes! The world of the play is alive with people. *The Journey of Mary Kelly* also had quite a large cast and it had to recreate street scenes in London. Doing *Little Sister* the actors had to double occasionally which worked well. I have written only one two-hander and it's a very intimate and internal piece but this was the exception.

HWD: *Are you now so much of an East Anglian girl that writing for theatre in Wales is no longer on the agenda?*

SE: I sometimes wonder where I might be if the arts scene had been different in Wales when I started writing. There were many reasons why I moved into London and started writing there, not least because in the late 1980s there seemed to be a flowering of women writing for the theatre, largely inspired by people like Caryl Churchill and Sarah Daniels in this country and Maria Irene Fornes in America. As well as The Women's Theatre Group, the director Jules Wright had started the Women's Playhouse Trust and there was a growing body of women directors, Nancy Meckler and Nancy Duiguid from America, and in London Hettie MacDonald, Katie Mitchell, Jude Kelly, Paulette Randall, Deborah Warner, Annie Castledene, Yvonne Brewster. Although 'women's theatre' received a tiny sliver of the funding cake there was interest from audiences and critics alike. When I attended my first Write On! festival in the mid 1980s at the Sherman in Cardiff I went to a talk by Elaine Morgan about women and theatre practitioners in Wales, and I attended other festivals and workshops. The first piece of work I had produced in Wales was a radio play called *Dancing On the Turf*, broadcast in 1990; it took another six years to get a play on. And no, I didn't do a lot of banging on the Welsh table as it were. As I've already said, theatre is part of a community and maybe this was even more true of Wales then. I wasn't living in that community and I didn't really want to. I was enjoying being in London with all the ethnic and social diversity that involved. Now of course I've moved further east again! I don't rule out moving back to Wales someday, I'm just not ready yet. None of this makes me any less of a Celt; like all exiles your sense of difference is more acute when you live outside your homeland, and no, writing for theatre is not off the agenda.

HWD: *Despite the absence of banging and shouting, you did come to the attention in the early 1990s of Ruth Caleb at BBC Wales. What work did she commission from you?*

SE: Yes, when Ruth ran BBC Wales she was pretty pro-active about seeking out women in the industry. She commissioned my first television play, a half hour piece called *Insect Life* which was broadcast by BBC Wales as part of the Wales Playhouse strand. She also funded my place on a masterclass with Andrew Davies and secured for me a writer's exchange to Los Angeles. This kind of patronage is invaluable when you're starting out. I don't think subsequent drama heads at

BBC Wales were so interested in hunting out female talent. I did one more project for BBC Wales, an adaptation of Brenda Chamberlain's book *Tide Race* for The Slate. The book's about the artist's time on the island Ynys Enlli and is full of the visual detail one might expect from an artist. The last few chapters however were chock full of amazing stories about the islanders; so I had to unpack this and restructure it to provide a narrative for the drama. At the end it was a shame we couldn't include more of her work in the film since she's a very underrated artist.

HWD: *I first met you two years ago at a 'Sorted Symposium' in London arranged by Sally Gritton to celebrate and discuss the plays of Welsh dramatists writing in the medium of English. The irony of it all struck me forcibly on the journey to London. I actually had to travel out of Wales to celebrate the works of our dramatists. Were you yourself aware of that irony?*

SE: I think many of us there that day were aware of it. I think there is a wider cultural issue here, above and beyond being 'a prophet in oné's own country'. Some working-class cultures collude in their own oppression. This is by no means exclusive to Wales, and a culture of anti-intellectualism, of philistinism is allowed to flourish. It doesn't appear to exist in France for example, nor it seems in Norfolk. My children go to a state school in Norwich and when asked by working-class mothers what I do I'm happy to say I'm a writer. The response is always curious and positive – what do you write, etc. I think if I were living in Wales I'd probably censor what I said, otherwise I don't think they'd ever speak to me again. Sadly there's 'Who does he/she think she is' attitude, a certain fear, a defensiveness that infects the culture. It may be an urban/rural thing, I'm not sure.

HWD: *In the field of the arts there may have been a time in Wales where you played down your achievements, though that has never been* *the case, of course, where rugby or 'celebrity' status is concerned. Do you think perhaps, in your case, the Bridgend you knew didn't take kindly to the intellectual interests or artistic ambitions of women in particular?*

SE: I'm not sure it even registered in the general consciousness. When a school friend didn't get the A level grades she desperately wanted, my neighbour's response was 'Well, she's a girl, it's not so important'. Those girls who did do well at school were seen as being hard-working, obedient and by and large tolerated. People assumed that they'd go to college, get married, have a family and that would be that. But the creative life is something else. You need a personal and intellectual vision, something unique to you and a sense that you have the right to express this vision to other people, that's it's worth something. It's not about passing exams, it's about challenging preconceptions and this requires a lot more confidence. The thought that there might be girls who not only wanted to get into college but be writers or artists was anathema, beyond comprehension. Young men had a different problem. They couldn't be thought to be doing anything that wasn't intrinsically macho. I always smile when I hear the expression 'muscular theatre'. I'm not sure what this means except to reassure the writer and the audience that what they're engaged in can in no way be described as actors 'poncing about'.

HWD: *Lastly, could you talk a little about the project you did for the company, Second Stride?*

SE: I'd long admired the work of Second Stride and other companies that integrated music and dance in such an innovative way. I was asked by them to adapt a book by the Israeli writer Aaron Appelfeldt called *Badenheim 1939*. It's a piece about the holocaust by someone who survived it (he actually jumped off one of the transport trains as a child and lived rough in the forests). It's a very delicately written, oblique work about a group of Jewish intellectuals attending a music festival and in total denial about what is happening around them. We all did a great deal of research around the subject and it was while I was doing this research that my parents volunteered the fact that I had two Jewish great-grandmothers, one on each side! The fact that they'd never thought this worth mentioning, or worse, that it was something not to be mentioned surprised me. Then I became fascinated. I've always loved cultural diversity, part of the reason I studied languages at university and spent so much of my life in the unique cultural mix that is London. It's a place where nobody belongs and therefore everyone belongs. However, recently I took some time out on the Isle of Mull in Scotland and felt a strong cultural affinity with the place which took me aback. In some ways I feel it's only now that my sense of cultural identity is beginning to settle and take shape.

The Journey of Mary Kelly by Siân Evans

Lewis Davies

Interview
June 2004

HWD: *You're a Welsh writer with roots firmly embedded in the Neath valley. Your published works celebrate that particular area of South Wales, but they also celebrate the customs and cultures of other countries. You're an author at ease with crossing borders. What prompted this love of travel and this live interest in peoples and places?*

LD: I've always been interested in world geography and in reading widely about other places and continents. After leaving university at twenty-one I didn't want a career job and I decided to opt for travelling and working in other countries and environments. Most of this travelling was funded by myself through certain scams or roofing jobs – call them what you will – and certainly those early travels were crucial to my development as a writer.

During my wanderings I kept diaries because travelling allows you time to think and to record. It also divests you of the ephemera that fixes you in one place and one time. You live cheaply, you read and you observe people. My travel book, *Freeways: A Journey West on Route 66* was the result of one of my wanderings, and it won me in 1994 the John Morgan Award. The patron of the award, which allowed me the freedom to travel across the Western States of America, was Jo Menell. I dedicated *As I was a Boy Fishing* to him because the months I spent in America, courtesy of that award, was of immense importance in terms of my writing. Apart from the opportunity it gave me to meet and talk with a wide variety of people, it also gave me a confidence boost, since it was the first time anybody had given me money to do what I was happiest doing, namely writing. I suppose I was also fortunate to have applied for the award in a year when the committee felt that it was important to support a young writer who sought to extend literal horizons in his writing. I had, prior to writing the travel book, completed my first novel *Work, Sex and Rugby* which is a four-day odyssey through the pubs, bedrooms and building sites of a smouldering town in South Wales. John Morgan himself had written one novel called *A Small Town* and had then decided to abandon novel writing altogether. Alun Richards told me several years ago that the critics had done a demolition job on *A Small Town* and that they'd done their job so thoroughly that they had succeeded in stifling every hope John Morgan had nurtured of writing a second novel.

HWD: *So was it the plight of the migrant worker that drew you to California?*

LD: The impetus was a literary one. What led me to California was John Steinbeck's *The Grapes of Wrath*, that great narrative of a people forced through poverty to go elsewhere.

Also, in his *Of Mice and Men* I'd found another treatment of uprooting. As a dramatist I was also fascinated by the fact that Steinbeck had written *Of Mice and Men* in a deliberately dramatic style with the intention of adapting it into a play which could tour the fields of California. With his wife as collaborator he eventually wrote the play and it was performed by a small profit-share company. What Steinbeck wrote about, however, was the plight of white American migrants from the Midwest who settled in California in the 1930s. What he missed and ignored was the fact that poor, deprived Mexicans, long before the 1930s, had been exploited while working the fields in California.

HWD: *The John Morgan Award was the first substantial funding you received to nurture your writing skills, but the Thatcher government, in the late 1980s, had also encouraged your ambition to become a writer.*

LD: After gaining my first degree I went to Law School for a week and decided it wasn't for me. I wanted to write and felt I had things to say. And so I applied to the Swansea Enterprise Scheme for funding. And, yes, that scheme was set up by Margaret Thatcher's government to get people off the dole. It allowed people to come up with business ideas and helped support them with £40 a week while they got that business into gear. My enterprise idea was well researched, and it was this: I would write short-stories, send them to Faber, get them published and make a fortune! It was a young man's enterprise, but it did give me the impetus to start writing. During that period I wasn't just sitting around in cafes wishfully thinking about being a author. I wrote for several months, delivered pizzas for three months and then caught a train to Morocco. So it was a good year. Later I won an Arts Council of Wales bursary, but that came after five years of development, when I was already a published author.

HWD: *Your work is sympathetically concerned with the underdog and with the deprived. Would I be right to assume that your period as an employee in the social services fed into your work?*

LD: In the late 1980s and early 1990s I was working for the social services in Cardiff. Before then, I had never come into contact with people who had learning difficulties. I had grown up in Neath and had enjoyed a very stable and happy home environment. I'd also benefitted from a good comprehensive school education. 'Mentally handicapped' children in Neath in my time were bussed to another school. They played no part in my life. Meeting and making friends within this world was a new experience for me, and it's no accident that it was during my time with the social services in Cardiff that I wrote my first play. It was at that time too that I decided I wanted to be part of the Cardiff theatre scene that was emerging about then.

HWD: *The late 1980s and early 1990s was, of course, an enabling period for dramatists and theatre artists in Cardiff. How did that ferment influence your work?*

LD: At that time there were two or three companies in Cardiff producing writer-led work. There was Ed Thomas's Y Cwmni and Ian Rowlands's Theatr y Byd. These two dramatists were word-sculptors. At that time, too, Made in Wales were putting on two or three different plays a year and Brith Gof were out in a wet warehouse. At the time, I was writing novels and short-stories that were dialogue-led. To see people on stage, speaking clever dialogue appealed to me, and it was at that time that I decided I wanted to write plays. One of the plays was *Waiting for the Fall*. The play was based on an accident in Blaenant mine where my grandfather was killed when a roof collapsed. It was also a story of family relationships and sibling rivalry. In a way the play was a trial run. It had a decent structure and dialogue, but it was over-written and had too many stage directions. But it was a play I needed to write before moving on to *My Piece of Happiness*.

I sent that play to Made in Wales and to a couple of theatres in London. I received some encouraging responses and a few detailed reports, although I have to say that some of the suggestions for improvements were clearly quite the opposite to what the play needed. Unfortunately, some theatre companies send out new plays to readers who are often themselves frustrated dramatists who have failed to get their plays staged. In their reports, therefore, what you're given is what *they* would do to your play. It's a recipe for failure, and it's not disinterested criticism. I read these unhelpful responses to *My Piece of Happiness* over two years, and wrote several drafts of the play, and all this without once being invited to meet any of the theatre companies who were responding to my work. By the time Made in Wales was imploding into apathy, I'd decided to re-write *My Piece of Happiness* as a novel since I'd had no encouragement and no follow-up from the company. It was good news for theatre in Wales when Jeff Teare took charge of Made in Wales because all at once he injected new life into the company. He was interested in developing multicultural and non-mainstream work and he was the one who saw the possibilities in my play. He and the actor James Westaway, during a workshop of the play, gave me encouragement and support.

HWD: *For the first time, therefore, you were collaborating with a company and an experienced mentor. What exactly, as a dramatist, did you gain from that collaboration?*

LD: What became increasingly clear to me during that collaborative process was that, in order to develop dramatic skills, a dramatist needs to work with a good director and with a group of artists. Theatre is, after all, in essence, a collaborative process. In writing a novel you are very much alone, or if you're with anyone, it's with those fictional characters that exist in your head, or maybe with those novelists who have influenced your imagination and narrative skills. Editors, of course, are also influential in terms of novel writing, but, it's generally two or three months before you hear from an editor, and then it's only a one-to-one response. In a theatre workshop, you get an immediate and live response from several people, and the advice of serious and perceptive actors. A Welsh actor who has, I'm certain, been crucial in developing several good plays during the workshop process is Dorien Thomas. In fact, he has been one of the key figures in Welsh drama, and has certainly not received the credit he deserves. In the 1980s and 1990s he was involved in all the major productions of Y Cwmni and was also central to many of the Made in Wales productions. The dramatist Alan Osborne actually dedicated the *Merthyr Trilogy* to Dorien Thomas. He's an actor with intelligence, insight and energy. As is Russell Gomer. The fact is that without their energy and input we wouldn't have had the stage-powerful performances and plays we enjoyed in the 1990s.

One of the memorable things Jeff Teare told me was that a dramatist, ideally, should have an idea of the kind of actor/actors for whom he's writing the roles, because then the script can be developed with a view to drawing on the particular actor's strength. That's another example of the kind of collaboration that theatre allows the dramatist.

HWD: *Those workshops also afforded you entry into an extended theatre family, and you were invited by Made in Wales to become tour manager of Roger Williams's play* Gulp.

LD: Jeff Teare and Rebecca Gould of Made in Wales were excellent at developing the sense of camaraderie between writers, directors, actors, designers and stage-managers. During the tour of Roger's play *Gulp* I was the guy driving the van to the Dublin Festival. As a writer you do need that energizing involvement with fellow-writers and theatre artists. Unfortunately, that kind of involvement isn't available to me now. I live in Aberteifi, which isn't exactly a theatrical centre. Theatr Mwldan is there, of course, so I get to see touring companies. But I feel that there is less opportunity now for me to be involved intimately with the process of theatre.

Gary Owen is one example these days of a dramatist who is involved on a regular basis with a theatre company. In the early and mid 1990s there indeed existed what you've called a theatre 'ferment' in Cardiff because there was a 'mass' there, not only of theatre practitioners but also of audiences eager to attend performances of new writing. The artists involved with those companies have now dispersed – many of them to sparsely-populated West Wales. Ian Rowlands lives in Carmarthen and Dic Edwards in Aberaeron. It seems to me that what is missing now is vigorous audience response, a response that can have a key influence on a dramatist's artistic development.

I myself am still working in the theatre, but at a distance. This summer I'm taking my show *Football* to the Edinburgh Festival, and last year I was lucky enough to be able to work with Theatr y Byd on my play *Sex and Power at the Beau Rivage*. But to be alive to theatre, you've got to go where it's happening and I'm not convinced that it's happening in Wales at the moment. I've read a couple of reviews recently that indicate that something is taking place and that Chapter and the Sherman in Cardiff have featured forty-minute slots for the work of new writers. I assume therefore that somebody is doing something, but the hard fact is that you can do work on limited money only for a limited time. Think for example of Ed Thomas and Ian Rowlands. Those two when they started to write put career, income and house on the line in order to get their plays on stage. They couldn't be expected to do that indefinitely. Ed moved on to television and film and Ian to directing.

HWD: *Where do you stand in that still ongoing 'national theatre debate'. Would an English-medium national theatre company create once again that all-important critical mass that existed in the 1980s and 1990s?*

LD: What I'd like to see in Wales is something akin to the Scottish Traverse model where you get a producing house that makes available to audiences a wide range of texts and where new writing has a proper home. That producing house needs to be in our capital city. What we mustn't have in Cardiff is yet another theatre that produces just English, European or American classical texts. What we need is the kind of theatre that would produce a wonderfully new production of one of Alan Osborne's plays, say *Bull, Rock and Nut*. Now that kind of production would certainly draw audiences.

The sad thing is that over the last ten years the major recipients of public drama funding have done hardly anything to encourage Welsh drama or writing. We've seen staging of Roald Dahl's books, adaptations of Dickens and popular musical theatre. But where's the reinterpretation of, for example, *East from the Gantry*, *Love in Plastic* or *In Sunshine and in Shadow*? Despite the fact that these plays exist in published form, directors have ignored them.

HWD: *I myself would travel a considerable distance to see a reinterpretation of one of the plays you've mentioned, and I agree with you that you'd be likely to get full houses at all the performances. Why, therefore, have directors ignored these plays?*

LD: 'New writing and Welsh plays in English don't attract audiences' – so the argument goes. Anyway, if that's the argument why doesn't a director, say Terry Hands, produce and tour a Frank Vickery play? That would get him his audience, especially if he toured South Wales. Frank Vickery has important things to say about the South Walian condition, and he's humorous and highly entertaining. His is good theatre and it draws the crowds.

HWD: *Nearly all the playwrights in this present volume are based in South Wales. What do you think accounts for that?*

LD: Again it's a question of a critical mass and the density of the population of the South Wales valleys. That dense population was bound to produce dramatists as well as poets and novelists. There is also the fact that this area was strongly socialist. The political and social ferment in South Wales was bound to produce and stimulate dramatists who, naturally, gravitated towards Cardiff.

HWD: *Do you think Cardiff, Wales's capital city, has come of age? Were you surprised that it failed in its bid to become a 'Culture Capital'?*

LD: No, it hasn't come of age, and no, I wasn't surprised that it wasn't nominated Capital of Culture. It hasn't got the depth and range of artistic work that is being produced in other metropolitan cities. Also, it hasn't got a producing theatre of any note. The Millennium Centre is due to open this year, and it's of the utmost importance that it's seen as a distinctly Welsh centre rather than a London adjunct where we import the equivalent of the FA cup now and then to draw people in. I assume, however, that it will take a huge, spectacular event to draw people from Anglesey, Bangor or Aberystwyth for a night out in the Millennium Centre.

HWD: *You've written that, for you, being Welsh is 'a state of mind, as well as a geographic reality'. What did you mean by that?*

LD: I grew up in Neath which is very consciously a Welsh place, and therefore I couldn't get away from the fact that Welshness was part me. Neath and Wales also defined who and what I was. So Welshness is coming from Neath and having my great-grandfather's farm sitting up there on the mountain above the town. It's a question of roots and continuity. My father's first language was Welsh and my children now speak it. But there's a gap in the continuum, and at home and in school my first language was English. The education system in Neath at that time didn't actively seek to promote the Welsh language. I did, however, hear it spoken by members of my family and I well remember how my grandmother would expertly use Welsh and English within the same sentence.

When I'm abroad I'm particularly aware of my nationality and my sense of being Welsh is considerably heightened. As I've said before, when I'm travelling I always feel homesick. Wales is that 'home'.

HWD: *You spent several weeks in the south of France working on the script of your play* Sex and Power at the Beau Rivage, *a play about the visit of Rhys Davies, the novelist and short-story writer, to Frieda and D H Lawrence's home on the Beau Rivage in the 1920s. What prompted you to write that play?*

LD: I'd always wanted to set a play of mine in the 1920s since I live imaginatively in that period anyway. And I'd always wanted to write about Lawrence. I've read almost everything he's written and in my travels around the world I always seem to be visiting places connected with Lawrence. There was so much drama in his life. Some time ago I'd started a play which was set in Taos where Lawrence's grave is. I wrote about fifty pages, then abandoned the play. It was around that time that Chris Morgan, director of Theatr y Byd, asked me if I'd be interested in writing a play, set in the South of France, about the meeting between the Lawrences and Rhys Davies. Davies had published one book; Lawrence had read and liked it, and through a mutual connection invited the Welshman, who was living in Nice at the time, to come and stay as his guest at the Beau Rivage. Rhys, of course, jumped at the chance.

I'd recently won the Rhys Davies Award and I, of course, jumped at the chance. While I was writing the play I too felt like a guest at the Beau Rivage. How could I fail to write on a terrace overlooking the Mediterranean? The play toured in 2003. I had an encouraging critical feedback from writers, and I'm told it was a performance from which people went away at the end of the night feeling that they'd been in the company of Rhys Davies, D H Lawrence and Frieda.

HWD: *You're at the moment fine-tuning* Football, *the play you'll be taking to Edinburgh this summer. What's it about?*

LD: *Football* has emerged as a forty-minute, quickfire piece. It could be called a comedy, but my partner Gill said she didn't laugh at any of it. The plot is that England has won the world cup and David Beckham's jersey has been sold for €137,000 at auction as a piece of art. When the play opens, three friends meet for dinner; two want sex and the other has just bought Beckham's shirt and wants it exhibited in art galleries. During the play the €137,000 shirt is replaced by another identical one and its owner is none the wiser. The play asks the questions, 'What is art?' and 'what is the value of celebrity?' Jeff Teare will direct it and it will be produced by Rebecca Gould in association with Made in Wales, Caribou House and Tinderbox. It's always been my ambition to take a play of mine to Edinburgh. It's an invigorating festival because of its eclecticism and the opportunity it gives you to meet and discuss theatre with other artists.

HWD: *Writing of course is only one of your interests. Would you enjoy the luxury of being a full-time writer?*

LD: No, there are too many other interesting things to do. Publishing is one of them. Fishing is another. In my time I've been a full-time creative writer and then a full-time creative roofer. Early on I was lucky that my father, who is a builder, could offer work while I was 'resting'. I've been happy cutting between different employments and maintaining my independence. Jonathan Raban has emphasised the importance to a writer of diversifying, and that advice had in turn been given to him by Malcolm Bradbury. If you maintain several sources of income, you're not beholden to any one of them in a major way.

HWD: *One of those sources of income is Parthian. What compelled you to establish the press in the first instance?*

LD: My initial aim was to set up a press so that my own work would see the light of day. At the time there was only one fiction house in Wales and its list was restricted, and London publishers weren't interested in Welsh contemporary products as they are now. I've been a front man and a publicity officer for Parthian but it has been, and remains, a collaborative effort. It's a publishing house with its own stamp, its own brand. It offers an opportunity for new and different voices to be heard, including the voice of the dramatist.

HWD: *Parthian has always been committed to publishing plays and to marketing them. Seren, unfortunately, decided to abandon our playwrights, and it's to Parthian's credit that the press has continued to support dramatists. When the press was established did you see the publication of plays as part of its remit?*

LD: Yes I did, because I was myself involved in theatre and a frequenter of plays. I'd also heard wonderful things about Alan Osborne's work, although I hadn't had the opportunity to see any of it. I wanted to read the plays and give them an opportunity for a re-run. I soon discovered that publishing them wouldn't be an easy matter since the plays existed in different forms in different places. Alan himself didn't have all the manuscripts so it was a rescue-operation from the start. Dorien Thomas's help was crucial in editing the work and analysing it in a perceptive essay. Gilly Adams, who had been a champion of Alan's work, wrote the introduction. The volume became a retrospective of Alan's various talents.

It's a fact, of course, that the print-run of plays is small because the potential market is limited and the officers of the Welsh Joint Education Committee don't seem to be aware of the existence or the range of published plays by English-medium dramatists in Wales. Why, for example, aren't pupils in Merthyr given the opportunity to study Alan Osborne's plays? Why not put Ed Thomas's plays on the A Level syllabus for young people in Cardiff or South Wales?

Publications of plays are of course 'add-ons' because, naturally, where the play really comes to life is in the theatre. But published plays can and do encourage audiences to attend performances. I remember, many years ago, buying a copy of *Death of a Salesman* from a bookstore in Sri Lanka, and after reading it I was determined to see a production of Miller's play. Published plays can also prompt re-runs. I'm pleased that Parthian a few years ago published Mark Jenkins's *Playing Burton*, a monologue that by now has won world-wide acclaim, and rightly so. Parthian will, in a few months, be publishing a volume of Mark Jenkins's plays. The press has also published the work of Welsh women dramatists. Indeed *One Woman, One Voice*, a collection of monologues by Lucinda Coxon, Lucy Gough, Gwenno Dafydd, Christine Watkins and Sharon Morgan, a collection you chose, edited and introduced for Parthian, is our best selling volume of plays. It sold out extremely quickly and is now being reprinted. It's a case of recognizing excellence and identifying and filling an important gap in the market.

HWD: *You are now working on yet another play, this time a commissioned piece for Hijinx, a company that tours to a wide variety of venues and plays to different kinds of audiences. How does that fact determine how and what you write?*

LD: That fact is of crucial importance. Within the Hijinx remit a writer has to be quite strict about the kind of material he presents to audiences. There can be no swearing, no overt sexual references, and very little that's political. So this is a real challenge for me since what I'm writing is a political play about a sexual relationship between three modern political figures! It's a modern take on the legend of King Arthur, with Tony Blair, probably, as Arthur.

It's excellent to be working with Hijinx and with Chris Morgan, the director. He's interested in the relationships within the play and I'm interested in the politics. That's a natural interest of mine since I grew up in a home where political issues, were analysed and discussed. I learned early on to value the free state education I enjoyed and I appreciated too the fairness that is inherent in the idea of socialism. That early radical background is part of my identity as a Welshman.

HWD: *Would you say that theatre has an important part to play in establishing also a nation's individual identity?*

LD: Without a vibrant and developing theatre culture it's very difficult to see how a country can itself be vibrant and developing. Wales should have the opportunity to see itself reflected and interpreted through performances of plays by indigenous dramatists. A healthy nation needs to see itself on the stage. We desperately need to be engaged by our theatre.

Lewis Davies

Spinning the Round Table by Lewis Davies

Roger Williams

**Interview
July 2004**

HWD: *Your career as a dramatist began early. At the age of fifteen you were runner-up in a playwriting competition at the 1990 Drefach Urdd National Eisteddfod for your Welsh-language play* Wedi'r Bom. *Were you writing plays in both languages during that period?*

RW: Yes I was. I was a pupil at Queen Elizabeth Cambria Secondary School in Carmarthen, a school which was a very enabling one in terms of theatre. I remember Jane Thomas, a most encouraging teacher setting the class an assignment that greatly appealed to me. She asked us to script a scene for the stage, and as I was a very conscientious pupil, I submitted my work the following week. No one else submitted a scene. After reading my effort Jane Thomas told me, 'You should write more.' I did, and at the age of fourteen

I was writing several short plays which she would comment on. She was a crucial support inasmuch as she encouraged me above all else to persevere. I also bombarded my Welsh teacher with short little pieces and it was she who advised me to submit *Wedi'r Bom* to the Urdd National Eisteddfod. I think my ambition to become a dramatist started there. My first contact with professional theatre also occurred while I was at school. My teacher submitted some of my work to Made in Wales, and Gilly Adams chose the monologue *The Star Stalker* for a reading by the actor Rhodri Huw as part of an evening showcasing the work of young writers.

HWD: *From Carmarthen you went to the University of Warwick to study American Literature. What prompted you to gravitate towards that particular degree course?*

RW: One of my A Level subjects was drama, and Edward Albee's *Who's Afraid of Virginia Woolf?* was on the syllabus. That play made a deep impression on me and made me want to know more about American culture and literature. That A Level Drama course, and a close study of Albee's dramatic skills, were crucially influential in my desire to write for the theatre and in my development as a dramatist.

HWD: *Did you pursue your career as a writer at Warwick?*

RW: While I was at university I was fortunate to receive my first professional commission. After the reading of *The Star Stalker*, Made in Wales presented another play of mine, entitled *Touched*, at one of their Write On! festivals. Phil Clark of the Sherman had seen these plays and he invited me in the early 1990s to participate in a project called 'A Generation Arises'. This was an exciting collaboration between seven or eight writers. Subsequently Phil Clark invited me to submit my work for the Sherman lunchtime plays programme. So, yes, while I was at university, I was already writing professionally.

HWD: *Did that early success mean that, after you graduated, playwriting was the only career you contemplated?*

RW: I graduated when I was twenty and, at the time, I was very naïve about possible careers. I suppose I could have trained as a teacher. I'd also done a great deal of work with the campus radio station, and I contemplated going into the production side of broadcasting. But, as fate would have it, Alison Hindell of BBC Wales invited me to attend a course on writing for the radio at Tŷ Newydd, Llanystumdwy. The course was run by Alison and by Jeremy Mortimer who used to be a producer with Radio 4. Writers from the different BBC regions and nations attended the course, and it provided me with a wonderful opportunity to appreciate the very specific skills that were required of a radio dramatist. It was a happy accident that at Tŷ Newydd I started writing a comedy, and that Alison Hindell at the time needed another comedy for a season of six live radio plays she was planning to present at the Sherman. And so, in the August after I graduated I was commissioned to complete the comedy for the Sherman programme. In my naivety I assumed that this was the regular way you got a commission. You met people and it followed that you were given work. Because I was young and naïve I also used to telephone people about work prospects. I remember ringing Bethan Jones of Dalier Sylw requesting a meeting, and also Jeff Teare when he arrived at Made in Wales to ask if I could send him some of my ideas for plays. These are things I wouldn't be happy to do now because I am aware that there are various procedures that must be followed. I now have an agent who represents me. Ten years ago I would short-cut by picking up the phone.

HWD: *Maybe your direct approach to directors wasn't so naïve after all. It certainly got results.*

RW: It did, and the feedback from Bethan Jones and Jeff Teare encouraged me to continue to write, but still, looking back at that direct approach makes me feel slightly embarrassed. However, it is a fact that the advice I received then shaped my career as a dramatist.

HWD: *And the rapport, as a dramatist, you have with Lewis Davies of Parthian has guaranteed that your plays have the support of a publisher who is particularly committed to publishing plays by Welsh writers.*

RW: I've been very fortunate that Lewis Davies has taken an interest in my plays. He is himself of course a professional dramatist, and his enthusiasm and determination to publish Welsh plays in English has contributed enormously in the past few years to assuring Welsh dramatists that at least one press in Wales recognizes the importance of the work they do. When a dramatist writes a play, I think I'm right in saying that they forget about publication. For me, at least, the *performance* is the thing. Why else would I write a play? I want to see it staged. But a performance, however imaginative and powerful it is, is of its very nature ephemeral. For a play to be re-performed and re-interpreted by directors and actors it needs to be in published form. It seems that Parthian is the only press in Wales now that has the will to publish English-language plays on a regular basis.

HWD: *It's not only the problem of publication in the first place, but also the problem of marketing, within and outside Wales. How often, for instance, do we see plays from Wales on sale in the National Theatre bookshop on the South Bank? Or, more to the point, in the bookstore chains in Wales? We've established that having a play published in Wales is extremely difficult. How easy, then, is it to have a play performed?*

RW: Unless the play is a direct commission from a company with an interest in producing it, it is more or less impossible

348

to have it produced in Wales. This is an extremely distressing situation for dramatists. As I said earlier, you write a play to be performed. Why else would you write it? Because the theatre situation in Wales at the moment is not an enabling one, it's not surprising that many writers have already stopped writing for the medium.

HWD: *How in your opinion should our dramatists be encouraged and fostered?*

RW: Many people believe that the Welsh Assembly Government should be persuaded to release more money for this purpose. I think there's a simpler solution. Artistic directors in Wales should be *required* to stage work by Welsh writers. That isn't happening at the moment in English-language theatre. It's certainly happening in the Welsh language, because artistic directors understand the culture from the inside as it were, and they have a deep-seated interest in what the writers have to say about the society and country in which we live. This may be a generalisation, but many of the directors who work in the English language in Wales have little or no interest in what the writers of Wales have to say. The first step is to insist, as a condition of funding, that those artistic directors produce Welsh works. I repeat that I believe the Arts Council of Wales should demand clearly that substantial funding be ring-fenced for the performance of works by Welsh dramatists. After all, Assembly and Arts Council money is public money. It's there to support the culture and the writers and artists of Wales. The work of our dramatists should be seen on those very stages that were built, and are supported, with public money.

HWD: *I myself have heard the director of a funded theatre company argue that there is no audience for new Welsh writing.*

RW: I would say to that director, 'Prove it.' I will not accept the 'no-audience' argument as an excuse. Audiences have to be fostered, and that should be one of the central aims of any self-respecting theatre company. I'm puzzled by the fact that some directors in Wales focus on the works of other cultures. They could of course counter by saying that the works of other cultures are infinitely better than works from Wales. But that isn't being specifically said. In the end it all comes down to a will and a desire to produce work from Wales. If you want to produce a work by a first-time writer from, say, Haverfordwest, you'll do it because you are the boss, the gatekeeper of a theatre company. You have access to your company's budget and you are the decision-maker. Many of our artistic directors at the moment aren't producing plays by writers from Wales because they simply don't want to. And they don't want to because they have no knowledge of, and no sympathy towards, the culture of Wales. They do not perceive themselves as belonging to Wales and its culture despite the fact that they carve out careers for themselves here in Welsh theatre. There are, of course, exceptions to the rule. I'm thinking of Jeff Teare, an Englishman with a Welsh heritage. He made it his business to commission plays from Welsh writers. But it makes me terribly angry, and I cannot forgive artistic directors who are spending Welsh public money on producing, almost exclusively, plays by dramatists who belong to other cultures.

HWD: *You mentioned there the responsibility of a company to appeal to and foster new audiences. Have you yourself had the sense and satisfaction of attracting to the theatre people who would not normally attend a performance?*

RW: Yes, I have. My play *Gulp*, produced by Made in Wales in Chapter Arts Centre Cardiff in 1997 certainly pulled in new audiences. I'm not saying that *Gulp* is a great play; indeed it's very naïve in many ways. I was only twenty-two when I wrote it. It was a new play that concerned itself with a minority subject and with an appeal to a largely gay audience. Yet the performances were sold out.

HWD: *What was* Gulp *about?*

RW: It's about five young people sharing a Cardiff flat. A gay man lives with his best friend who is a woman. On a very simple level the play is a love story. But it also deals with the fear among the gay community of being infected with HIV. It confronts the way twenty-year-olds in Cardiff, who are relishing their youth in the city, live with the fear of infection and death. *Gulp* attracted an audience who either had not been near a theatre before or hadn't been near a theatre for years. Made in Wales, in its last years, was adept at identifying and attracting new audiences to swell the company's core following. I remember walking round clubs and pubs in Cardiff handing out flyers to people I knew would enjoy the play, because the play was about them. By the end, we were turning people away. We can have full houses for new writing, but identifying the audience needs a great deal of dedication and hard work.

HWD: *You have, of course, had the opportunity of working in countries that do appreciate their indigenous writers. It must be disheartening to return to a Wales that does not have a clear policy for fostering its own writers.*

RW: It's been an eye-opener and a wonderfully energizing experience to work with other theatre cultures. In 1998-99 I was Writer in Residence with the Sydney Theatre Company and the Australian National Playwrights' Centre. The Sydney Theatre Company is seen as the State Theatre of New South Wales and the unofficial National Theatre Company of Australia. On its main stage it produces ten to twelve performances a year, 50% of which are plays by

Australian writers, because the funding bodies insist that it does so. If they fail to produce a substantial number of plays by indigenous writers, funding will be withheld or reduced. This is because the company itself and the funding bodies have the will to create and develop a distinctive Australian voice and theatre culture. In Sydney classic English, European and American texts are there onstage alongside new Australian works, and these Australian plays pull in enthusiastic audiences.

HWD: *In view of the lack of enthusiasm and financial support for new writing in Wales these past years what has prompted you to continue to write plays when so many other writers have turned their backs on the theatre?*

RW: When I started as a schoolboy to come into contact with professional theatre in Wales, there was far more goodwill towards new writing. There was then at that time a desire to create a canon of Welsh texts in English. That desire isn't there anymore. When I started on my writing career there was the enabling Made in Wales and there was Phil Clark at the Sherman commissioning and supporting writers. In time, it will be realized how influential Phil's input has been to the development of Welsh writers. I'm thinking specifically of the HTV Sherman plays and the BBC Sherman radio plays. Indeed that particular theatre has been a catalyst for Welsh writers because it gave them their first break. We no longer, for a variety of reasons, have those wonderful initiatives or the ferment in the field of new writing which I experienced when I started. What killed all this good work was the 1999 Arts Council drama strategy. I don't think, on the writing side, that we have ever recovered from that blow. After 1999 uncertainty poisoned the theatre scene in Wales, with companies having no idea whether they'd still be in existence in twelve months' time. The commissioning of new writers stopped altogether. Indeed, the Arts Council specifically ordered Made in Wales to stop commissioning well before officially informing the Company that its funding would cease. At that time, then, a great many companies lost contact with writers and we've never got back to where we were before that damaging drama strategy.

HWD: *Most Welsh-language companies, however, maintained the close contact they had with writers, and the National Eisteddfod also remained loyal to its commissioning practice.*

RW: Welsh-language theatre has a more supportive culture, and I decided some time ago that in the immediate future I would be writing for the theatre only through the medium of Welsh. It is too frustrating to find, time and again, that the plays I write in English cannot find a stage here in Wales. I've written a play in English entitled *Lingua* which I believe is my best play yet. It's been read in London, New Zealand and New York but I cannot find a producer for it here in Wales, and that is demoralizing. I believe in this play. It has relevance to Wales and beyond. Because the situation here with regard to new writing is so desperate I have now also decided to concentrate on my work for radio and television. I write for the theatre only when there is something I desperately want to say. I'm lucky because I feel comfortable with all three mediums. I relish the flexibility of radio. It allows the writer to jump in and out of worlds very quickly, and its elasticity allows you to travel rapidly from the jungle to New York city – and very cheaply too. In another sense radio is the most alien medium to me as a writer because I have to dispense with the visual. So much of television work on the other hand is involved with imagining what a particular person looks like in place and time and in imagining how the final picture will appear. I particularly enjoy theatre because it allows me the picture and the word. Language is very important to me and my plays tend to be dialogue-heavy. It's no accident that I chose the title *Lingua* for one of my plays.

HWD: *You mention* Lingua*'s relevance to Wales. What is the play about?*

RW: It's about four linguists – from America, Scotland, aboriginal Australia and Polynesia. The four come to Cardiff to discuss the plight of endangered languages. There is a pot of money on offer to support the continuance and growth of one of those languages, and the characters have to argue the case for the preservation of the particular language they represent.

HWD: *Which one wins in the end?*

RW: You'll have to wait and see. It's certainly a play that received an enthusiastic response when it was read by the Lark Theatre Company in New York in 2003 and by the audience at the New Zealand International Theatre Festival in Wellington in 2004. *Lingua* is essentially a play of ideas, and New York audiences are hungry for such plays at the moment. Many of the themes are about globalisation and how it erodes minority languages. The play gained support in New Zealand because of the debate there concerning the Maori language. White New Zealanders, the *pakeha*, see the continuance of Maori as a threat to unity.

HWD: *In the new millennium your plays have had an increasingly international appeal. Would you say that there is a definite pattern of development in your work in that sense?*

RW: There is. My early works, *Gulp* and *Saturday Night Forever* are about sexuality and what it means to be gay in Wales. I didn't know of any play that dealt with this subject and, at the time, this was what I needed to write about. I've now said all I have to say about that. It was while I was a writer in residence in Sydney that I realised I had other topics and arguments to present on stage. In Sydney I gained international perspectives on Wales. There I was, thousands of miles from home, and having conversations with people who had no idea where Wales was on a map. That led me to write *Killing Kangaroos*, a play which deals with the way we perceive ourselves in Wales and also the way we perceive Australians. I used soap opera techniques precisely because it is from soap operas that we get our mistaken and over-generalised idea of Australia. There has been an international element in all my other recent plays, either in subject matter or through collaboration with artists from other cultures.

HWD: *You saw yourself in the 1990s as first a gay writer, and secondly a Welsh writer. How do you see yourself now?*

RW: Now I see myself first as a bilingual Welsh writer who is also a gay writer. This year I was at an event in the Hay-on-Wye festival where John Sam Jones, the short-story writer, was telling the audience that he too sees himself first and foremost as a Welsh writer and secondly as a gay writer. Wales is inherently homophobic with a macho culture: one thinks of rugby, heavy industries, male voice choirs and men drinking together down the pub. But as I mentioned earlier, I have other subjects that I need to address now other than sexuality.

HWD: *You are one of the very few bilingual writers we have in Wales. Do you tend to deal with very different topics as between your Welsh-language and English-language plays?*

RW: This is the way I work. I start with an idea for a play, and, if it's not a commissioned piece, I've got to decide which language I'm going to use. On a couple of occasions I've written in both Welsh and English. Take *Calon Lân* which I wrote for Made in Wales and the Royal Welsh College of Music and Drama and which was produced at St Fagans. That play started in Welsh but ended in English.

There are certain topics such as issues concerning the Welsh language and its culture which I'm more comfortable to deal with in Welsh. In those plays I specifically address a Welsh-speaking audience. It is of prime importance that you acknowledge the nature of your audience. In this view I was influenced by Jeff Teare, who, after working for so many years with Stratford East, realised that to be successful, a writer had to answer two questions, 'For whom are you writing this play?' and 'Why are you writing this play?' I think of my own answers to these questions consciously throughout the period of writing. It comes back to the point that playwrights write for the purpose of having their plays performed, and during a performance an audience has to be entertained.

HWD: *Most of your plays are comedies. Is that because you rate the entertainment factor highly?*

RW: I think its extremely important. If you're asking people to hand over £8 to sit and watch your play, I can't imagine why you shouldn't want to entertain them. And by 'entertain' of course, I don't mean a laugh a minute. What we need to do is to stimulate an audience. Ideally, the audience should leave the theatre believing that they have taken something away with them, whether it be entertainment, intellectual stimulus or just a sense that they are pleased with what they have seen. Not that you can please everybody, of course. I've had interesting and varied responses from audiences. Take *Gulp*. We did three or four British sign-language performances of that play during the first and second run. That was a happy accident. An employee at Chapter knew someone who had partial hearing, who interpreted and was gay. He brought Cardiff's gay, deaf community with him. It's one thing being Welsh and gay; it's quite a different thing to be Welsh, gay and deaf. Word got round about the interpreted performances and people were travelling from as far away as Swindon and

Birmingham to see the play. Something that affected me greatly was the effect *Gulp* had on the audience. I was told that after the run there had been a rush for HIV tests by Cardiff's gay community who for the first time understood the issue.

HWD: *During this interview you've referred to 'public money'. Public money for theatre comes of course from the Welsh Assembly Government which has its own political agenda. Recently it has emphasised the importance of theatre for Young People and Community Theatre. Do you think that prioritising particular kinds of theatre is inimical to the overall good health of theatre in Wales?*

RW: All kinds of theatre can co-exist and flourish. I seriously dislike the kind of snobbery that goes hand in hand with statements such as, 'Oh, that play is only for young people and the community.' The only experience I've had of working with the community was in Aberdare where *Love in Aberdare* was commissioned by Made in Wales and RCT Youth Theatre. There I witnessed the power and ability of theatre to bring people together to enjoy working on a project. I was an incomer to that community so I don't know if it had a regenerative effect. I enjoyed writing for young people too when I worked for Made in Wales and Sherman Theatre Company. When I write for young people I like to give the play a happy ending. The resolution of a play is tremendously important for a young audience who need to feel that they've been on a journey with a very definite beginning and a satisfactory ending. For me writing for the theatre is a job, and I would hugely enjoy a commission to write a play for young people. But I do realize also the importance of having in Wales a successful, large professional theatre. There is a professional theatre here of course and millions of pounds are poured annually into funding that theatre. But as I say, Welsh playwrights are generally not welcome there.

HWD: *The Welsh-language National Theatre Company is a different matter, and a foretaste of its programme shows that the work of Welsh-language dramatists will be celebrated there.*

RW: I would love the opportunity to work with the company. I've written one large-stage play, and I enjoyed the large canvas which the seven-character *Killing Kangaroos* allowed me. I don't have any strong opinions about the fact that it is designated a 'national' company. It will stand or fall by the quality of its product, not by its 'national' status. I am very pleased that, as part of its remit, it will be commissioning new writing, and I hope it will make the works a central part of its repertoire. But, of course, it's early days yet.

Frank Vickery

Interview
November 2004

HWD: *To date you have written over thirty plays, many of which have been published by Samuel French. These plays are extremely popular with amateur companies all over Britain, and some have won prestigious awards. How early did this interest in, and aptitude for, playwriting begin?*

FV: I first started writing in junior school. For some unexplained reason (I hadn't seen a playscript at that point) my writing always took the form of dialogue. It was never descriptive or novelish. I always wrote what came out of people's mouths. At the age of fourteen I joined the local boys-club and it was there that I saw a playscript for the first time. The boys-club led to youth-club, and eventually I joined an adult drama group. I was more interested in acting at that time but I was still writing, for myself mainly. It wasn't until 1978, when I was asked if I had anything a church group could produce, that I showed them my comedy *After I'm Gone*. When they were reading it they fell about laughing. They produced it and ended up winning the Howard de Walden Trophy for the Best One Act Play in Great Britain in 1978. For me, that is where it all began.

It was after this 1978 success that I went on to form The Parc and Dare Theatre Company at Treorchy with Brian Meadows. It was specifically for this company that I learned the craft of playwriting. In the early years I was also encouraged by my friend Einon Evans, himself a veteran Valleys playwright. My association with the Parc and Dare Theatre Company lasted for over fifteen years during which time the company became one of the best, if not *the* best in the country. Writing for the company led to other commissions including writing for the Sherman and for radio and television. One of the most prestigious things the Parc and Dare Theatre Company did was to take my plays to the London West End, once a year. It was a huge challenge for everyone and our efforts were recognized when we were given a London Weekend Television Plays on Stage Award for being the most prestigious company in 1993.

HWD: *You have been described as 'the Welsh Alan Ayckbourn.' What relationship do you yourself see between your work and Ayckbourn's?*

FV: I have been described many times by many people as 'the Welsh Alan Ayckbourn'. The first time this was said was by an adjudicator at the Welsh Finals of the Drama Association of Wales Competition held at the Sherman in Cardiff. The name of the person now escapes me but he was editor of the *Sunday Times* at the time. He said, before awarding my production first prize, that I reminded him of Alan Ayckbourn mainly because I run my own small theatre company, similar to the one Ayckbourn ran in Scarborough.

This I think was subsequently taken out of context by many people who then likened Ayckbourn's work to mine. I think it's fair and pretty accurate to say that his work differs vastly from my work. He writes about and for the middle classes and I undoubtedly write for and about the working-class of Wales – people who wouldn't under most circumstances ever be seen in a theatre. This is a fact I am particularly proud of.

HWD: *In a Kaleidoscope broadcast on BBC4 in 1994 it was reported that 'Vickery... has a relationship with his audiences that Ayckbourn, Godber, Russell or Bleasedale might envy.' What is the nature of that relationship?*

FV: The nature of my relationship with my audiences is identification. I hold up characters and situations that most people can identify with. It's just like showing a mirror to the audience, and consequently this is a good part of the reason they turn out to see my work in large numbers. I make them forget they are sitting with hundreds of other people, and help them feel the characters are talking for them personally. In the Kaleidoscope broadcast for BBC4, the producer decided to chat with some of the audience as they were coming out of the theatre at the end of the play. One woman was approached to say something about the play she had just seen, and she said in a wonderfully low and rich Valleys accent, 'Oh it was marvellous, absolutely marvellous. It was just like listening to people in their front room'. What more can I ask from my audience than that!

HWD: *How would you describe the 'essence' of a Frank Vickery play?*

FV: That's a difficult one. I'd have to mention 'identification' again. My plays contain characters and situations that are immediately identifiable. Comedy too must play a part. Even my most serious plays have comedy in them, and the challenge for me as a writer is to deal with a highly serious subject and find a way of playing it through humour. I am also interested in writing about taboo subjects such as death, infidelity, homosexuality and possessiveness. My intention is to bring onto the public stage subjects that are usually discussed in private. But I've always written about taboo subjects with humour.

HWD: *Would you say that what we encounter in many of your plays are characters who laugh in the face of adversity?*

FV: Laughing in the face of adversity? I suppose the play that does that best is *A Kiss on the Bottom* which is a very funny play set in a cancer ward of a hospital. Not a place for a comedy one would think, but in fact it's not the place that's important in the play, but the people that inhabit it. Over and above the usual challenges of writing comedy, with *A Kiss on the Bottom* I deliberately set myself some difficult obstacles, but I knew from the beginning that it was a challenge I would enjoy overcoming. The word 'cancer' is never mentioned, but I felt I had to make it pretty clear from the beginning where we were and what illness the characters were suffering from. But at the same time I had to make the audience feel comfortable and not let them lose their trust in me. My technique is to make them laugh and make them laugh as early as possible. And so I had to make the first line as funny as I could. If I could capture the audience with that, then I'd be on my way.

There is one moment in this play of which I'm particularly proud. Grace, one of the characters, has been in hospital for a long time and her demise is pretty near. Earlier on in the play a wedding photograph had been taken in the ward and Grace was one of the persons in the group. When Bev, one of the nurses, brings the developed photographs to the ward, all the patients crowd round to have a look. Grace asks who one particular person is, but the rest are so excited they don't hear the question. Grace asks again and this time they all realise that the illness has taken such a toll on Grace's appearance that she doesn't recognize herself in the photograph. The other characters react by exchanging looks. The audience's empathy at this moment is almost tangible. To punctuate the moment I place it at the end of a scene. The lights fade to black-out and the audience are left momentarily in a very emotional state. It's not comedy, it's not pathos but a mixture of the two. It's pure magic, pure theatre. Moments like that highlight my stagecraft.

HWD: *After* A Kiss on the Bottom *I understand that many people asked you to write 'a bloody good laugh again'. Did you oblige?*

FV: I don't usually listen to the taste of my audience. If I were to listen to them they'd restrict me and not let me grow and develop. If I let them control me I would create a monster. When I wrote *Biting the Bullet* I knew that because people wouldn't be rolling in the aisles with laughter it wouldn't be a play that would be staged often. Nevertheless it was a play I wanted to write and I'm reasonably proud of it. And so I don't deliberately target an audience. I write the play I want to write. Take my comedy *Tonto Evans*. I knew when I was writing it that it would please a great many of my audience. I knew this for two very good reasons. It was a deliberate nod back to my earlier work and, yes, many people had asked me to go and write 'a bloody good laugh again'. But I wrote *Tonto Evans*, not for the audience, but for myself, because I wanted to prove to myself that I could actually write that kind of comedy again. In my experience an audience will react more (I don't mean in terms of laughter or applause, but in terms of discussion after the play, in the bar or outside the theatre) to a play that has amused them than to one that has moved them.

HWD: *Have you had particular actors in mind when you are writing a play?*

FV: I certainly wrote plays specifically for Menna Trussler. *A Kiss on the Bottom* was the first play I wrote for her. She has been a huge inspiration and I hope to continue to write for her for some years to come. Many writers have identified with actors and actresses who understand their work totally. Alan Bennett had Thora Hird and I had Menna Trussler. A good writer can write for anyone, but when he finds someone who is in tune with his work, then something special and magical happens and his work takes on another dimension. I'm sure I'd have written other plays but certainly not that half a dozen or so inspired by Menna. It's a good way of working and seems to get the best out of the actor/actress and the writer and director.

HWD: *You've enjoyed a particularly successful collaboration with the Sherman Theatre Company. How did that association come about?*

FV: Back in the 1980s when The Parc and Dare Theatre Company were making a name for themselves they started hiring the Arena Theatre at the Sherman for three nights at a time. This became so successful that performances were soon extended to a full week. The theatre was run at this time by a lady whose name escapes me, but by and large we as a company were ignored by her. Eventually she was replaced by a gentleman called Jeffrey Axeworthy and he too, for some reason, took no interest in our popularity, even when soon after his appointment we had moved from the 160 seater arena to the 447 seats in the main house. We were enjoying great success there when the post of Artistic Director was suddenly filled by a guy called Phil Clark. Immediately he took notice of my work and started offering me writing commissions. The collaboration proved to be very successful. When the Sherman lost some funding, the Grand Theatre Swansea, because of my popularity with audiences there, came on board with funding. By that time the Parc and Dare Company had folded and been replaced by my own semi-professional company, Grass Roots Production.

HWD: *You have acted in your own plays and have recently played Aguecheek in Michael Bogdanov's production of* Twelfth Night *and Philario in his production of* Cymbeline. *To what degree has the fact that you're an actor influenced the way you write?*

FV: I'm sure I am a better writer because I am also an actor. Because I am an actor I have a natural instinct of what will work on stage and what won't. And I must confess that as I am writing I am acting out all the parts in my head. The danger is because I am an actor and have acted out all the male parts as I wrote them, you think you are capable of playing any of them, and that is not true. Often in the past I have written a part that I thought I would play, but when Brian Meadows from the Parc and Dare Company cast it he would cast me as something different, and he would usually be proved right to do so.

HWD: *You have written over thirty stage plays and about fifteen scripts for radio. Have you found it difficult to write variations on a character or theme?*

FV: I've never encountered that difficulty. Someone told me once that a playwright only ever writes one play and all the rest are variations on it. I'm not sure I agree totally with that, but there's something in it. I think maybe if you are lucky you have a dozen or so subjects that interest you and everything usually stems from there. You may start out with only two or three subjects that interest you, but as you grow as a person and a writer the list grows with you.

HWD: *Your plays travel well and have been translated into other languages. How would you analyse the appeal they have for audiences from different cultures?*

FV: Many of my plays have been translated into several languages including Welsh, Gaelic, Spanish and Frisian. I think the reason for their popularity in those countries is that, if you take the Welshness out of the dialogue, the basic situations are not particularly Welsh at all. Their themes are pretty universal. In Wales we tend, even now, to have strong Welsh Mams. It's the same in Spanish and Italian culture, as in most cultures. It's the same, too, for the taboo subjects I mentioned earlier. I am a Welshman living and writing in Wales, but the situations I write about are not parochial in the least.

HWD: *You mentioned earlier that you won the Lord Howard de Walden Trophy. Howard de Walden of course was a great patron and advocate of the amateur theatre in Wales and of writers who wrote for that theatre. How healthy is the amateur theatre in Wales today?*

FV: Sadly, I don't think the amateur theatre in Wales is anywhere near as strong as it was, say, twenty years ago. The amateur operatic companies are doing quite well, but I think it's fair to say that the standard is nowhere near as high in some places as it used to be. Part of the reason for this, I think, is that when young people come along with an obvious talent, it's not long before they leave to go and train for the professional stage, which is as it should be of course. But, on the whole, the amateur theatre in Wales has lost a great deal of its old impetus.

On The Black Hill by Charles Way

Drowned World by Gary Owen

Biographies

Greg Cullen

Greg Cullen has worked as an actor, director and writer with the East End Theatre Group; Harlow Theatre Van; Chats Palace Community Arts Centre, Hackney; and The Grove Theatre, Hammersmith. In 1983 he moved to Wales as Writer in Residence at Theatr Powys and for twelve years was writer and artistic director for Mid-Powys Youth Theatre. He has written for radio, film and television as well as for theatre and his work has won several awards. *Past Caring* (1984) was featured by ASSITEJ as an outstanding play for young audiences; *Taken Out* (1985) was part of a season of new radio plays to win a Sony Award; and *Mary Morgan* (1988) won the City Limits Award for New Expressionism. In 1989 *Frida and Diego* won the Fringe First Award at the Edinburgh Festival and was selected in 1994 for the BT National Connections Festival. In 1996 *Birdbrain* was winner of the Wales Film Council/BBC Competition for a Short Film to celebrate a hundred years of cinema. In 2003 he completed the radio play *Mudcrawlers* for BBC Radio Wales. Amongst his numerous large-cast stage plays are *Tarzanne* (1988), *An Informer's Duty* (1991-2), *The Ark* (1992), *Little Devils* (1994), *Ice Cream* (2003), *Whispers in the Woods* (2004). Amongst his adaptations are *Hard Times* (1980), *The Snow Queen* (1986), *Lysistrata* (1992) and *Silas Marner* (1996). His publications include *Greg Cullen: Three Plays* (Seren, 1998) and 'The Graveyard of Ambition?' in Anna-Marie Taylor's (ed.) *Staging Wales* (University of Wales Press, 1997). 2004 saw a new touring production of *Paul Robeson Knew My Father* and the completion of his first opera, *The Tailor's Daughter*, for the WNO-Max. In 2005 he completed *Botticelli's Bonfire* for the National Youth Theatre of Wales. He has worked for several theatre companies, the Royal Welsh College of Music and Drama and the University of Wales, Aberystwyth. He is currently Director of the National Youth Theatre of Wales and is developing three new musicals, in New York and Miami.

Hazel Walford Davies

Hazel Walford Davies has held posts at the University of Wales, Aberystwyth and at the University of Glamorgan, along with Visiting Professorships in Theatre at various American universities. Her main area of research is Welsh-language and English-language theatre in Wales. She was a member of the Drama panel of the Arts Council of Wales (1991-4), theatre advisor to the *New Welsh Review* (1994-2002) and a member and Chair of the periodical's Editorial Board. Between 1994 and 2004 she was Chair of the Wales Advisory Board of the North American Association for the Study of Welsh Culture and History, and in 2000 she was appointed a member of the Arts Council of Wales and Chair of its Literature Committee. She is currently a member of the Council and Court of the National Library of Wales, a trustee of the Wales Theatre Company, and a member of the Advisory Board of the Wales media journal, *Cyfrwng*. Amongst her publications are *O M Edwards* (University of

Wales Press, 1988), *Saunders Lewis a Theatr Garthewin* (Gomer, 1995), *State of Play: Four Playwrights of Wales* ed. (Gomer, 1998), *Llwyfannau Lleol* ed. (*Local Stages*) (Gomer, 2000). She has published an essay on the performance history of Saunders Lewis's *Blodeuwedd* in the *Cambridge History of Twentieth-Century Theatre* (2005). She is also the editor of a volume of commissioned critical essays on the Welsh-language national theatre movement, *Theatr Genedlaethol Cymru* (*The Welsh National Theatre*), to be published by the University of Wales Press in 2005. Her own contribution to this volume is an essay on the theatre patronage of Lord Howard de Walden.

Lewis Davies

Lewis Davies is a novelist, short-story writer, publisher and playwright. Amongst his plays are *Without Leave* (1998), *My Piece of Happiness* (1998), *Sex and Power at the Beau Rivage* (2003) and *Football* (2004). His travel book *Freeways, A Journey West on Route 66* won the 1994 John Morgan Award and in 1999 he won the Rhys Davies Prize for *Mr Rooprantna's Chocolate*. His novels include *Work, Sex and Rugby* (1993), *Tree of Crows* (1996), and *My Piece of Happiness* (2000). *As I was a Boy Fishing*, a collection of essays, vignettes and poems, was published in 2003. He is currently preparing an edition of Welsh fiction entitled *Urban Welsh*. He lives in Cardigan 'where he is trying to write, publish and fish.'

Dic Edwards

Dic Edwards was born in Cardiff and has been a playwright since 1981 when his first play, a one-acter, *Late City Echo* was produced at the Sherman Arena. As a result of the successful one-night performance Made in Wales Theatre Company was formed and it commissioned his first full-length play *At the End of the Bay* (1982). He has been Writer in Residence at Theatr Clwyd and Theatr Powys and at various schools in South and West Wales. His plays have been produced by Made in Wales, the Sherman Theatre Company, Spectacle,

Castaway and Sgript Cymru. His plays *Long to Rain Over Us* (1986) and *Low People* (1989) were produced at Leicester Haymarket Theatre. The Citizens Theatre, Glasgow produced *Casanova Undone* (1992) and *Wittgenstein's Daughter* (1993). The last two plays were also produced at The White Bear Theatre, London in 1993 and 1994 respectively. He wrote the libretto for *The Beggar's New Clothes* (1993) and *The Juniper Tree* (1995). Both were performed at the Broomhill International Opera Festival in Kent. A new opera, *Manifest Destiny* had a concert production at The Cockpit in 2003 and was produced at The Tricycle in 2004 as a benefit performance for the Guantanamo Human Rights Commission. Amongst his other stage plays are *Canned Goods* (1983), *Looking for the World* (1986), *Little Yankee* (1987), *The fourth world* (1990), *Regan* (1991), *Utah Blue* (1995), *Lola Brecht* (1996), *The Man Who Gave His Foot for Love* (1996), and *Franco's Bastard* (2002). He has written several plays for Theatre in Education productions. *Welshing*, his new play for Volcano will be produced in 2005 and his play about Baudelaire's *The Pimp* will be produced in London shortly. His publications include *3 Plays* (Oberon Books, 1992), *Wittgenstein's Daughter* (Oberon Books, 1993), *The Shakespeare Factory, Moon River: The Deal, David* (Seren, 1997), *Americana* (Oberon Books, 2000), *Franco's Bastard, Lola Brecht* (Oberon Books, 2000), *Sobre el Bosc Lacti* (*Over Milk Wood*) (Arola, Barcelona, 2003) and an essay in *The Professions in Modern Theatre* (Intellect Books, 2000). He holds a lectureship in Creative Writing at the Department of English, University of Wales, Lampeter and he also teaches scriptwriting at the Theatre Department, University of Wales, Aberystwyth.

Siôn Eirian

Siôn Eirian is a poet, novelist and dramatist. After graduating from the University of Wales Aberystwyth he was appointed in 1978 to Theatr Clwyd as its first playwright in residence. At Clwyd he adapted Daniel Owen's *Rhys Lewis* into an English-language stage play. He has written numerous plays for companies such as Moving Being, Made in Wales, Bara Caws and the Royal Welsh College of Music and Drama. He was co-writer of the 1994 film *Gadael Lenin* (*Leaving Lenin*) which won the Audience Award at the London Film Festival, and his film thriller *A Mind to Kill* has been shown on US prime time TV. In the 1994 BBC Wales Arts Award he received the prize 'Artist of the Year' at the London Film Festival for his contribution to theatre and film. Amongst his television credits are *Marwolaeth yr Asyn o Fflint* (*The Death of the Donkey from Flint*) (1983), the series *Bowen a'i Bartner* (*Bowen and his Partner*) (1984-88) and the films *Noson yr Heliwr* (*The Night of the Huntsman*) (1991). His stage plays include *Wastad ar y Tu Fas* (*Always on the Outside*) (1986), *Elvis, Y Blew a Fi* (*Elvis, Y Blew and Me*) (1988), and *Epa yn y Parlwr Cefn* (*An Ape in the Back Parlour*) (1994). Over the last three years he has written and set up an eight-part drama series, *Mostyn Fflint 'n Aye!* which features Cadfan Roberts as an alcoholic failed club comedian. He has also translated scripts for Theatr Iolo, Gwent Theatre, the Royal Welsh College of Music and Drama and the Sherman, and he has written librettos for Music Theatre Wales and Theatr na n'Og.

Siân Evans

Siân Evans was born and brought up in Bridgend. Her stage plays include *Badenheim 1939* (1995), *Little Sister* (1996), *Asleep Under the Dark Earth* (1997), and *The Journey of Mary Kelly* (1998). Her work for radio and television includes *Dancing on the Turf*, BBC Radio 4 (1993), *Insect Life*, BBC Wales (1993), *Tide Race*, BBC Wales, *The Slate* (1996). She has also written episodes for Carlton Television's *Peak Practice*, ITV's *Touching Evil* and *Where the Heart Is* and her own six-part series, *Hereafter*. Her translations include *The Memoirs of Elizabeth Vigee Lebrun*, Racine's *Britannicus* and Denise Chalem's *A Cinquante Ans Elle Decouvrait La Mer*. *Asleep Under the Dark Earth* was published by Faber and Faber in 2001 and *Little Sister* was published by Parthian in *New Welsh Drama II*. In

1992 she won the Arts Council of England Translation Award and the Caloust-Gulbenkian Bursary. She lives in Norfolk and is working on various film and television projects. She teaches scriptwriting at the University of East Anglia.

Lucy Gough

Lucy Gough was born in London and spent her early years in Beddgelert before the family settled in Bath. She returned to live in Wales in 1974. She graduated in Drama at the University of Wales, Aberystwyth and gained an MA in Playwriting at Birmingham University. Her stage plays include *Joanna* (1989), *Catherine Wheel* (1991), *By a Thread* (1992), *As to be Naked* (1994), *Stars* (1995), *Rushes* (1995), *Wolfskin* (1997), *Mapping the Soul* (2001) and *Gryfhead* (2003). In 1994 *Crossing the Bar* was shortlisted for both the BBC Writer of the Year Award and the John Whiting Award. Amongst her commissioned radio plays are *Our Lady of Shadows*, BBC Radio 3 (1994), *Head*, BBC Radio 4 (1990), *The Prophetess of Exeter*, BBC World Service (1997), *The Red Room*, BBC Radio 4 (1999), *The Mermaid's Tail*, BBC Radio 4 (1999), *The Raft*, BBC Radio 4 (2002) which was nominated for the Prix Europa, and *Wuthering Heights*, BBC Radio 4 (2003). Since the mid 1990s she has been script-writer for *Hollyoaks*. She teaches Radio Drama for the University of Wales at Aberystwyth and Lampeter. Her publications include *Lucy Gough: Crossing the Bar*, *Head*, *Our Lady of Shadows* (Seren, 2000) and *The Red Room* and *The Tail* in *One Woman, One Voice* (Parthian, 2000).

Mark Jenkins

Mark Jenkins was born and educated in London and moved to Wales in 1980 to take up an appointment as Principal Lecturer in Public Sector Management at the University of Glamorgan where he currently teaches scriptwriting. His monograph *Bevanism* was published in 1979 by Spokesman University Press and republished in 1981. His plays include *Birthmarks*

(1987), *Strindberg Knew My Father* (1991), *Playing Burton* (1992), *Downtown Paradise* (1996), *Nora's Bloke* (2003) and *Rosebud* (2004). He wrote the filmscript for *The Scarlet Tunic* which was premiered at the Odeon, Leicester Square in 1998 and his teleplay *Er Gwell, Er Gwaeth* (*For Better, For Worse*) was shown on S4C in 1985. His publications include *Strindberg Knew My Father* (Aurora Metro, 1998), *Playing Burton* (Parthian, 2001), and *More Lives Than One*, a collection of five of his plays, including *Playing Burton* (Parthian, 2004). *Rosebud* was awarded a Fringe First Award as well as the Carol Tambor Edinburgh to New York Award at the Edinburgh Festival, 2004.

Gareth Miles

After twelve years as a schoolteacher of French and English and eight years as National Organizer for the Welsh-language teachers' union UCAC, Gareth Miles in 1982 became a freelance writer. His work includes political pamphlets, short stories, novels and plays. He has translated plays by Lope de Vega, Marivaux, Ionesco and Daniel Danis and has adapted Webster's *Duchess of Malfi*, Mikhaill Bulgakov's *Heart of a Dog* and Alfred Jarry's *Ubu Roi*. Amongst his plays are *Trotsci* (1973), *Diwedd y Saithdegau* (*The End of the Seventies*) (1983), *Unwaith Eto, 'Nghymru Annwyl* (*Once Again, In Dear Wales*) (1986), *Chwiorydd* (*Sisters*) (1987), *Hunllef yng Nghymru Fydd* (*Nightmare in Wales 2030 AD*) (1990), *Dyrnod Branwen* (*Branwen's Grief*) (1993) and *Byd y Banc* (*The World of the Bank*) (1996). He has published collections of short stories and novels and also writes for radio and television.

Alan Osborne

Alan Osborne was born in Merthyr and after a period as teacher in London and Faringdon, near Oxford, he returned to Wales in 1975 to teach art at Afon Taf, Troed-y-Rhiw. He has written for radio and television as well as for theatre. In 1981 his play *Bull, Rock and Nut* won the Play for Wales Competition. He has written and illustrated *Plans for the*

Great Trapeze Act (1974), *Terraces* (1979), *Johnny Darkie* (1981). *In Sunshine and in Shadow* toured Wales in 1985 and was also performed at the Battersea Arts Centre, London. He wrote *Tiger! Tiger! Burning Bright* (1985), *The Rising* (1987), *The Redemption Song* (1987), *The Tuscan* (1988) and *The Forbidden Hymn* (1989). In 1993 Made in Wales performed a retrospective of his work at the Sherman Theatre. His television dramas include *The Whistling Boy* (1994) and *The Beach Inspector* (1996). He composed *Give us the Flowers Now* for the BBC Symphony Orchestra and his choral libretto *Spirit of Our Distant Fathers* toured the United States with Brecon High School. He has worked with the WNO and contributed to Fire Tree/Coeden Dân at the International Celtic Festival in Brittany in 2002. In 1998 *The Merthyr Trilogy*, a collection of three of his plays was published by Parthian.

Gary Owen

Gary Owen's plays include *Crazy Gary's Mobile Disco*, *The Shadow of a Boy*, *The Drowned World*, *Amser Canser* and *Ghost City*. *Crazy Gary's Mobile Disco* opened in Chapter, Cardiff in 2001, played for a month at the Lyric, Hammersmith and then toured Britain. It has since been produced in Germany, Holland, Italy, Sweden and Canada. *The Shadow of a Boy* was joint winner of the 2002 George Devine Award, and winner of the 2003 Meyer Whitworth Award. *The Drowned World* won a Fringe First at the 2002 Edinburgh Festival and was joint winner of the 2003 Pearson Best Play Award. *Amser Canser* was first performed in Welsh by students of the Royal Welsh College of Music and Drama in 2003 and in 2004 was produced in English translation by the Caird Company at Theatre 503 in Battersea. *Ghost City* was part of the inaugural festival in 2004 of new British work at the 59E59 Street Theatre in New York. For young people he has written *The Green*, a short for the National Theatre's Assembly project, and *SK8*, a hip-hop musical for the Theatre Royal, Plymouth. A collection of his work will be published by Methuen in 2005.

Ian Rowlands

Ian Rowlands was born in Porth in the Rhondda Fach and trained as an actor at the Royal Welsh College of Music and Drama. He is currently Artistic Director of Llwyfan Gogledd Cymru (North Wales Stage). He was founder of Theatr y Byd and has been Artistic Director of Bara Caws and Theatr Gwynedd. His stage plays include *The Sin Eaters* (1992) which was nominated 'Best Regional Play' for the year by the Writers' Guild of Great Britain, *Solomon's Glory* (1993), *Glissando on an Empty Harp* (1994), *Love in Plastic* (1996), *Marriage of Convenience* (1997), which won two awards at the Dublin Festival, *Blue Heron in the Womb* (1998), *New South Wales* (1999), *Pacific/Môr Tawel* (2000). His television work includes *A Light in the Valley*, BBC Wales, which won the Royal Television Award for 'Best Regional Programme' in 1998, *Men*, Teliesyn Films/BBC and *The Ogpu Men*, HTV. For radio he has written *3 o'clock at Ponty*, BBC Radio Wales, 1996 and has contributed to *Station Road* and *The Dough Boys*. Several of his plays have been published by Bydbooks and *The Ogpu Men* was published in *Act 1 Wales* (Seren, 1997). In 2000 Parthian published *Trilogy of Appropriation* (*Glissando on an Empty Harp*, *Love in Plastic* and *Blue Heron in the Womb*). In 2001 *Marriage of Convenience* appeared in *One Man, One Voice* (Parthian) and in 2002 Gwasg Carreg Gwalch published *Môr Tawel* in *Llais Un yn Llefain*, a collection of monologues edited by Ian Rowlands.

Ed Thomas

Ed Thomas is director of Fiction Factory Ltd, a film and TV production company based in Cardiff. His stage plays include *House of America* (1988), *Adar Heb Adenydd* (1989), *The Myth of Michael Roderick* (1990), *Flowers of the Dead Red Sea* (1991), *East from the Gantry* (1992), *Envy* (1993), *Hiraeth/ Strangers in Conversation* (1993), *Song from a Forgotten City* (1994), *Gas Station Angel* (1998) and *Stone City Blue* (2004). His work as writer, director and producer in theatre, film and television has won numerous awards including Time Out/01 for London (1989), BBC Writer of the Year (1994), Arts Foundation Fellowship Award (1994), Celtic Film and Television Festival Awards (1993, 2004) and BAFTA Cymru Awards (1994, 1997, 1998, 2002, 2004). His plays have been performed world-wide and have been translated into eight languages. His publications include *East from the Gantry* in Pamela Edwardes (ed.), *Frontline Intelligence* (Methuen, 1993), *Edward Thomas, Three Plays* (Seren, 1994), *Hiraeth/Strangers in Conversation* in *One Act Wales* (Seren, 1997), *Gas Station Angel* (Methuen, 1998), and *Ed Thomas: '95-'98 Selected Work* (Parthian, 2002).

Frank Vickery

Frank Vickery lives in the Rhondda Valley where he works as playwright, producer and actor. He gave up his job at the Chrystie Taylor furniture factory in 1989 to work full-time as a writer and actor. He has his own theatre company, Grassroots Productions, and also writes for radio and television. Amongst his many plays published by Samuel French are *A Night on the Tiles* (1987), *Trivial Pursuits* (1990), *Spanish Lies* (1993), *Erogenous Zones* (1994), *The Drag Factor* (1994), *Loose Ends* (1995), *A Kiss on the Bottom* (1995), *Biting the Bullet* (1997), and *Roots and Wings* (1997). His first play, *After I'm Gone* won the Howard de Walden Trophy for Best One Act Play in Great Britain in 1978. Other nominations include the London Weekend Television Plays on Stage Award and the Writers Guild of Great Britain Award for *Erogenous Zones* (1993), The Lloyds Bank Playwright of the Year Award for *Loose Ends* (1994) and BAFTA Cymru nominations for *Green Farms* (1994) and *The Drag Factor* (1995). He is currently writing a new musical, *Amazing Grace*, for the Wales Theatre Company and in 2005 he will tour a production of his popular comedy *One O'Clock From the House* and a production of his new play *Grannie Annie*.

Charles Way

Charles Way, a Devonian, moved to Wales in 1980 and was appointed Resident Writer for Gwent Theatre. He has worked closely with Hijinx, Spectacle, Made in Wales and the Sherman. He also works with key theatre companies for young people in England. His plays for children and young people have been performed world-wide, and have been translated into several languages. Amongst his many plays are *She Scored for Wales* (1981), *In Living Memory* (1983), *Paradise Drive* (1989), *The Flood* (1990), *Dead Man's Hat* (1992), *The Search for Odysseus* (1993), *Ill Met By Moonlight* (1994), *The Dove Maiden* (1995), *Playing from the Heart* (1998), *The Night Before Christmas* (1999), *Beauty and the Beast* (2001), *One Snowy Night* (2002), *Red Red Shoes* (2003), *The Long Way Home* (2004), *Merlin and the Cave of Dreams* (2004). He has worked for radio and television and is the author of several community projects and stage adaptations. In 1985 Made in Wales staged his adaptation of Bruce Chatwin's *On the Black Hill* which was later broadcast on BBC Radio 4. His publications include *Charles Way: Three Plays* (Seren, 1994), *Charles Way: Plays for Young People* (Aurora Metro, 2001) and *The Classic Fairytales* (Aurora Metro, 2002), *A Spell of Cold Weather* (Aurora Metro, 2003), *Alice in the News* (Barrington Stokes, and NT, 2004). He is winner of the Writers Guild Best Children's Play Award and in 2004 *Red Red Shoes* won the Arts Council of England's 'Children's Award'.

Roger Williams

Roger Williams writes for theatre, radio and television. He has directed several of his plays and has worked with Made in Wales, RCT Youth Theatre, the Sherman and the Sherman Youth Theatre, the Royal Welsh College of Music and Drama and Sgript Cymru. In 1998-99 he was playwright-in-residence at Sydney Theatre Company and the Australian National Playwrights' Centre. In 2000 he won the Arts Council of Wales's Playwright's Bursary for his play *Lingua* which has had readings in New York and at New Zealand's International Theatre Festival, Wellington, and the Pleasance Theatre, London. A reading of *Killing Kangaroos* was featured at the Australian Playwrights' Conference, Canberra, 2001. His plays include *Love in Aberdare* (1997), *Gulp* (1997), *Calon Lân* (1998), *Saturday Night Forever* (1998), *Killing Kangaroos* (1999), *Pop* (2000), *Y Byd (A'i Brawd)* (2004). For BBC Wales he has written *Shelf Life* (1996), *Carmarthen Cowgirls* (1998), and *Pushy* (2001). For Radio Cymru he wrote *Dechrau Cerdded* (1996) and *Duckie* (2003) for Radio 4. He has also contributed to several series for CBBC, BBC2, BBC Wales and S4C. His published plays include *Surfing Carmarthen Bay* (Drama Association of Wales, 1996), *Gulp* in *New Welsh Drama 1* (Parthian 1998), *Killing Kangaroos* in *New Welsh Drama II* (Parthian 2001) and *Saturday Night Forever* in *One Man, One Voice* (Parthian 2001).

Index

Arden, John 252
Argentina 151
Aristotle 81
Armstrong, Gareth 216
Arts Centre, Aberystwyth 247, 268
Arts Council of Wales 13, 14, 40, 43, 45, 61, 76, 97, 101, 115,
 129, 140, 159, 163, 164, 180, 199, 204, 233, 241, 244,
 247, 264, 288, 332, 349
 'Drama Strategy' (1999) 46, 129, 241, 246, 352-53
ASSITEJ 168
Attlee, Clement 276
Auden, W H 102
Aurora Metro Press 140, 284
Australia 33, 76, 179, 285, 290, 315, 354, 355
Australian National Playwrights' Centre 351-52
Axeworthy, Jeffrey 364
Ayckbourn, Alan 360-61

Bachae, The 152
Badenheim 1939 326
BAFTA Award 260
Baines, Menna 1
Baker, Michael 1, 43
Baker, Tim 71
Baker-Sperry, Lori 134
Bala, Iwan 35
Baldwin, James 149
Balkans 308
Bara Caws Theatre 235, 243, 244
Barcelona 27, 31
Barclays New Stages Award 13, 14
Barker, Howard 20, 69, 257, 263
Barn (Welsh-language periodical) 1, 42n
Barr, Jean-Marc 288
Barnes, Peter 320

410